Family and Child Welfare

FAMILY AND CHILD WELFARE

Ajit K. Singh

CENTRUM PRESS
NEW DELHI-110002 (INDIA)

CENTRUM PRESS
H.O.: 4360/4, Ansari Road, Daryaganj,
New Delhi-110002 (India)
Tel: 23278000, 23261597, 23255577, 23286875
B.O.: No. 1015, Ist Main Road, BSK IIIrd Stage,
IIIrd Phase, IIIrd Block, Bengaluru-560085 (INDIA)
Tel: 080-41723429
Email: centrumpress@gmail.com
Visit us at: www.centrumpress.com

Family and Child Welfare

First Edition, 2011

ISBN 978-93-81293-70-6

PRINTED IN INDIA

Printed at Tarun Offset, Delhi

Contents

Preface

Indian women were given liberties and rights such as freedom of expression and equality, as well as right to get education. But still today, we are fighting for crisis such as dowry, female infanticide, sex selective abortions, health, domestic violence, etc. Women today are educated but illiterate in terms of knowing their rights properly. Another harmful practise is the Dowry system where gift of money or valuables given by the bride's family to the groom's at the time of their marriage. This is the new harassment in the name of wedding gift. Women are killed if they bring less dowry after marriage. The term Bride Burning is criticized within India itself. India has a low sex ratio, the chief reason being that many child die before reaching adulthood.

They are abated in the womb itself as many people do not want a girl child because they cannot pay dowry. This is a vicious circle which is linked to one another. It is somewhere a criticism that highest female ratio lies in Kerala and Tribal societies in India knowing the fact that tribal communities have far lower levels of income, literacy and health facilities. Female infanticide (killing of girl infants) is still prevalent in some rural areas. Dowry has been one of the main reasons for female infanticides in India.

Sati, as the practice of self-immolation, is a long-standing tradition among upper caste Hindus. Although legitimized through myth, it is a violent practice against women. It is complicated by the fact that it is often used against women to take control of land that they might inherit as widows. Widows have very little status in Hindu India and are often seen as bad omens. Therefore, they are treated miserably. Some do commit suicide rather than be subject to daily torture and humiliation and some are killed.

Child labour and child abuse could be treated separately due to its magnitude and shame they leave on the society. But for convenience, they are being dealt with together. These are major problems of children which need special attention by development workers. Besides, the entire society has the responsibility to provide for the establishment of a better society where children are treated with care, bye and dignity. The suffering, despair and the resignation that are part of the children of slums are enormous and frightening. They have deep-seated lack of confidence in adults, even though they have great deal of patience in coping with tremendous adversity. They can overcome the existing social, educational and even economic chaos that can be immediately felt by a conscious person who visits any slum. Children are the future of the community. But child labour destroys the vitality of children and they become old without enjoying the charms and joys of childhood.

This book makes it an ideal text for a wide range of disciplines including Family and Child Welfare.

—*Editor*

1

Situation and Status of Women in India

The status of women in India has been subject to great many changes over the past few millennia. From a largely unknown status in ancient times through the low points of the medieval period, to the promotion of equal rights by many reformers, the history of women in India has been eventful.

WOMEN IN ANCIENT INDIA

It is said that women enjoyed equal status with men in all fields of life in ancient India. In the early Vedic period women were educated. We can see this in the works of Grammarians such as 'Patanjali' & 'Katyayana'. Women got married at a mature age and were also free to select their husbands. Scriptures such as Rig Veda and Upanishads mention many women sages and seers, notably Gargi and Maitreyi. There are some kingdoms in ancient India, which had customs such as 'nagarvadhu' i.e. the bride of the city. According to this custom women competed to win the prestigious title of 'nagarvadhu'. Amrapali is the most famous example of a 'nagarvadhu'. Women in fact had superior position than their male counterparts. It is truly in this period that women were really treated as Durga and Parvati.

There was a special thread ceremony in which girls were tied threads of honour based on merit. Later this ceremony was replaced by 'child-marriage'. Child-Marriage by this time was started on a large scale because of many holy books. Girls were married when they were infants. They were send to their husbands house when they attained puberty. Girls were not permitted to gain education. Although many Jain institutions admitted girls but it was of no use as only few number of girls attended these institutes.

WOMEN IN MEDIEVAL INDIA

The condition of Women in society was deteriorated more during the medieval period. At this point of time child-marriage, sati, female infanticide was practiced largely. The Muslim seclusion in India introduced the 'purdah' system by and large on Muslim women. These women were also forced to practice 'zenana'. The Rajput women of Rajasthan who are known to place a high premium on honour practiced 'jauhar'. Jauhar refers to the practice of the voluntary immolation of all the wives and daughters of defeated warriors, in order to avoid capture and consequent molestation by the enemy. Polygamy i.e. husband marrying more than once was practised by most Hindu Kshatriyas. At the same time many women excelled in arts, literature, music. Women were also rulers in the medieval period. Some of the great women rulers were Razia Sultan, the only women monarch to rule the throne of Delhi.

The Gond queen Durgavati ruled for fifteen long years, before she lost the battle to Mughal emperor Akbar's general Asaf Ali. Chand Bibi also fought the mughals in 1590's. Nur Jehan the only Mughal women ruler is still today considered the most effective ruler. Inspite of all these successful women the condition of a poor Indian women was the same. At this time, girls were married at an early age say 5-6 years. Sati was also practised where women were forced to jump in the burning funeral of their dead husband.

Purdah was practised among Muslim women i.e. to cover their heads fully with a 'veil'. Devdasi was prevalent in south India where girls were married to deity or trees. This practise had destoyed the lives of many girls as they were physically molested and sexually exploited by many pundits.

WOMEN IN MODERN INDIA

Modern India witnessed improvements in the Status of Women There were many women reformers who worked for the betterment and upliftment of their other female counterparts. The begum of Bhopal discarded the purdah and fought in the revolt of 1857. Many reformers like Ishwarchandra Vidyasagar, Jyotiba Phule with his wife Savitribai Phule undertook various measures to eradicate social stigmas from the society. Sir Sayyed Ahmad Khan established the Aligarh Muslim University for the spread of education among the Muslims. He also abolished the purdah system among Muslim women. Many Acts were passed for the upliftment of women among those Widow Remarraige Act of 1856 was important.

In the modern times, Indian women were given liberties and rights such as freedom of expression and equality, as well as right to get education. But still today, we are fighting for crisis such as dowry, female infanticide, sex selective abortions, health, domestic violence, etc. Women today are educated but illiterate in terms of knowing their rights properly. Another harmful practise is the Dowry system where gift of money or valuables given by the bride's family to the groom's at the time of their marriage. This is the new harassment in the name of wedding gift. Women are killed if they bring less dowry after marriage. The term Bride Burning is criticized within India itself. India has a low sex ratio, the chief reason being that many child die before reaching adulthood. They are abated in the womb itself as many people do not want a girl child because they cannot pay dowry.

This is a vicious circle which is linked to one another. It is somewhere a criticism that highest female ratio lies in Kerala and Tribal societies in India knowing the fact that tribal communities have far lower levels of income, literacy and health facilities. Female infanticide (killing of girl infants) is still prevalent in some rural areas. Dowry has been one of the main reasons for female infanticides in India.

The level of Domestic violence is also high in India. Husbands beat their wives in a drunken state to get rid of their frustration. Domestic violence is also prevalent because of 'dowry'. Trafficking is also a big reason for female abuse. Trafficking means girls are sold to big people for satisfying their sexual needs or kidnapped to make them prostitutes. In many rural families, girls and women face nutritional discrimination within the family, and are anaemic and malnourished.

The maternal mortality in India is the second highest in the world. Only a few percentage of births in the country are supervised by doctors. Most women deliver with the help of traditional nurses in the village who often lack the skills and resources to save the mother's life if it is in danger. Women suffer many health problems because of abuse and other malnourishments. The average Indian woman has little control over her own fertility and reproductive health. So women today in short are suffering from various other problems but still thanks to the reformer's like Jyotiba Phule, Dayanand Saraswati, Swami Vivekananda that they still can live to an extent on their own & fight for their Rights

CHRONIC HUNGER AND WOMEN IN INDIA

Introductory Quotes

You can tell the condition of a nation by looking at the status of its women. — Jawaharlal Nehru

However much a mother may love her children, it is all but impossible for her to provide high-quality child care if she herself is poor and oppressed, illiterate and uninformed, anaemic and unhealthy, has five or six other children, lives in a slum or shanty, has neither clean water nor safe sanitation, and if she is without the necessary support either from health services, or from her society, or from the father of her children. — Vulimiri Ramalingaswami, "The Asian Enigma"

The women who participate in and lead ecology movements in countries like India are not speaking merely as victims. Their voices are the voices of liberation and transformation... The women's and ecology movements are therefore one, and are primarily counter-trends to a patriarchal maldevelopment. — Vandana Shiva

Amartya Sen-The Unheeded Conscience: We will lionise him, but will we ever listen to what he's saying?

Sen points out that when he took up issues of women's welfare, he was accused in India of voicing "foreign concerns." "I was told Indian women don't think like that about equality. But I would like to argue that if

they don't think like that they should be given a real opportunity to think like that."
— *Parmita Shastri, Outlook India, 1998*

The persistence of hunger and abject poverty in India and other parts of the world is due in large measure to the subjugation, marginalization and disempowerment of women. Women suffer from hunger and poverty in greater numbers and to a great degree then men. At the same time, it is women who bear the primary responsibility for actions needed to end hunger: education, nutrition, health and family income.

Looking through the lens of hunger and poverty, there are seven major areas of discrimination against women in India:

- *Malnutrition*: India has exceptionally high rates of child malnutrition, because tradition in India requires that women eat last and least throughout their lives, even when pregnant and lactating. Malnourished women give birth to malnourished children, perpetuating the cycle.
- *Poor Health*: Females receive less health care than males. Many women die in childbirth of easily prevented complications. Working conditions and environmental pollution further impairs women's health.
- *Lack of education*: Families are far less likely to educate girls than boys, and far more likely to pull them out of school, either to help out at home or from fear of violence.
- *Overwork*: Women work longer hours and their work is more arduous than men's, yet their work is unrecognized. Men report that "women, like children, eat and do nothing." Technological progress in agriculture has had a negative impact on women.
- *Unskilled*: In women's primary employment sector-agriculture-extension services overlook women.
- *Mistreatment*: In recent years, there has been an alarming rise in atrocities against women in India, in terms of rapes, assaults and dowry-related murders. Fear of violence suppresses the aspirations of all women. Female infanticide and sex-selective abortions are additional forms of violence that reflect the devaluing of females in Indian society.

- *Powerlessness*: While women are guaranteed equality under the constitution, legal protection has little effect in the face of prevailing patriarchal traditions. Women lack power to decide who they will marry, and are often married off as children. Legal loopholes are used to deny women inheritance rights.

India has a long history of activism for women's welfare and rights, which has increasingly focused on women's economic rights. A range of government programs have been launched to increase economic opportunity for women, although there appear to be no existing programs to address the cultural and traditional discrimination against women that leads to her abject conditions.

WOMEN'S STATUS AT THE TIME

When Gandhiji assumed India's leadership the average life span of an Indian woman was only twenty seven years. Babies and the pregnant women ran a high risk of dying young. Child marriage was very common and widows were in very large number.

Only 2% of the women had any kind of education and women did not have an identity of their own. In North India, they practiced the purdah (veil) system. Women could not go out of the house unless accompanied by men and the face covered with cloth. The fortunate ones who could go to school had to commute in covered carts (tangas).

It is in this context that we have to recognize the miracle of Gandhi's work. Gandhiji claimed that a woman is completely equal to a man and practiced it in strict sense. Thousands and millions of women, educated and illiterate, house wives and widows, students and elderly participated in the India's freedom movement because his influence.

For Gandhiji, the freedom fight was not political alone; it was also an economic and social reform of a national proportion. After a couple of decades, this equality became very natural in India. After India's freedom (in 1947) and adoption of constitution (1950), emphasized equality of women, when Hindu code was formulated, the population was not even impressed. They said- "Of course, it had to be done."

WOMAN AND PROGRESS

Gandhiji always advocated a complete reform which he called "Sarvodaya" meaning comprehensive progress. He believed that the difference between men and women was only physical and has expressed several times in his writings that in many matters especially those of tolerance, patience, and sacrifice the Indian woman is superior to the male. You will discover this when you read his articles from "Young India" and "Harijan". During the 40 years of his political career, he only found more reasons to deepen his faith in what he wrote. He never had a specific program for women, but women had a integral role to play in all his programs. I feel that this is one of the reasons why women participated in his programs so overwhelmingly.

Gandhiji declared that there is no school better than home and there is no teacher better than parents. He said men and women are equal, but not identical. "Intellectually, mentally, and spiritually, woman is equivalent to a male and she can participate in every activity." Indian society is a male dominated one. Gandhiji has illustrated in his autobiography (The stories of my experiments with truth) how early in his marriage he too wanted to dominate his wife. He often said that paternal society is the root cause of inequality. In his book, there is a very touching chapter about when he asked his wife to clean a public toilet and the resulting conflict between him and his wife. He has written how ashamed he was of himself, and how he took care not to hurt her anymore for the rest of his life. Even though there was big gap between him and his wife intellectually, it did not affect their family life. He has said that Kasturba followed her husband more than was expected of her.

Gandhiji followed Bramacharya (strict discipline of food, drinks, and of celibacy) from a very young age, but when his wife passed away, Gandhi grieved that without Ba, his life would have been meaningless. That was the bondage of his 62 years of marriage.

WOMAN AND SOCIAL SERVICE

Gandhiji struggled very hard to understand a woman's physical and mental pain. From a young age he introduced his wife and children to social sacrifice and service. He believed that service has to be performed for self-fulfilment, not for public consumption or exhibition. He believed that the publicity given to one's social service actually decrements the value of the service. He tried very hard to eliminate job indignity and bias based on caste system. He tried to do the work of a barber, dhobi (washer man), and janitor to understand them and demonstrate that the work one does has no impact on one's status in the society.

For me, the fact that he contributed a great deal in raising his children is very modern concept. On one occasion the white midwife would not show up for his wife's delivery and Gandhiji himself delivered his child. He helped wife with feeding, bathing, and toiletries of the infant. In western countries these days men are encouraged to be with their wives during the delivery and the men are supposed to pitch in with diaper changing, etc. Gandhiji practiced this very modern concept 90 years ago in his own family.

ROLE OF WOMEN

"Womanhood is not restricted to the kitchen", he opined and felt that "Only when the woman is liberated from the slavery of the kitchen, that her true spirit may be discovered". It does not mean that women should not cook, but only that household responsibilities be shared among men, women and children. He wanted women to outgrow the traditional responsibilities and participate in the affairs of nation. He criticized Indian's passion for male progeny. He said that as long as we don't consider girls as natural as our boys our nation will be in a dark eclipse.

Child Widows

Gandhiji was especially considerate of the young widows. In the last 80 years, as a nation, if we have made any progress on the matter of child widows (girls used get married very early and after untimely deaths of their husbands, they were condemned to a life of great agony, shaving heads, living in isolation, and shunned by the society.) it is due to the reformers like Gandhiji and his contemporaries. Gandhiji once noted during his legendary travels across India that he never came across 13 year old who was not married. He declared the marriages in which the girls were not consulted were unholy.

At that time in Madras presidency, the number of child widows were alarmingly large. He called upon the young to marry the widows and also to boycott child marriages. (It may be noted here that Gandhiji himself married when very young; he was thirteen.) The history of India knows of many such young men who married widows and went on to work as social reformers.

Temple Women and Prostitutes

Gandhiji was very disturbed by the plight of this low caste untouchable section of the society, namely the Devadasis. He was hurt by the miserable way the children of brothels were treated. He had made elaborate plans for their rehabilitation. He declared that protecting women's honour was important and as holy as protecting cows. His book "Women and Social Injustice" contains discussions of very deep thoughts and solutions on the topic. He felt that after India became free, the system of temple women and brothels must be abolished. Even though on paper we have abolished the system of Devadasis, rampant exploitation of women as sex servants has continued. There was no way Gandhiji could have predicted modern ways and means of prostitution (call girls, phone sex etc.) but he certainly identified its social evil and tried to fight it.

Gandhiji's Contribution for Betterment of Women

As we look back at the Indian history and compare the conditions of women before Gandhi's rise, and now, the progress we have made is quite enormous. A whole generation of women leaders came up influenced by Gandhi's vision. If today in India so many women can go to work in offices, educational institutions, and factories without fear or hesitation, the roots for such system were laid 90 years ago by Gandhiji and his followers.

As mentioned earlier, Gandhiji formulated India's freedom struggle as a comprehensive plan for women's development. Even though a lot of inequalities remain in our society, there is a fundamental agreement that men and women are equal. As Indians, we can be very proud that the same cannot be claimed even by so called "advanced nations". In Britain as well as in the U.S.A., women could not vote 75 years ago. But women's voting came very naturally to us from the beginning. About 100 years ago, the western woman could not own property, get a divorce or take the custody of her children. We just have to look at the life and struggles of Dr. Annie Besant to understand the status of western women during Gandhiji's time. The western women had to take to streets, overcome many stereotypes to establish themselves voting and other rights. But for us, political, economic and voting rights came so naturally through the constitution!

Legacy

Today, if Gandhi's agenda has fallen apart, it is due to Indian politics. The continued exploitation of women can be attributed to the degradation in moral values of the society, and utter poverty of our nation. We ignored the role of social service, job dignity, and self reliance. Once in a while we run into true volunteers who believe in Gandhiji's ideals and have implemented his programs. I hope that at least a few of the younger generation take up Gandhiji's unfinished manifesto and work to eliminate social barriers facing women.

A Synopsis by India

- Contrary to sensational reports sometimes appearing in the news-hungry media in both India and other countries, female infanticide, bride burning (for reasons of dowry) and 'sati' (widow burning) are NOT normal in India. Each of these acts is a criminal act and an extremely rare occurrence.
- Enron Corporation's (Power Division) CEO Rebecca Mark, a woman, has inadvertently highlighted that women are taken at a par with men in government and business. She managed to rescue a contract her company had won but had run into trouble with a state government in India.
- India has the world's largest number of professionally qualified women.
- India has more female doctors, surgeons, scientists and professors than the United States.
- India has more working women than any other country in the world. This includes female workers at all levels of skill-from the surgeon and the airline pilot to bus conductors and menial labourers.

- On an average however, women in India are socially, politically and economically weaker than men.
- Moves are underway to empower women. The most news-making development was the introduction of the Women's Bill in Parliament in late 1998: the Bill seeks to reserve a certain percentage of seats in Parliament for women. This Bill is most likely to be passed by Parliament in 1999.
- There is a National Human Rights Commission for Women that handles all human rights violations against women. There is a National Council for Women that advocates policy for Women. There is an entire ministry for women that formulates and implements policy for them.

ROLE MODELS FOR FEMINISTS IN INDIA

Gargi Vachaknavi

Gargi Vachaknavi was an ancient Indian female philosopher, born in the family of Garga. She was daughter of sage Vachaknavi. Gargi is mentioned in the Brihadaranyaka Upanishad. In Vedic literature, she is honoured as one of the great natural philosophers. She was the daughter of sage Vachaknu. Gargi composed several hymns that questioned the origin of all existence. At brahmayajna, a philosophic congress organized by King Janak of Videha, she challenged the sage Yajnavalkya with perturbing questions on the atman (soul).

Maitreyi

Maitreyi was an ancient Indian female philosopher. She was one of the two wives of the sage Yajnavalkya, the other being Katyayani. Maitreyi was well-versed in the Hindu scriptures and was a brahmavadini. About ten hymns in Rig Veda are accredited to Maitreyi.

According to legend, Maitreyi really did not want to marry Yajnavalkya, but she wanted to live with him as a disciple and a spiritual companion to do sadhana. She went to Yajnavalkya's wife, Katyayani and expressed her desire to live with the sage. With Katyayani's consent, she became his companion.

Razia Sultana

Razia al-Din, "throne name" Jalalat ud-Din Raziya, usually referred to in history as Razia Sultan or Razia Sultana, was born in 1205 and died in 1240. She was of Turkish Seljuks ancestry and like some other Muslim princesses of the time, she was trained to lead armies and administer kingdoms if necessary. She succeeded her father Iltutmish to the Sultanate of Delhi in 1236. Iltutmish became the first sultan to appoint a woman as his successor when he designated his daughter Razia as his heir apparent. (According to one source, Iltumish's eldest son had initially been groomed as his successor, but had died prematurely.) But the Muslim nobility had no intention of acceding to Iltutmish's disregard of tradition in appointing a woman as heir, and after the sultan died on April 29, 1236, Razia's brother, Ruknuddin Feroze Shah, was elevated to the throne instead.

Ruknuddin's reign was short. With Iltutmish's widow Shah Turkaan for all practical purposes running the government, Ruknuddin abandoned himself to the pursuit of personal pleasure and debauchery, to the considerable outrage of the citizenry. On November 9, 1236, both Ruknuddin and his mother Shah Turkaan were put to death--after only six months in power. With reluctance, the nobility next agreed to allow Razia to reign as sultana of Delhi. As a child and adolescent, Razia had little contact with the women of the harem, so she had little opportunity to learn the customary behaviour of women in the Muslim society that she was born into. Even before she became queen--during her father's reign--she was reportedly preoccupied with the affairs of state. As sultana, Razia adopted men's dress; and contrary to custom, she would later show her face when she later rode an elephant into battle at the head of her army.

A shrewd politician, Razia managed to keep the nobles in check, while enlisting the support of the army and the populace. Her greatest accomplishment on the political front was to manipulate rebel factions into opposing each other. At that point, Razia seemed destined to become one of the most powerful rulers of the Delhi sultanate. But the sultana miscounted the consequences that a special relationship with one of her Assyrian slaves, Jalal-ud-din Yaqut, would have for her reign. According to some accounts, Razia and Yaqut were lovers; other sources simply identify them as close confidants. In any case, before long she had aroused the jealousy of the Muslim nobility by the favouritism she displayed toward Yaqut. Eventually, the governor of Bhatinda, a childhood friend named Malik Ikhtiar-ud-din Altunia, rebelled, refusing any longer to accept Razia's authority.

A battle between Razia and Altunia ensued, with the result that Yaqut was killed and Razia taken prisoner. To escape death, Razia agreed to marry Altunia. Meanwhile, Razia's brother, Muiuddin Bahram Shah, had usurped the throne. After Altunia and Razia undertook to take back the sultanate from Bahram through battle, both Razia and her husband--neither one more than 30 years of age--were both killed on October 14, 1240 (some sources say October 13). Bahram, for his part, would later be dethroned for incompetence.

Razia's Legacy

As sultana, Razia reportedly sought to abolish the tax on non-Muslims but met opposition from the nobility. By way of response, Razia is said to have pointed out that the spirit of religion was more important than its parts, and that even the Muslim Prophet spoke against overburdening the non-Muslims. On another occasion, Razia reportedly tried to appoint an Indian Muslim convert from Hinduism to an official position but again ran into opposition from the nobles. In this case she yielded, having concluded that the bonds of Islam were weaker than old prejudices. Razia was reportedly devoted to the cause of her empire and to her subjects. There is no record that she made any attempt to remain aloof from her subjects, rather it appears she preferred to mingle among them. Her tolerance of Hinduism would later bring her criticism from Muslim historians.

Razia established schools, academies, centres for research, and public libraries that included the works of ancient philosophers along with the Koran and the Traditions of the Prophet. Hindu works in the sciences, philosophy, astronomy, and literature were reportedly studied in schools and colleges.

Razia's Tomb

Today Razia's unpretentious tomb lies among the narrow lanes of Old Delhi in Northern India. Crumbling and covered by dust and grime, the tomb has clearly suffered the ravages of time. The grave is surrounded on all sides by unattractive residential buildings. Meanwhile modern-day encroachers have placed plastic sheets around the tomb and started to live in it, turning it into an urban ghetto. In the thirteenth century, the site of the tomb was a jungle, and no one knows how Razia's body ended up where it lies today. Though a second grave accompanies Razia's, the identity of the occupant is unknown. Some of the local residents have turned the tomb into a place of worship, where prayers are conducted five times each day. Razia refused to be addressed to as Sultana because it meant "wife of a sultan". She would only answer to the title "Sultan".

Jijabai

Jijabai was the mother of Shivaji, founder of the Maratha Empire. She was a daughter of Lakhuji Jadhav, a prominent grandee of Sindkhed in the present-day Buldhana district of Maharashtra State. As per the customs of that age, she was wed at an early age to Shahaji Bhosale, a nobleman and military commander under the Adil Shahi sultans of Bijapur in present-day Karnataka. She was his second wife. Jijabai was the mother of eight children, six daughters and two sons. Shivaji was the younger of her sons. Jijabai was well known for her chivalry and character.

On Mission

She wholeheartly supported her husband's cause. Shahaji had tried to establish maratha state on the ruin of the erstwhile Nizamshahi sultanate. However he was defeated by the combined forces of Mughals and Adilshahi. As per the treaty he was forced to move south. In order to continue the struggle, he deputed her as queen regent. She was chosen for this because of her ability as a warrior and administrator. This has been the tradition of Maratha women since time immemorial. At that time Shivaji was 14 years old and so accompanied his mother. The elder son Sambhaji remained with their father. Shivaji left Bangalore along with her mother, a council of ministers and chosen military commanders. Against this background, Shivaji took oath at the temple of lord Raireshwar. The rest of the story is well known. Her elder son Sambhaji was killed in a battle with Afzul Khan of the Adil Shahi court.

Shivaji killed Afzul Khan and took revenge. When Shahaji died Jijabai tried to committ suttee but Shivaji stopped her from doing so by request. Jijabai is widely credited with raising Shivaji in a manner that led to his future greatness. She gave a human touch to Shivaji's personality. His policy towards captured women reflects her influence. She died immediately after the coronation of Shivaji, fulfilling her mission. It is worth mentioning that apart from her, Rukmini (wife of Krishna), Damayanti (wife of Nala), Lopamudra (wife of sage agasti) were princesses from Bhoj Yadavas of Vidarbha. All four princesses are well known for their versite personality and character.

Rani Lakshmibai

Lakshmibai, The Rani of Jhansi (c. 1828 – 17 June 1858), the queen of the Maratha-ruled princely state of Jhansi in North India, was one of the leading figures of the Indian rebellion of 1857, and a symbol of resistance to British rule in India. She was born at Kashi and died at Gwalior. Her childhood name was Manikarnika. She is sometimes referred to as the Boudicca of India.

Lakshmi Bai was a Maharashtrian born sometime around 1828 at Kashi (presently known as Varanasi). An alternate date of 19 November 1835 was asserted by D. B. Parasnis in his biography of the Rani. However, no other credible historian agrees with this date and all the evidence points to 1828. The simplest and most direct evidence comes via John Lang. In his account of his meeting with the Rani in 1854 he mentions that her vakil said she was a woman of about 26 years. Her father Moropanth Tambey was a Karhade Brahmin and her mother Bhagirathibai was cultured, intelligent and religious. Born Manikarnika, she was affectionately called Manu in her family. Manu lost her mother at the age of four, and responsibility of looking after the young girl fell to her father. She completed her education and martial training, which included horse riding, fencing and shooting, when she was still a child.

She was married to Raja Gangadhar Rao Newalkar, the Maharaja of Jhansi in 1842, and became the queen of Jhansi. After their marriage, she was given the name Lakshmi Bai. The ceremony of the marriage was performed at the Ganesh

Mandir, the temple of Lord Ganesha situated in the old city of Jhansi. Rani Lakshmi Bai gave birth to a son in 1851, but this child died when he was about four months old. In 1853 Gangadhar Rao fell very ill and he was persuaded to adopt a child. To ensure that the British would not be able to contest the adoption, the Rani had it witnessed by the local British representatives. Maharaja Gangadhar Rao expired the following day, 21 November 1853.

Annexation

At that time, Lord Dalhousie was the Governor General of British India. Though little Damodar Rao, adopted son of late Maharaja Gangadhar Rao and Rani Lakshmi Bai, was Maharaja's heir and successor under Hindu tradition, the British rulers rejected Rani's claim that Damodar Rao was their legal heir. Lord Dalhousie decided to annex the state of Jhansi under the Doctrine of Lapse. The Rani then did the unprecedented: she sought the advice of a British lawyer, John Lang, and appealed her case in London. Although these petitions were well-argued, they were ultimately rejected. The British Indian authorities clearly sought to punish Rani for her presumptuous Behaviour. They confiscated the state jewels and deducted her husband's debts from her annual pension of Rs. 60,000. She was required to leave Jhansi fort for the Rani Mahal in Jhansi town, as well. But Rani Lakshmi Bai was determined to defend Jhansi. She proclaimed her decision with the famous words: Mi mahji Jhansi nahi dehnar (I will not give up my Jhansi).

The war

Jhansi became a centre of the rebellion upon the outbreak of violence in 1857. Rani Lakshmi Bai started strengthening the defence of Jhansi and assembled a volunteer army. Women were recruited as well as men and given military training. Rani was accompanied by her generals. Many from the local population volunteered for service in the army ranks, with the popular support for her cause on the rise. In September and October of 1857, the Rani led the successful defence of Jhansi from the invading armies of the neighbouring rajas of Datia and Orchha.

In January of 1858, the British Army started its advance on Jhansi, and in March laid siege to the city. After two weeks of fighting the British captured the city, but the Rani escaped in the guise of a man, strapping her adopted son Damodar Rao closely on her back. She fled to Kalpi where she joined Tatya Tope. During the battle for Gwalior the Rani met her death on 17 June. During this battle the Rani's original horse was mortally wounded. He had to be replaced by a younger, more energetic, but less trained horse.

The folklore surrounding her during the war is that during the battle the Rani was trying to escape and two British officers followed her. The horse reached a cliff and being insufficiently trained, could not pass over it. The British set upon her by surrounding her. As she was cornered, she knew there was only one option to take was to jump off which she did. A Brahmin, who found her, carefully took her into his ashram. She lay there unconscious for a moment then her last words were "Jai Hind!", meaning victory to India. In actual fact, most sources have the Rani being shot or run through with a saber and there is no mention of a cliff. It is also unlikely that the many princes who led the Mutiny were in any way more than peripherally concerned with the concept of a united India.

All were uniformly concerned with the loss of their personal powers and privileges, and at most, with regional issues. Indeed Laksmi Bai's main objective throughout the Mutiny seems to have been to secure the throne of Jhansi for her adopted son. For a considerable length of time after the start of the Mutiny, she was in correspondence with the British and professed to be on the British side, stating in her letters that she hoped in return that the East India Company would eventually restore all privileges to her son. There are also allegations that Lakshmi Bai did not do enough to prevent the massacre of the British garrison at Jhansi. It is probable that soldiers in her pay took part in the massacre.

The British captured Gwalior three days later. In his report of the battle for Gwalior, General Rose commented that the Rani had been "the bravest and the best" of the rebels. Because of her unprecedented bravery, courage and wisdom and her progressive views on women's empowerment in 19th century India, and due to her sacrifices, she became an icon of Indian nationalist movement.

Epilogue

The fall of Jhansi and the death of Rani Lakshmibai was the last series of the resistance to British Raj under the Sepoy Mutiny. Its immediate effects included:

* Due to her bravery, she became a national hero and the epitome of female bravery in India. When the Indian National Army, formed by Subhash C. Bose of Indian prisoners of war to fight the British created its first female unit, it was named after her.
* Her father, Moropant Tambe, was captured and hanged a few days after the fall of Jhansi.
* Her adopted son, Damodar Rao, was given a pension by the British Raj, although he never received his inheritance.
* The administration of an undivided India passed on from the East India Company to the British crown.
* The Rani was memorialized in bronze statues at both Jhansi and Gwalior, both of which portray her in equestrian style.

Chandramukhi Basu

Chandramukhi Basu, who was a Bengali speaking Christian from Dehradun, which was located in the (then known as) United Provinces of Agra and Oudh, was one of the first two female graduates of the British Empire. Along with Kadambini Ganguly, she received her Bachelor's degree in Arts from the Bethune College, an affiliate college of the University of Calcutta, India in 1883.

Early Life

The daughter of Bhuban Mohan Bose, she passed the First Arts examination from Dehradun Native Christian School in 1880. Till then Bethune School did not admit non-Hindu girls. The rule was relaxed and she was admitted for the degree course, along with Kadambini Ganguly. After her graduation, she was the only and first woman to pass MA from Calcutta University in 1884.

Career

She started her career as a lecturer in Bethune College (it

was still part of Bethune School) in 1886. The college was separated from the school in 1888. She became the principal, thus becoming the first female head of an undergraduate academic establishment in South Asia. She retired in 1891 because of bad health and spent the rest of her life in Dehradun.

Sisters

Two of her sisters, Bidhumukhi and Bindubasini, were also renowned. Bidhumukhi Bose and Virginia Mary Mitra (Nandi) were the first two woman medical graduates from Calcutta Medical College. They passed out in 1890. Thereafter, Bindubasini Bose passed out from Calcutta Medical College in 1891.

Kadambini Ganguly

Kadambini Ganguly (1861 – 3 October 1923) was one of the first female graduates of the British Empire and the first female physician of South Asia to be trained in European medicine.

Early Life

The daughter of Brahmo reformer Braja Kishore Basu, she was born at Bhagalpur, Bihar in British India. The family was from Chandsi, in Barisal which is now in Bangladesh. Her father was headmaster of Bhagalpur School. He and Abhay Charan Mallick started the movement for women's emancipation at Bhagalpur, establishing the women's organisation Bhagalpur Mahila Samiti in 1863, the first in India. Kadambini started her education at Banga Mahila Vidyalaya and while at Bethune School (established by Bethune) in 1878 became the first woman to pass the University of Calcutta entrance examination. It was partly in recognition of her efforts that Bethune College first introduced FA (First Arts), and then graduation courses in 1883. She and Chandramukhi Basu became the first graduates from Bethune College, and in the process became the first female graduates in the country and in the entire British Empire.

Medical Education and Profession

Ganguly studied medicine at the Calcutta Medical College. In 1886, she was awarded a GBMC (Graduate of Bengal Medical

College) degree, which gave her the right to practise. She thus became the first Indian woman doctor qualified to practice western medicine. Abala Bose passed entrance in 1881 but was refused admission to the medical college and went to Madras (now Chennai) to study medicine but never graduated. Kadambini overcame some opposition from the teaching staff, and orthodox sections of society. She went to the United Kingdom in 1892 and returned to India after qualifying as LRCP (Edinburgh), LRCS (Glasgow), and GFPS (Dublin). After working for a short period in Lady Dufferin Hospital, she started her own private practice.

Social Activities

In 1883 she married the Brahmo reformer and leader of women's emancipation Dwarka Nath Ganguly. They were actively involved in female emancipation and social movements to improve work conditions of female coal miners in eastern India. She was one of the six female delegates to the fifth session of the Indian National Congress in 1889, and even organized the Women's Conference in Calcutta in 1906 in the aftermath of the partition of Bengal.

In 1908, she had also organized and presided over a Calcutta meeting for expressing sympathy with Satyagraha-inspired Indian labourers in Transvaal, South Africa. She formed an association to collect money with the help of fundraisers to assist the workers. In 1914 she presided over the meeting of the Sadharan Brahmo Samaj, which was held in Calcutta to honour Mahatma Gandhi during his Calcutta visit.

As the mother of eight children she had to devote considerable time to her household affairs. She was deft in needlework. The noted American historian David Kopf has written, "Ganguli's wife, Kadambini, was appropriately enough the most accomplished and liberated Brahmo woman of her time.

From all accounts, their relationship was most unusual in being founded on mutual love, sensitivity and intelligence... Mrs. Ganguli's case was hardly typical even among the more emancipated Brahmo and Christian women in contemporary Bengali society. Her ability to rise above circumstances and to realize her potential as a human being made her a prize attraction to Sadharan Brahmos dedicated ideologically to the liberation of Bengal's women."

Anandi Gopal Joshi

Anandi Gopal Joshi (or Anandibai) (March 31, 1865-February 26, 1887) was the first Indian woman to obtain a medical degree in the Western hemisphere. She was one of the first Indian women to be trained in Western system of medicine. Many sources claim that she was the first India's first woman doctor. A fictionalized account of her life has been depicted in the novel "Anandi Gopal", written by SJ Joshi.

Early Life

Joshi was born as Yamuna Joshi (Yamunabai) at Thane near Mumbai, in an orthodox wealthy Brahmin family. She suffered from pockmarks. Aged 9, she was married to a postal clerk, Gopalrao Joshi. Gopalrao, also a Brahmin, was a widower and almost twenty years her senior. After the marriage, Yamuna was renamed as Anandi, according to Maharashtrian traditions. Gopalrao worked as a postal clerk in Kalyan. Later, he was transferred to Alibag, and finally to Calcutta (now Kolkata). He was a progressive thinker, and supported the education of women-then not very prevalent in India. It was common for Brahmins to learn Sanskrit, but Lokhitawadi's Shat Patre had convinced Gopalrao that Sanskrit was no longer of much use. He considered English to be more important. He noticed his wife's interest in learning and helped her to learn English. At the age of 14, Joshi gave birth to a boy. The child survived only for ten days, owing to the paucity of medical care available. This incident was a turning point in Joshi's life and inspired her to become a doctor.

Towards a Medical Career

Gopalrao encouraged his wife to study medicine. In 1880, he sent a letter to Royal Wilder, a well-known American missionary, expressing Anandi's interest in studying medicine in the United States, and inquiring about a suitable post there for himself. Wilder offered to help if the couple converted to Christianity. This was not acceptable to the Joshis. Wilder published the correspondence in his publication, Princeton's Missionary Review. It was read by Theodicia E. Carpenter, a resident of Roselle, New Jersey, while waiting to see her dentist. She was impressed by Joshi's desire to learn medicine, and by Gopalrao's support for his wife. She wrote to them, offering accommodation to Joshi in America. This began a series of letters between Joshi and Carpenter, in which they discussed Hindu culture and religion, among other things.

While Gopalrao and Joshi were in Calcutta, Joshi's general health was declining. She suffered from weakness, constant headaches, occasional fever, and sometimes breathlessness. Carpenter sent her medicines from America, without results. In 1883, Gopalrao was transferred to Serampore. It was here that he decided to send Joshi to America alone. Joshi was apprehensive, but Gopalrao convinced her by saying that she should set an example for other women. A Dr. Thorborn and his wife, who was also a doctor, suggested Joshi apply to the Woman's Medical College of Pennsylvania. When Joshi's decision became known, she was rejected by Hindu society. She was spat at in public and had stones thrown at her. Many Christians supported her decision, but they wanted her to convert to Christianity.

Eventually, Joshi addressed the community at Serampore College Hall, explaining her decision to go to America and obtain a medical degree. She discussed the persecution she and her husband had endured. She stressed the need for Hindu female doctors in India, and talked about her goal of opening a medical college for women in India. She also pledged that she would not convert from Hinduism. After her speech was published, financial contributions started coming in from all over India. The Viceroy of India contributed 200 rupees towards funds for her education. However, the money was not enough, and Joshi had to sell her gold bangles to fund her travel and education.

In America

Joshi travelled to New York from Calcutta by ship, chaperoned by two English female acquaintances of Dr. Thorborn. In New York, Carpenter received her in June 1883. Joshi wrote to the Women's Medical College of Pennsylvania, asking to be admitted to their medical program, which was the first women's medical program in the world. Rachel L. Bodley, the dean of the college, enrolled her. Joshi began her medical education at the age of 19. In America, her already declining health was worsened by the cold weather and unfamiliar diet. She contracted tuberculosis. Her friends sent her to Colorado Springs for her health, but it failed to improve her condition. She submitted a thesis on "Obstetrics among the Aryan Hindoos". When she graduated with an M.D. on March 11, 1886, Queen Victoria sent a congratulatory message.

Return to India

Joshi's husband and her friends advised her to settle in the United States, but she insisted on returning to India. Before she returned to India, the princely state of Kolhapur, appointed her the Physician-in-charge of the female ward of the Albert Edward Hospital. On October 9, 1886, she sailed from New York. She returned to India, and was met with a hero's welcome. The newspapers closely monitored her health. Joshi died in Poona at any early age of 22, in her mother's arms. Her death was mourned throughout India. Her ashes were sent to Carpenter, who placed them in her family cemetery in Poughkeepsie, New York. A fictionalized account of her experiences was depicted in the Marathi novel Anandi Gopal, written by Shrikrishna Janardan Joshi.

Bhikaiji Cama

Bhikaiji Rustom Cama (Madam Cama, Madame Cama) (September 24, 1861-August 13, 1936) was a prominent figure in the Indian Nationalist Movement. Bhikaiji Rustom Cama was born Bhikai Sorab Patel on 24th September, 1861 in Bombay (now Mumbai) into a large, well-off Parsi family. Her parents, Sorabji and Jaijibai Patel, were well-known in the city, where her father Sorabji Framji Patel-a lawyer by training and a merchant by profession-was an influential member of the Parsi community. The father doted on his little girl, and affectionately called her "Munni".

Like many Parsi girls of the time, Bhikaiji attended Alexandra Native Girl's English Institution. Bhikaiji was by all accounts a diligent, disciplined child, with a flair for languages and an interest in the personalities of the nationalist movement(s). On August 3, 1885, she married Rustom Cama, a wealthy, pro-British lawyer with a desire to enter politics.

It was not a happy marriage, and Bhikaiji spent most of her time and energy in philanthropic activities and social work.

In October 1896, the Bombay Presidency was first hit by famine, and shortly thereafter by bubonic plague. Bhikaiji joined one of the many teams working out of Grant Medical College (which would subsequently become Haffkine's plague vaccine research centre), in an effort to provide care for the afflicted, and (later) to inoculate the healthy. She contracted the plague herself, but survived. Severely weakened, she set sail for Europe for subsequent medical care and recuperation in 1902. In London, she received word that her return to India would be prevented unless she sign a statement promising not to participate in nationalist activities. She refused, and remained in exile in Europe until shortly before her death (at Parsi General Hospital in Bombay) in 1936. While in London, she served as private secretary to Dadabhai Naoroji, the first Asian to be elected to the British House of Commons, and the first to publicly demand independence from Great Britain.

In Paris she came in contact with other notable members of the movement for Indian sovereignty, and would come to clandestinely (in Holland) publish and distribute revolutionary literature for the movement. While in France, the British Government requested her extradition, but the French Government refused to cooperate. In return, the British Government seized Cama's inheritance. Lenin reportedly invited her to reside in Russia, but she did not accept. Influenced by Christabel Pankhurst and the Suffragette movement, Bhikaiji Cama was vehement in her support for gender equality. Speaking in Cairo, Egypt in 1910, she asked, "I see here the representatives of only half the population of Egypt. May I ask where is the other half? Sons of Egypt, where are the daughters of Egypt? Where are your mothers and sisters? Your wives and daughters?"

Bhikaiji Cama is best known for having unfurled a "Flag of Indian Independence" on August 22, 1907, at the International Socialist Conference in Stuttgart, Germany. That flag, a slight modification of the Calcutta Flag, was co-designed by Cama, Veer Savarkar and Shyamji Krishna Varma, and would later serve as a template upon which the current national flag of India is based. At the conference, she described the devastating effects of a famine that had struck the subcontinent, and made an appeal for human rights, equality and for Indian independence: "This flag is of India's independence. Behold, it is born. It is already sanctified by the blood of martyred Indian youth. I call upon you, gentlemen, to rise and salute the flag of Indian independence. In the name of this flag I appeal to lovers of freedom all over the world to cooperate with this flag in freeing one-fifth of the human race".

One nationalist legend involving Bhikaiji Cama goes like this:

> *Veer Savarkar was in custody (aboard the "Morena") for his nationalist stance. As the story goes, Savarkar evaded his captors and jumped overboard in an attempt to escape. Cama saw him go overboard, but misunderstood it to be an accident. She jumped in after him (to save him as she thought), and attracted enough attention to result in Savarkar's recapture.*

Another variation of the story (possibly true), goes like this: Veer Savarkar had been arrested in London for nationalist activities and was on his way back to India for trial. Aboard the "Morena" in Marseilles Harbour, he wiggled out of a porthole window and jumped into the sea. Reaching shore, he expected to find Cama and others waiting for him (who got there late), but ran into the local constabulary instead. Unable to communicate his predicament to the French authorities without Cama's help, he was returned to British custody. Several Indian cities have streets and places named after Bhikaiji Cama. On January 26th 1962, the Indian Posts and Telegraphs Department issued a stamp in her honour. The Indian Coast Guard has a ship named after her.

Sucheta Kriplani

Sucheta Kriplani (born Sucheta Mazumdar) (1908-1974) was an Indian freedom fighter and politician. She became the first woman to be elected Chief Minister of a state.

Early Life

She was born in Ambala, Haryana to a Bengali family. Her father, S.N. Majumdar though a government doctor was a nationalist. Educated at Indraprastha College and St.Stephen's

College, Delhi she became a lecturer at the Banaras Hindu University. In 1936, she married socialist, Acharya Kriplani and became involved with the Indian National Congress.

Freedom Movement and Independence

Like her contemporaries Aruna Asaf Ali and Usha Mehta, she came to the forefront during the Quit India Movement. She later worked closely with Mahatma Gandhi during the Partition riots. She accompanied him to Noakhali in 1946. She was one of the few women who were elected to the Constituent Assembly and was part of the subcommittee that drafted the Indian Constitution. On 15th August, 1947 she sang Vande Mataram in the Independence Session of the Constituent Assembly.

Post Independence

After independence she remained involved with politics in U.P. She was elected to the Lok Sabha in 1952 and 1957 and served as a Minister of State for Small Scale Industries. In 1962, she was elected to the U.P Assembly from Kanpur and served in the Cabinet in 1962. In 1963, she became the Chief Minister of Uttar Pradesh, the first woman to hold that position in any Indian state. The highlight of her tenure was the firm handling of a state employees strike. The first-ever strike by the state employees which continued for 62 days took place during her regime. She relented only when the employees' leaders agreed for compromise. Although the wife of a socialist, Kriplani cemented her reputation as a firm administrator by refusing their demand for pay hike. She retired from politics in 1971 and remained in seclusion till her death in 1974.

Pritilata Waddedar

Pritilata Waddedar was an anti-British pro-India revolutionary in East Bengal, (then part of Province of Bengal in pre-independence India), now in Bangladesh. Born in Chittagong in 1911, she was a meritorious student at the Dr. Khastagir Government Girls' School of Chittagong and passed the matriculation examination in the first division in 1927. She continued her education in Eden College, Dhaka and in 1929, she passed the Intermediate examinations securing the first place among all the candidates from Dhaka Board. Two years later, Pritilata graduated in Philosophy with distinction from

Bethune College of Kolkata. In early 1930s, Pritilata joined Mastarda Surya Sen's armed resistance movement.

In 1932, Surya Sen planned an attack on the Pahartali European Club, which bore the notorious sign 'Dogs and Indians not allowed'. He assigned Pritilata to lead a team that would attack the Club on September 23, 1932. Members of the team were instructed to carry potassium cyanide with them so that in case they were caught by police they could swallow it before the arrest. The raid was successful but Pritilata, dressed as a man was trapped without a way of escape on that fateful night. She committed suicide by swallowing the cyanide, thus ending her short endeavour in fighting for freedom of her country.

Vijaya Lakshmi Pandit

Vijaya Lakshmi Nehru Pandit (1900-1990) was an Indian diplomat and politician, sister of Indian Prime Minister Jawaharlal Nehru, and the first female President of the United Nations General Assembly. In 1921 she married Ranjit Sitaram Pandit. She was the first Indian woman to hold a cabinet post. In 1937 she was elected to the provincial legislature of the United Provinces and designated minister of local self-government and public health. She held the latter post until 1939 and again from 1946 to 1947. In 1946, she was elected to the Constituent Assembly from the United Provinces.

Following India's independence from the British in 1947, she entered the diplomatic service and became India's ambassador to several different countries: the Soviet Union from 1947 to 1949, the United States and Mexico from 1949 to 1951, Ireland from 1955 to 1961 (during which time she was also the Indian High Commissioner to the United Kingdom), and Spain from 1958 to 1961. Between 1946 and 1968 she also headed the Indian delegation to the United Nations. In India, she served as governor of Maharashtra from 1962 until 1964, after which she was elected to the Indian Lok Sabha from Phulpur, her brother's former constituency. She held office from 1964 to 1968. Pandit was a harsh critic of her niece, Indira Gandhi, after Gandhi became Prime Minister in 1966, and she retired from active politics after relations soured between them. Upon retiring, she moved to Dehradun in the Doon Valley in the Himalayan foothills.

In 1979 she was appointed the Indian representative to the UN Human Rights Commission, after which she retired from public life. Her writings include The Evolution of India (1958) and The Scope of Happiness: A Personal Memoir (1979). Her daughter Nayantara Sahgal, who later settled in her mother's house in Dehradun, is a well-known novelist.

Rajkumari Amrit Kaur

Rajkumari Amrit Kaur (2nd February 1889, Lucknow – 2nd October 1964) was the first female Indian Cabinet Minister. She was born into the princely family of Kapurthala of undivided India and became an eminent Gandhian, social activist and freedom fighter. Lakshmi N. Menon had described her, as "the master craft of Gandhi is conspicuously visible in the case of Amrit Kaur who gave up her princely ways and habits in favour of service for the nation." For many years she remained close to the select group of leaders fighting for the freedom of India, and after India's independence she became the health minister of India. She also remained active in many social activities.

Early Life

Rajkumari Amrit Kaur was born on 2nd February 1889 in Lucknow (Uttar Pradesh, India), and belonged to a princely family. She was the only daughter of her parents, Raja Harnam Singh and Rani Harnam Singh. Her mother was a Bengali Presbyterian Christian. She had seven brothers, and the environment in her home was generally strict and disciplined one. Rajkumari inherited Christianity as her religion, and her early education was in England in a school at Sherborne, Dorsetshire, and later studies at the Oxford. She was also a good player of tennis and won several prizes. With her family and educational background, she could have led a life of affluence and luxury. However, when she returned to India, She got attracted towards the freedom movement and became a social worker. Her father Raja Sir Harnam Singh was reputed as a "pious and pure" Christian. Harman Singh was the last ruling prince of Kapurthala in the Punjab region, and enjoyed the goodwill and confidence of many leaders of the Indian National Congress party, including Gopal Krishna Gokhale, one of the most prominent leaders of his time. Many other political leaders also visited the Raja, and Amrit Kaur became interested in the freedom struggle and learnt about the activities of the freedom fighters and about Mahatma Gandhi. She saw Mahatma Gandhi for the first time in Bombay (now called Mumbai), and was immensely influenced by his words.

The Jallianwala Bagh Massacre of 1919 resulted into killing of unarmed civilians by the troops of the British Raj, and this incidence convinced her about necessity for India to become a free nation. Although her parents were against her joining Mahatma Gandhi at his ashram due to a life of austerities there, she remained convinced to be part of the struggle for the freedom of India. She started spinning khadi, and participated in social work in Jallandhar and later among the Harijans of Simla. Inspired by Mahatma Gandhi, she joined the Indian National Congress party, and became socially and politically active. She participated in a number of movements initiated by Mahatma Gandhi for the freedom of India, including a 240 mile march led by Gandhi in March 1930, known as the Dandi march. During the march, Rajkumari was arrested and imprisoned by the authorities of the British Raj.

As a Gandhian

After her father's death, she left her home and came to live in Mahatma Gandhi's ashram in 1934. She started wearing clothes made of khadi, and became an active disciple of Mahatma Gandhi. Sometime, visitors from Europe and the USA would be amazed to learn an Indian princesses living in the ashram in an environment of austerities. She was assigned the role of Mahatma Gandhi's English language secretary, and it was a challenging assignment. Mahatma Gandhi received and enormous quantity of mails, and he himself used to write more than 160 notes in own hands, and his other secretaries (namely, Mahadev Desai and Pyarelal) handled thousands of mails every week. Beside these, the secretaries were also required to manage innumerable editorials, essays, and public statements. Generally Mahatma Gandhi was tender to her in the early days, but was a strict disciplinarian.

She once recalled that she delivered a note written by Mahatma Gandhi to a wrong person, and this made the Mahatma very unhappy. However, at the same time Mahatma

Gandhi used to care for all the people around her, and on her birthday she received a hand written note from Mahatma Gandhi which read: "an ideal secretary keeps her chief straight when he is going astray. She hovers over him, watches all movements about him... picks up his papers, even those torn... lest he might have torn something important, by mistake. She leaves after him and seeks what he left behind... and if not owned by anyone else, collects it. Follow the spirit of this note and you will be the ideal secretary. This is my birthday present, which goes loaded with all the good wishes that I am capable of conveying... Love, Bapu." She continued to serve Mahatma Gandhi as one of his secretaries for sixteen years.

As a representative of the Indian National Congress, she was sent on a mission of goodwill to Bannu, Northwest Frontier Province. The British government of the Raj arrested her, charging her with sedition, and she was convicted and imprisoned on 16th July 1937. In 1942, she again became active in the Quit India Movement; led many protest rallies, and in one of such rallies in Kalka (Punjab) suffered injuries when the troops charged the protesters. She was arrested and imprisoned again. She was a co-founder of the All India Women's Conference in 1927, and became its secretary in 1930. During 1931-33 she served as the president of the Women's Association. She also championed the cause of universal suffrage, and espoused and testified before the Lothian Committee on Indian franchise and constitutional reforms, and before the Joint Select Committee of Parliament on Indian constitutional reforms.

In 1938 she was elected as the president of All India Women's Conference. She had also served as the Chairperson of the All India Women's Education Fund Association and as a member of the Executive Committee of Lady Irwin College, New Delhi. She was an appointed as a member (the first women to be so appointed) by the British Raj to the Advisory Board of Education, a position which she resigned in the wake of the Quit India Movement. She was sent as a member of the Indian delegation to participate in UNESCO's conferences in London (1945), and in Paris (1946). She also served as a member of the Board of Trustees of the All India Spinners' Association.

She was committed to Mahatma Gandhi's objective of making India a free nation, and at the same time continued to be active in elimination of several bad practices of the Indian society, and such practices included early or child marriage, system of purdah both among the Muslim and Hindu women, illiteracy.

She articulated her views on these issues in these words: "the abolition of earl marriage and purdah, therefore, will not only improve the health of millions of women but will remove two of the main obstacles in the way of the spread of female education. Needless to say that the position of the widows in Hindu homes, marriage laws and the laws relating to the inheritance of property by women need radical alteration."

She also actively espoused the cause of female education, and believed in reforms in the education of Indian women. In one of the women's conferences, she had presented her views as follows: "in the realm of educational reform, we have urged ever since our inception that there should be free and compulsory education. Again, as far as proper facilities for the female education are concerned until such time as universal, free and compulsory primary education as well as an adequate supply of infant and girl's schools equipped with trained women teachers are introduced, we must continue to do our utmost to have the system of education in our exiting institutions changed."

Post-independence

After India's independence, Amrit Kaur became part of Jawaharlal Nehru's first Cabinet; she was the first woman to hold Cabinet rank. She was assigned the Ministry of Health, and was the only Indian Christian in the Cabinet. She was also elected the president of World Health Assembly in 1950, a position held by only two women in the first 25 years of the WHO's history. She was also the moving force behind the conceptualization and building of the All India Institute of Medical Sciences in New Delhi, and for establishing this institute she secured aid from New Zealand, funds form the West Germany for books, equipments form the Sweden, and assistance for a rehabilitation centre from the Vocational Rehabilitation Centre of US to establish a rehabilitation centre. She also secured aid from the Rockefeller Foundation and Punjab Government for the medical Community Block.

She and her brother even donated their ancestral property and house named Manorville (Simla, Himachal Pradesh, India) to serve as a holiday home for the staff and nurses of the institute. She functioned as the Chairperson of the Indian Red Cross society for fourteen years, and during her leadership, the Indian Red Cross did a number of pioneering works in the tribal belts and hinterland of India. She continued to be the Health Minister of India until 1957, after which she retired from ministerial activity but remained a member of the Rajya Sabha until her death on 2nd October, 1964. However, until her death, she continued to hold charge of the Presidentship of the All India Institute of Medical Sciences, and the Tuberculosis Association and the Chairperson of the Indian Red Cross and St. John's Ambulance Corps. Rajkumari Amrit Kaur remained a spinster all her life.

Quotes

About Harijans: "It is a crying shame that the people who cater for our services are relegated in most towns to live in the most abominable dwellings—if, indeed we can call their hovels by this name."

About Child Marriage: "Child marriage is eating as a canker into the vitality of our national life. Girls become mothers while they are children themselves, and bring into the world off—springs, who are, in the very nature of things, the victims of disease and ill health."

Sarojini Naidu

Sarojini Naidu (February 13, 1879-March 2, 1949), known as Bharatiya Kokila (The Nightingale of India), was a child prodigy, freedom fighter, and poet. Naidu was the first Indian woman to become the President of the Indian National Congress and the first woman to become the governor of a state in India.

Early Life and Family

Sarojini Chattopadhyaya was born in Hyderabad, India as the eldest daughter of scientist-philosopher, Aghornath Chattopadhyaya, and Varada Sundari Devi, a poetess. Her father was the founder of the Nizam College. She learnt to speak Urdu, Telugu, English, Persian and Bengali. Her favourite poet was P.B. Shelley. She attained national fame for entering

Madras University at the age of twelve. At sixteen, she travelled to England to study first at King's College London, and Girton College, Cambridge.

At the age of 17, she met Dr. Muthyala Govindarajulu Naidu and fell in love with him. He was from South India. After finishing her studies at the age of 19, she married him during the time when inter-caste marriages were not allowed. Her marriage was a very happy one. They were married by the Brahmo Marriage Act (1872), in Madras in 1898. They had 4 children: Jayasurya, Padmaja, Randheer, and Leelamani.

In the Freedom Struggle

She joined the Indian independence movement, in the wake of the aftermath of partition of Bengal in 1905. During 1903-17 Sarojini came into contact with Gopal Krishna Gokhale, Rabindranath Tagore, Muhammad Ali Jinnah, Annie Besant, C. P. Ramaswami Iyer, Mohandas Gandhi and Jawaharlal Nehru. From 1915 to 1918 she lectured all over India on welfare of youth, dignity of labour, women's emancipation and nationalism. After meeting Jawaharlal Nehru in 1916, she took up the cause of the indigo workers of Champaran. In 1925 she was elected as the President of the Congress, the first Indian woman to hold the post.

In March 1919, the Britain | British government passed the Rowlatt Act by which the possession of seditious documents was deemed illegal. Mohandas Gandhi organized the Non-Cooperation Movement to protest and Naidu was the first to join the movement which the government worked to suppress. In July 1919, Naidu became the Home Rule League's ambassador to England. In July 1920 she returned to India and on August 1, Mahatma Gandhi declared the Non-Cooperation Movement. In January 1924, she was one of the two Indian National Congress delegates at the East African Indian Congress.

Naidu arrived in New York in October 1928 and was concerned with the unjust treatment of the African Americans and the Amerindians. Upon her return to India she became a member of Congress Working Committee. On January 26, 1930 the National Congress proclaimed its independence from the British Empire. On May 5, Mohandas Gandhi was arrested.

Naidu was arrested shortly thereafter and was in jail for several months. She, along with Gandhi, was released on January 31, 1931. Later that year, they were again arrested.

Naidu was eventually released due to her poor health and Gandhi was released in 1933. In 1931, she participated in the Round Table Summit, along with Gandhiji and Pundit Malaviyaji. In 1942, she was arrested during the "Quit India" protest and stayed in jail for 21 months with Gandhiji. Naidu shared a warm relationship with Mohandas Gandhi, even calling him "Mickey Mouse". At the Asian Relations Conference of March 1947, Naidu presided over the Steering Committee. On August 15, 1947, with the independence of India, Naidu became the Governor of Uttar Pradesh, India's first woman governor and she died in office in 1949.

Poetry, Writings and Quotes

In 1905, the first volume of her collection of poems was published as The Golden Threshold. Two more volumes were published: The Bird of Time (1912) and The Broken Wing in (1917). Sarojini Naidu is also well acclaimed for her contribution to poetry. Her poetry had beautiful words that could also be sung. Her collection of poems was published in 1905 under the title "Golden Threshold". She published two other collections called "The Bird of Time", and "The Broken Wings". Later, "The Magic Tree", "The Wizard Mask", and "A Treasury of Poems" were published.

Naidu writes:

Shall hope prevail where clamorous hate is rife,

Shall sweet love prosper or high dreams have place

Amid the tumult of reverberant strife

'Twixt ancient creeds, 'twixt race and ancient race,

That mars the grave, glad purposes of life,

Leaving no refuge save thy succoring face ?

Naidu said, "When there is oppression, the only self-respecting thing is to rise and say this shall cease today, because my right is justice." Naidu adds, "If you are stronger, you have to help the weaker boy or girl both in play and in the work." In 1916, Naidu published the first biography of

Muhammad Ali Jinnah, The Ambassador of Hindu-Muslim Unity.

Kiran Bedi

Kiran Bedi is an Indian police officer and is the first woman to join the Indian Police Service (IPS) in 1972. She was born on 9th June 1949 in Amritsar, Punjab state, India, and is one of the most celebrated and widely known police officers who ever served the Indian Police Force.

Kiran Bedi is the second of the four daughters of her parents, Prakash Lal Peshawaria and Prem Lata Peshawaria. She has been recently appointed as Director General of India's Bureau of Police Research and Development. Earlier, she was Police Advisor in the United Nations peacekeeping department, and has also been honoured with the UN medal for outstanding service. In May 2005, she was awarded an honorary degree of Doctor of Law In recognition of her "humanitarian approach to prison reforms and policing".

Education

She completed her schooling from the Sacred Heart Convent School, Amritsar, and obtained her B.A. degree (1964-68) in English from the Government College for Women, Amritsar. She then earned a Master's degree (1968-70) in Political Science from Punjab University, Chandigarh. Even while in active service in the Indian Police, She continued her educational pursuits, and obtained a Law degree (LLB) in 1988 from Delhi University, Delhi. She was also awarded a Ph.D. in 1993 in Social Sciences by the Department of Social Sciences, the Indian Institute of Technology, New Delhi. The topic of her thesis was Drug Abuse and Domestic Violence. Kiran Bedi is also a former all-India and all-Asian tennis champion, and had won the Asian Ladies Title at the age of 22.

Contributions

She began her career as a Lecturer in Political Science (1970-72) at Khalsa College for Women, Amritsar, India. In the year 1972, she was selected for the Indian Police Service. On her web site, she states that she joined the police service "because of my urge to be OUTSTANDING". She served in a number of tough assignments ranging from Traffic

Commissioner of New Delhi, Deputy Inspector General of Police in insurgency prone Mizoram, Advisor to the Lieutanent Governor of Chandigarh, Director General of Narcotics Control Bureau and also on a United Nationsdeputation. She is popularly referred to as Crane Bedi for towing the Prime Minister Indira Gandhi car for parking violation. (the PM was on tour of United States then)

Kiran Bedi influenced several decisions of the Indian Police Service, particularly in the areas of control over narcotics, traffic management, and VIP security. During her stint as the Inspector General of Prisons, Tihar Jail (Delhi), she instituted a number of reforms in the management the prison, and initiated a number of measures such as detoxification programs, yoga, vipassana meditation, and redressing of complaints by prisoners. Navajyoti (which literally means New Enlightenment), set up in 1988, and India Vision Foundation, set up in 1994, are the two major voluntary organizations established by her with the objectives of improving the condition of the drug addicts and the poor people.

Her efforts have won national and international recognition, and her organizations was awarded the Serge Soitiroff Memorial Award for drug abuse prevention by the United Nations.

Awards

Kiran Bedi has received a number of Awards, including the following:

* President's Gallantry Award (1979)
* Women of the Year Award (1980)
* Asia Region Award for Drug Prevention and Control (1991)
* Magsaysay Award (1994) for Government Service
* Mahila Shiromani Award (1995)
* Father Machismo Humanitarian Award (1995)
* Lion of the Year (1995)
* Joseph Beuys Award (1997)
* Pride of India (1999)
* Mother Teresa Memorial National Award for Social Justice (2005).

WOMEN IN PANCHAYATI RAJ

At the start of the new millennium, there are really two Indias. Together they comprise one-sixth of all humanity. The first India-the modern India-has a remarkable record of accomplishment. Since independence in 1947, India has taken its place as a power on the global stage. It is the world's largest democracy and the 10th largest industrial power, with solid and consistent economic growth. It has the largest middle class of any nation, with the third largest scientific and technical workforce. Indian engineers hold top jobs in computer corporations on every continent. In agriculture, India is the number one producer in sugar, groundnuts (peanuts), tea and fruit. It is the number two producer in rice, wheat, vegetables and milk.

India's diverse and ancient religious traditions, its languages and its arts, are all part of its greatness. No nation has contributed more spiritual richness and truth to humanity. The list of winners of the major international prizes in literature, including the Nobel, Booker and Pulitzer Prizes, is filled with Indian writers and poets. The second, and much larger, India is an entirely different world. Of the one billion people living in India today, 720 million-nearly three-quarters-live in rural areas characterised by grinding poverty and social injustice. This India has been bypassed by progress and opportunity.

At the dawn of the twenty-first century, most rural Indians live with the technology of a thousand years ago. In the age of the Internet, the majority cannot read and few have ever seen a computer. Living and voting in a democracy with constitutional guarantees, they remain powerless, locked in an oppressive system of economic exploitation, class division, caste prejudice and pervasive corruption. While the economy of modern India grows, the people lack access to education, nutrition and health care, sanitation, land and other assets that could enable them to escape the trap of poverty. Rural India has an infant mortality rate of 85, compared with 53 in the cities-and a life expectancy of only 54 years, compared with 63 in urban areas. There is a truth that many would like to ignore: India's future will be determined in this "second India". Concern for the people of the second India is not merely humanitarian. Modern India has chosen to join the emerging global, information-based economy. To thrive in that economy, it must enter as one nation, with broadly based participation, productivity and prosperity. It cannot survive with rafts of wealth floating in a sea of poverty, and with the instability that comes with that condition. The nations that prosper in the global economy are those with a healthy and educated workforce, stable population growth and relative freedom from corruption and conflict.

India's recent history demonstrates that action from the top alone cannot meet the challenge. It will take the creativity, resources and participation of the entire population, many of whom have never before had a meaningful role or voice. For India, this means a two-fold revolution: the creation and nurturing of genuine participatory local democracy, and a profound transformation in the status and leadership of women.

In the critical areas for the well-being of the nation, women are on the "front lines". The future of rural India depends on overcoming enormous challenges in health, education, nutrition, population and environment.

Women bear primary responsibility in every one of these areas-day after day after day. It is women who know best what needs to be done, and it is women who are most committed to taking those actions. Yet, for thousands of years, India's rural women have been systematically denied the freedom, resources, information and decision-making power they need to carry out these responsibilities. In India, women have been kept in an almost unimaginable state of powerlessness, illiteracy, isolation and malnutrition.

India today faces an historic opportunity. As local democracy and expanded opportunity flourish around the world, India must not be left behind. The first step has been taken with the unprecedented 73rd amendment to India's constitution. This amendment mandates the transfer of decision-making power and resources in the rural areas to local democratic councils known as panchayats. Most revolutionary of all, one-third of all panchayat seats are to be reserved for women-guaranteeing them a role in determining the future of their communities. If fully implemented, women will, for the first time in India's history, have a voice in the decisions that affect their lives.

The struggle has only begun. Passage of the constitutional amendment on paper does not guarantee implementation in practice. Deeply entrenched interests oppose local democracy and women's rights, and are working to undermine this process directly and indirectly. There is a prevailing public cynicism regarding the possibility of grass-roots women's leadership. Removing these obstacles requires a social transformation of unprecedented proportions, demanding a concerted campaign lasting many years. The first generation of women panchayat leaders will need to possess enormous courage. Those supporting them will require great endurance.

The most strategic action that can be taken for India's future is to strengthen the hand of women panchayat leaders. The strategies and actions required to accomplish this are being shaped even now by an emerging network of committed individuals and organisations at all levels of society. The transfer of power to one million women elected local representatives-many of whom are malnourished and illiterate-is the greatest social experiment of our time. These women are struggling against enormous odds to improve the lives of their families, their villages and their nation. They are the key change agents for a new future for India. By ensuring that they gain access to the resources and information they need-and by allowing their voices to be heard-India can finally become one nation. In doing so, it will fulfil its destiny and reveal its true greatness.

EMPOWERING WOMEN

The last five decades have witnessed some basic changes in the status and role of women in our society. Today this process has been further accelerated with some women becoming increasingly self-conscious of their discrimination in several areas of the family and public life. They are also in a position to mobilise themselves on issues which affect them vitally, and constitute a significant segment in the electoral politics of the nation. Inspite of all these efforts, it is revealed that during the past decades the sex ratio in the country has been continually worsening.

Promoting Awareness

A large number of women are either ill-equipped or not in a position to propel themselves out of their traditionally unsatisfactory socio-economic conditions. They are poor, uneducated and insufficiently trained. Some tend to be ill-nourished anaemic and burdened by domestic chores and child care responsibilities. They are often absorbed in the struggle to sustain the family physically and emotionally and as a rule are discouraged from even taking an interest in affairs outside the home. There is an urgent need to encourage them to face the problems of illiteracy, lack of information and lack of skills, and try to find solutions to these problems. They should be made aware of their shortcomings in terms of education, nutrition and health.

There are many issues that require to be taken up for betterment of women in India. The recently announced national population policy is built on the correct premise that population stabilisation is a matter of human development. It is also important to look at this in the broader context of women's health and enhancement of their capabilities. Success will depend upon a number of related factors including simultaneous improvements in education, child health care, how effectively women get empowered to gain access to education, to make the right choices, and to influence decisions.

Education

Education of women is a critical input for improving nutrition levels, raising the age at marriage, acceptance of family planning, improvement in self-image, and their empowerment. In India female literacy rate is as low as 39.42 per cent as compared to 63.86 per cent of men. The need of the hour is to improve female literacy. With the exception of Kerala where the female literacy is 86.9 per cent, in the states like Bihar, Rajasthan, Uttar Pradesh and Madhya Pradesh less than 30 per cent women are literate. The recent UNDP report placed India 103 out of 174 in the rank of 'gender-related development index'. Education is the key to development. For educational development of women, a vigorous drive for universalisation of elementary education, retention of girl child in school, reduction in drop out rate and promotion of adult literacy was taken up by Government in the Five-Year Plans. Some of the special initiatives were, review of school text books to remove gender bias, re-orientation of school teachers to present gender equality and setting up of Women's Development Centre in Universities and colleges to bring about social awareness on women's issues.

Education is the basic tool for empowering a woman. This is where the NGOs and Social Service Sector people need to work. There are phases of empowerment. Once a girl undergoes the first phase of information, education and communication she becomes aware of her surroundings. Then comes the phase of accountability, where she is given the ability to rationalise and take informed decisions for which she is accountable. Once she is educated and empowered, she is in a better position to take care of herself and this needs to be sustained.

On one side where there is a need to educate girls, it is also necessary that the other sex be sensitised towards her. Cultural patterns tend to impose male superiority by assigning males with the roles of producers and heirs. It is important to usher in changes in societal attitudes and perceptions with regard to the role of women in different spheres of life. Adjustments have to be made in traditional gender specific performance of tasks. Mass media and inter-personal communication techniques should be utilised to achieve these ends.

Health Care

Equal status of women is difficult, as women are physically smaller in size and strength as compared to their male counterparts. To make woman physically healthy and may be able to take challenges of equality, she needs special health care and diet. NGOs/Social Service Sector people should look into this aspect and help the women to be enlightened about this. To be useful to the family, community and the society, they must take care of their own health. They must not only think of their husbands, children and in-laws but also think of themselves. The seventies brought women to the forefront of development concerns. This happened with publication of the report of the committee on Status of Women in India, the observance of the International Women's year in 1975, preparation of a National Plan of Action for women and introduction of the Medical Termination of Pregnancy Act 1971.

Thirty years have gone by and a look at indicators of Maternal & Child Health (MCH) care, shows the poor current status of health of women. India like other South East Asian countries has a very high maternal mortality rate of 4.6 per 1,000 live births, Bangladesh 6, Nepal 8.3 where as USA 0.08 and Switzerland 0.05. Magnitude of the problem of anemia for pregnant women in South East Asian countries is high – 60 per cent in India, 77 per cent in Bangladesh and 68 per cent in Nepal in comparison to 29 per cent in America and 20 per cent in Europe. The sex ratio in India was 1,000 males to 978 females in 1901, which has come down to 1000 males to 927 females in 1991. Where as in developed countries like USA, Canada and Britain the ratio is 1000 males to 1080 females. How is it that the population of females in India is going down? Ultra sound, Amniocentesis to detect the sex of the foetus is followed by female foeticide. Besides other causes, female foeticide is one of the main causes for decrease in female population in India.

A girl is discriminated from the very childhood. At birth she is unwanted, she is not sent to school, she is given less food to avoid her to grow fast. After sad experiences of childhood in a woman's life come three phases that could be remembered with 3 Ms. These are – Menarche, Motherhood and Menopause.

At Menarche, she should be educated to take high protein diet and food items containing iron. She must also be educated about sexuality, teenage pregnancy (17 per cent of pregnancies are in age group of 15-18 years) complications of abortions. The next phase is motherhood. It is also important that she is aware about the do's and don'ts of pregnancy. Access to good health facility for check ups, extra diet rich in protein, calcium and iron, and the power to decide as to how many children she should have. Maternal Care Indicators show that only 62.3 per cent of pregnant women receive antenatal check ups, 53.8 per cent doses of Tetanus Toxoid, 50.5 per cent iron/folic acid tablets, and only 25.5 per cent deliver with propers health care facilities. Lastly comes the phase of Menopause, when a woman reaches the age of 45 and generally stops menstruating. If she has an understanding of menopause and an understanding partner/husband and family, she gets over this phase smoothly. With the physical changes in this phase comes the need for self-respect and feeling of being wanted. Many a time family members are unable to show these in their behaviour.

The discrepancy in the ideology and practice of the empowerment policy of women in India constitutes its continued social, economic and cultural backwardness.

As empowerment of women in a society is the most effective index of measuring modernisation and development, it should be ensured therefore that at every phase of life, a woman needs to be given special inputs in terms of school education, higher education, health education, sex education, population education and education on self development, so that these may improve her status in the society and better the quality of her life.

IMPACT OF POLLUTION ON WOMEN

Women's health is further harmed by air and water pollution and lack of sanitation. The impact of pollution and industrial wastes on health is considerable. In Environment, Development and the Gender Gap, Sandhya Venkateswaran asserts that "the high incidence of malnutrition present amongst women and their low metabolism and other health problems affect their capacity to deal with chemical stress.

The smoke from household biomass (made up of wood, dung and crop residues) stoves within a three-hour period is equivalent to smoking 20 packs of cigarettes. For women who spend at least three hours per day cooking, often in a poorly ventilated area, the impact includes eye problems, respiratory problems, chronic bronchitis and lung cancer. One study quoted by WHO in 1991 found that pregnant women cooking over open biomass stoves had almost a 50 percent higher chance of stillbirth.

Anaemia makes a person more susceptible to carbon monoxide toxicity, which is one of the main pollutants in the biomass smoke. Given the number of Indian women who are anaemic-25 to 30 percent in the reproductive age group and almost 50 percent in the third trimester-this adds to their vulnerability to carbon monoxide toxicity. Additionally, with an increasing population, diseases caused by waste disposal, such as hookworm, are rampant. People who work barefooted are particularly susceptible, and it has been found that hookworm is directly responsible for the high percentage of anaemia among rural women.

Women are Uneducated

Women and girls receive far less education than men, due both to social norms and fears of violence. India has the largest population of non-school-going working girls. India's constitution guarantees free primary school education for both boys and girls up to age 14. This goal has been repeatedly reconfirmed, but primary education in India is not universal. Overall, the literacy rate for women is 39 percent versus 64 percent for men. The rate for women in the four large northern states-Bihar, Uttar Pradesh, Rajasthan and Madhya Pradesh-is lower than the national average: it was 25 percent in 1991. Attendance rates from the 1981 census suggest that no more than 1/3 of all girls (and a lower proportion of rural girls) aged 5-14 are attending school.

Although substantial progress has been achieved since India won its independence in 1947, when less than 8 percent of females were literate, the gains have not been rapid enough to keep pace with population growth: there were 16 million more illiterate females in 1991 than in 1981. Sonalde Desai in Gender Inequalities and Demographic Behaviour asserts that "parents' reluctance to educate daughters has its roots in the situation of women. Parents have several incentives for not educating their daughters. Foremost is the view that education of girls brings no returns to parents and that their future roles, being mainly reproductive and perhaps including agricultural labour, require no formal education. As more and more boys are engaged in education, there is a growing reliance on the labour of girls. Girls are increasingly replacing their brothers on the farm while carrying on their usual responsibilities in housework. A large proportion of the roughly 40 million "nonworking" girls who are not in school are kept at home because of responsibilities in housework."

The role of parents is to deliver a chaste daughter to her husband's family. Sonalde Desai goes on to point out that "another disincentive for sending daughters to school is a concern for the protection of their virginity. When schools are located at a distance, when teachers are male, and when girls are expected to study along with boys, parents are often unwilling to expose their daughters to the potential assault on their virginity."

There is little response to counter these obstacles: school hours remain inflexible to the labour demands of girls; many villages do not have a school; and fewer than 1/3 of India's primary and middle-school teachers are women.

According to Mapping Progress, "educational funds were cut by 801.3 million rupees in the 1991-92 budget. Funds for the mass literacy movement, in which women participate enthusiastically, have been reduced by 5 percent from the previous year. Budgetary provisions for non-formal education have been cut by 17 percent, leading to closure of many night schools and adult education programs in which working-class women participate. Reduction in government expenditures on higher education and encouragement to private colleges will reduce women's opportunities for higher education since privatization in education promotes only male-dominated professional and technical courses, as they are lucrative."

Women are Overworked

Women work longer hours and their work is more arduous than men's. Still, men report that "women, like children, eat and do nothing."

Hours Worked

Women work roughly twice as many as many hours as men. Women's contribution to agriculture-whether it be subsistence farming or commercial agriculture-when measured in terms of the number of tasks performed and time spent, is greater than men. "The extent of women's contribution is aptly highlighted by a micro study conducted in the Indian Himalayas which found that on a one-hectare farm, a pair of bullocks works 1,064 hours, a man 1,212 hours and a woman 3,485 hours in a year." In Andhra Pradesh, (Mies 1986) found that the work day of an woman agricultural labourer during the agricultural season lasts for 15 hours, from 4 am to 8 pm, with an hour's rest in between. Her male counterpart works for seven to eight hours, from 5 am to 10 am or 11 am and from 3 pm to 5 pm.

Another study on time and energy spent by men and women on agricultural work (Batliwala 1982) found that 53 percent of the total human hours per household are contributed by women as compared to 31 percent by men. The remaining contribution comes from children. The linking of agricultural activities to male dominance is described by Roy Burman (in Menon 1991):

> *The anxiety of man to monopolize his skill in plough culture is reflected in the taboo that is observed almost all over India, against the women's handling the plough. In many societies, she is not even allowed to touch it.*

Mies further observed that "whereas operations performed by men were those that entailed the use of machinery and draught animals, thereby using animal, hydraulic, mechanical or electrical energy, women almost always relied on manual labour, using only their own energy." Rice transplantations, the most arduous and labour intensive task in rice cultivation, is carried out entirely by women without the help of any tools.

> *"Girls learn to assist their mothers in almost all tasks, and from the age of 10 years participate fully in the agricultural work done by women. Mies cites the case of Laxmi, a three-year-old infant who, along with her mother, pulled seedlings for transplanting. Boys on the other hand were seldom seen transplanting or weeding though they did help out in ploughing or watering the fields."*

"Not only do women perform more tasks, their work is also more arduous than that undertaken by men. Both transplantation and weeding require women to spend the whole day and work in muddy soil with their hands. Moreover, they work the entire day under the intensely hot sun while men's work, such as ploughing and watering the fields, is invariably carried out early in the morning before the sun gets too hot. Mies argues that because women's work, unlike men's, does not involve implements and is based largely on human energy, it is considered unskilled and hence less productive. On this basis, women are invariably paid lower wages, despite the fact that they work harder and for longer hours than do men."

In contrast, a study in Uttar Pradesh reports that men "only reluctantly conceded that their womenfolk really work. The researchers in this area were repeatedly told that women, like children, simply eat food and do nothing."

THE IMPACT OF TECHNOLOGY ON WOMEN

The shift from subsistence to a market economy has a dramatic negative impact on women. According to Sandhya Venkateswaran, citing Shiva, the Green Revolution, which focused on increasing yields of rice and wheat, entailed a shift in inputs from human to technical. Women's participation, knowledge and inputs were marginalized, and their role shift from being "primary producers to subsidiary workers."

Where technology has been introduced in areas where women worked, women labourers have often been displaced by men. Threshing of grain was almost exclusively a female task, and with the introduction of automatic grain threshers-which are only operated by men-women have lost an important source of income. Combine harvesters leave virtually no residue. This means that this source of fodder is no longer available to women, which has a dramatic impact on women's workload. So too, as cattle dung is being used as fertilizer, there is less available for fuel for cooking.

> *"Commercialization and the consequent focus on cash crops has led to a situation where food is lifted straight from the farm to the market. The income accrued is controlled by men. Earlier, most of the produce was brought home and stored, and the women exchanged it for other commodities. Such a system vested more control with the women."*

Women are Unskilled

Women have unequal access to resources. Extension services tend to reach only men, which perpetuates the existing division of labour in the agricultural sector, with women continuing to perform unskilled tasks. A World Bank study in 1991 reveals that the assumption made by extension workers is that information within a family will be transmitted to the women by the men, which in actual practice seldom happens. "The male dominated extension system tends to overlook women's role in agriculture and proves ineffective in providing technical information to women farmers." Mapping Progress, states, "in the farm sector, the process of mechanization of agricultural activities has brought in tendencies for gender discrimination by replacing men for a number of activities performed by women and also by displacing the labour of women from subsistence and marginal households. Women are employed only when there is absolute shortage of labour and for specific operations like cotton-picking.

> *"To supply food-processing industries being set up with foreign collaboration, there has already been a major shift from subsistence farming method of rice, millet, corn and wheat to cash-crop production of fruit, mushrooms, flowers and vegetables. This shift has led to women being the first to lose jobs."*

A number of factors perpetuate women's limited job skills: if training women for economic activities requires them to leave their village, this is usually a problem for them. Unequal access to education restricts women's abilities to learn skills that require even functional levels of literacy. In terms of skill development, women are impeded by their lack of mobility, low literacy levels and prejudiced attitudes toward women. When women negotiate with banks and government officials, they are often ostracized by other men and women in their community for being 'too forward.' Government and bank officials have preconceived ideas of what women are capable of, and stereotypes of what is considered women's work.

Women are Mistreated

Violence against women and girls is the most pervasive human rights violation in the world today. Opening the door on the subject of violence against the world's females is like standing at the threshold of an immense dark chamber vibrating with collective anguish, but with the sounds of protest throttled back to a murmur. Where there should be outrage aimed at an intolerable status quo there is instead denial, and the largely passive acceptance of 'the way things are.'

Male violence against women is a worldwide phenomenon. Although not every woman has experienced it, and many expect not to, fear of violence is an important factor in the lives of most women. It determines what they do, when they do it, where they do it, and with whom. Fear of violence is a cause of women's lack of participation in activities beyond the home, as well as inside it. Within the home, women and girls may be subjected to physical and sexual abuse as punishment or as culturally justified assaults. These acts shape their attitude to life, and their expectations of themselves.

The insecurity outside the household is today the greatest obstacle in the path of women. Conscious that, compared to the atrocities outside the house, atrocities within the house are endurable, women not only continued to accept their inferiority in the house and society, but even called it sweet. In recent years, there has been an alarming rise in atrocities against women in India. Every 26 minutes a woman is molested. Every 34 minutes a rape takes place. Every 42 minutes a sexual harassment incident occurs. Every 43 minutes a woman is kidnapped. And every 93 minutes a woman is burnt to death over dowry.

One-quarter of the reported rapes involve girls under the age of 16 but the vast majority are never reported. Although the penalty is severe, convictions are rare.

Selective Abortions

The most extreme expression of the preference for sons is female infanticide and sex-selective abortion. A study of amniocentesis in a Bombay hospital found that 96 percent of female fetuses were aborted, compared with only a small percentage of male fetuses.

> *"Government officials event suspect that the disproportionate abortion of female fetuses may be a major underlying cause of the recent decline in the nation's sex ratio. In 1971 there were 930 females for every 1,000 males. A decade later this figure had increased to 934, but by 1991, instead of continuing to rise, the ratio dropped to 927, lower than the 1971 figure. This sex ratio is one of the lowest in the world."*

Sonalda Desai reports that there are posters in Bombay advertising sex-determination tests that read, "It is better to pay 500 Rs. now than 50,000 Rs. (in dowry) later." Government has passed legislation to curb the misuse of amniocentesis for sex selection and abortion of female fetuses. Women activists have been critical of this act because of its provision that calls for punishing the women who seek the procedure. These women may be under pressure to bear a male child.

Women are Powerless

Legal protection of women's rights have little effect in the face of prevailing patriarchal traditions. Women are subordinate in most marriages. Exposure to and interactions with the outside world are instrumental in determining the possibilities available to women in their daily lives. The situation of women is affected by the degree of their autonomy or capacity to make decisions both inside and outside their own household.

> *"The position of women in northern India is notably poor. Traditional Hindu society in northern rural areas is hierarchical and dominated by men, as evidenced by marriage customs. North Indian Hindus are expected to marry within prescribed boundaries: the bride and groom must not be related, they have no say in the matter, and the man must live outside the woman's natal village."*

"Wife givers" are socially and ritually inferior to "wife takers", thus necessitating the provision of a dowry. After marriage, the bride moves in with her husband's family. Such a bride is "a stranger in a strange place." They are controlled by the older females in the household, and their Behaviour reflects on the honour of their husbands. Because emotional ties between spouses are considered a potential threat to the solidarity of the patrilineal group, the northern system tends to segregate the sexes and limit communication between spouses-a circumstance that has direct consequences for family planning and similar "modern" Behaviours that affect health. A young Indian bride is brought up to believe that her own wishes and interests are subordinate to those of her husband and his family. The primary duty of a newly married young woman, and virtually her only means of improving her position in the hierarchy of her husband's household, is to bear sons." Sonalde Desai points out that the perception that sons are the major source of economic security in old age is so strong in the north that "many parents, while visiting their married daughters, do not accept food or other hospitality from them. However, given women's low independent incomes and lack of control over their earnings, few can provide economic support to their parents even if parents were willing to accept it."

2

Situation of Girl Child in India

TRAFFICKING OF GIRLS FOR COMMERCIAL EXPLOITATION

Trafficking of girls for commercial exploitation, domestic labour and forced early marriages continues to be a serious problem in India. For a vast number of trafficked women and children, who are subsequently rescued, rehabilitation and repatriation mechanisms are scarce and their reintegration in society is also very difficult. Buying and selling of girls for prostitution is a shameful and serious concern both for the country and the society at large. Importation of girls has increased by 93.5 per cent (NCBR 2005). Most of these cases are reported from Bihar and Jharkhand. There are lot of poor girls being trafficked from Nepal too. There has been a significant increase in the number of cases registered under the Immoral Trafficking Prevention Act, 1956 (ITPA) and most of these have been registered in Tamil Nadu as compared to other states.

For the crimes of immoral nature committed against children, only a few arrested offenders could be convicted representing only about a 30 per cent conviction rate. 85 per cent of the trafficked victims have been below the age of 30 years. It is important to note that offenders were known to the victims in as many as 85 per cent cases.

Reasons Behind Trafficking

A variety of conditions compel women and children to take up immoral work. These range from acute poverty, family's inability to pay dowry, desertion or widowhood or being lured into the profession by promise of a job, to an overall lack of skills as a result of little or no education. While many families live in remote areas with very few livelihood options, others are caught up in unrelenting cycles of migration in search of work. Still other families consist of single-parent households where survival itself is at times a formidable struggle. Violence and sexual abuse in some of these settings fail to provide children with an environment where their rights are protected. Such children are often pushed either into immoral work or low-paid labour. Often families with little or no income are compelled to sell their children to others who offer the child work. There are estimated more than 12 million child labourers in India. Most have never been to school or have dropped out before completing primary school. In Bihar, Nagaland, Mizoram, Rajasthan and Uttar Pradesh, 60 per cent or more girls dropped out before completing their first five years of education.

Poverty can force children out of school, into work and drive them from home on to the streets. The presence of a large number of street children, who receive no protection either from the family or the state, makes the situation more complex and one accepts or not they are invariably sexually exploited irrespective of their sex.

Roughly 20 per cent of the Indian population is considered migrant, 77 per cent of whom are women and children. They are often at greater risk of exploitation and tend to accept jobs on unfair terms. Forced relocation in conditions of distress, natural disasters or conflict also affect them psychologically and economically. Reports collected across the country brought out the fact that a significant number of cases registered against trafficked children and women were in the age group of 10-20 years. This is a fluid age group with the fine line dividing between major and a minor. Knowing the correct age of the trafficked person is critical to the outcome of a case, because very often the trafficked person may actually be below 18 years but is declared as above 18 years in the age-determination report.

Inaccurate age determination makes a crucial difference in the conduct of the proceedings in a court of law and can result in a miscarriage of justice, as according to the ITPA, trafficking of minors is a more heinous offence warranting more stringnent punishment as compared to adults (less than 18 years). In most cases the trafficked victims do not have birth/school registration certificates to prove their age and therefore the medical examination report submitted by the Medical Officer to the court is an important and crucial document, which assist the Judicial Officer in rendering justice to the victim by prosecuting the trafficker and sending the victim to a protective home.

Possible Solution

Government of India and UNICEF in collaboration with the district administration and local NGOs, are trying to set up a data base of trafficking routes, traffickers, and trafficked minors and women in order to make effective interventions. It is believed that well organised trafficker groups are operating in the country and have patronage of bigwigs in the country. There is need to focus on community sensitisation and mobilisation for prevention of trafficking. Village based anti-trafficking committees comprising of local youth, self-help group members and elected representatives at panchayat level should be established. These committees in vulnerable villages need to monitor, follow up and counsel girls and women who are approached by relatives or friends in the guise of offering employment. The committees should initiate action against traffickers by registering police cases against them. Motivated volunteers and local administration should link vulnerable women and girls to development schemes. Minors and women need to be trained in livelihood skills and facilitated to find alternative options.

Trafficking of children for commercial exploitation is a heinous crime. It is on increase and should be curbed. Civil society should come forward to root it out from society. Rape crisis centre should be made in all districts where these trafficked victims are delit at one place. Secondly coordination of various government agencies and various stake-holders is badly needed, which is totally lacking, with the result that no body is accountable in the system.

GIRLS FOR SALE

India has become one of the biggest slave bazaars for minor girls. Other than as sex workers, they are also exploited as labourers, drug peddlers and for their organs. Terror is the only emotion that registers on Champa's drawn face. Sitting on the stained floor of a dingy hut in the Chakalisher village of Punjab, this 14-year-old with matted, grimy hair and dirty nails sobs uncontrollably. "He will hurt me," she blurts out in Bengali. Across the floor, under heaps of smelly clothes hanging on a clothesline, two other girls sit huddled together. One is fidgeting with a torn picture of a goddess; the other keeps readjusting her dupatta. In the dim light of a bulb hanging from a loose electric wire, all three look like mirror images of one another. A Murshidabad truck driver paid their parents Rs 3,000 each and brought them to Punjab. He raped Champa on the way. In the courtyard, an old lady, with parchment skin and bent back, sits on her charpoy. "Bachalo unko (save them)," she says feebly before a burly, bearded man storms in and bellows, "Bebe (mother) you keep out of this." He turns to us. "Get out, who are you?" Outside the mud walls, we bump into five men and a woman. "They have come to "see" the girls, whispers a local. The bargaining is about to start.

What was once a scattered trade run by petty pimps is now an organised crime with international gangs involved, some with underworld links. Earlier, touts used PCOs to make calls and chloroform-laced handkerchiefs to make the girls unconscious. Now they carry mobile phones, video cameras and mood-altering depressant drugs. Dayawati, 15, rescued in Mewat in Haryana was found carrying a strip of tranquilisers which she said were pills for energy given to her by her "chacha". The city traffickers are not paan-chewing men with bulging bellies or garish women wearing red lipstick. Cultured, English-speaking voices picked up phones, when numbers given by rescued girls were called by India Today. One woman said she ran an agency that supplied "crowds" for film shootings. In Kolkata, girls below 10 years are "groomed" for the sex trade by making them work in brothel bars. "They bars as part of the "grooming" for the sex trade. "They are taught to be coquettish with the customers," informs Prabir Basu of NGO span. Traffickers also trade in mentally challenged and blind girls by first befriending them.

It is a huge, unscrupulous bazaar with its own rules and ratings. Girls between nine and 15 years of age fetch the highest price depending upon their physical attributes. As traffickers change hands, the price of girls bought for Rs 2,000-4,000 from their native villages appreciates to Rs 50,000 in the beer bars of Mumbai where pimps invest in attractive girls. So on an average a healthy, good-looking girl will fetch a profit of over Rs 30,000. Some pimps work on regular, monthly commissions with an additional fee per girl sold. "Undoubtedly, the organised nexus has strengthened and spread over the years," agrees Inspector-General of Police P.M. Nair, nodal officer of the National Human Rights Commission (NHRC) in Delhi for its project, the Action Research on Trafficking in Women and Children. This soon-to-be-released research is the first of its type commissioned by NHRC. Sponsored by UNIFEM (United Nations Development Fund for Women), the research is being done at Delhi's Institute of Social Sciences with inputs from key agencies in 11 states.

The problem needs to be seriously studied because the changing demands have altered the supply dynamics of this age-old trade. Last week, 13-year-old Jamila was rescued from the house of Hasan, a trafficker in the notorious Nuh village in Haryana's Mewat region. Hasan, 35, had brought Jamila from a village in West Bengal after paying Rs 3,000 to her mother. There is a huge spurt in the demand for minor girls like her. A comparison of various estimates reveals that trafficking in minor girls from and within India has increased by about 45 per cent in the last decade. Unwanted by poor parents, they come cheap. Illiterate, deprived of care and too innocent to resist force of any kind, they are ideal subjects to be abducted or ensnared. Like the battered and pregnant 15-year-old Nagi of Hori village in Jharkhand, who was sold for Rs 2,000 in Haryana. Then there's the haggard, Mita Gurung of Beheliya, Nepal, whose buyers in Saudi Arabia poked fingers in her eyes while she slaved as a domestic help for 15 hours a day. Or shockingly, eight-year-old Anu with sunburnt hair and jagged hands who was rescued from a circus-the jingle Paisa pheko tamasha dekho forever haunts her. And the ghost-like Samira, 14, of Hooghly in West Bengal, who was duped and drugged only to wake up in Mumbai's Kamatipura. "Touts force girls into drug addiction so that they are manipulated into following orders," says Tapati Bhowmick of Kolkata NGO

Sanlaap. Also, the myths that virgins can cure venereal diseases or that pre-pubescent girls cannot carry the HIV virus have increased their saleability in sex markets multifold. On the contrary, new studies reveal that the disease has passed on from infected men to these girls. Many are HIV positive, some have full-blown aids. The practice of young girls being married off to ageing Arab sheikhs continues in Hyderabad, but with a dangerous twist. "The traffickers pose as Arabs. The parents are led to believe that their daughters are in the Middle East, when actually they are pushed into the flesh trade," says Dr. Sunitha Krishnan of Prajwala, a Hyderabad-based anti-trafficking organisation.

Murshidabad district of West Bengal which once supplied minor boys for camel jockeying to the Middle East, is now the biggest supplier of minor girls for clandestine prostitution rackets involving Haj tourists. The Bedia community of Uttar Pradesh, which traditionally sells daughters to brothels, now gives them away to rich clients abroad. Jamtala Daspara village in South 24 Parganas, West Bengal, has no more teenaged girls. Sitala began this trend by being the first girl to become a sex worker who sent her earnings back to poor villagers. From an outcast, she became a village matriarch when in 1963, she funded the only school there-a decrepit, one-storey building with four classrooms, now called the Sitala Devi Primary School. Today, almost every family in Jamtala sells its girl children.

This is modern India where, as India Today's investigations showed, hundreds of similar tragedies are being enacted every day. Of minor girls being abducted, lured, beaten black and blue, raped and abused, sold and resold till they give in to slavery. Trafficking is just a constitutional description for the slave trade in girls, now a billion-dollar industry in south Asia. The UN and the NHRC term it as the fastest growing criminal enterprise in the world. India has emerged as a big transit point on the world map of human trafficking. About 89 per cent of the total trafficked girls are sold within the country. Researchers warn that instead of going by the hype that numbers create, it is important to look at the changing patterns in female trafficking. The gangs have an extensive network and the trade works in three tiers. Salim Khan, 19, of Deoria in eastern Uttar Pradesh, is a link in one such chain. With a vicious expression he says he seduces young girls, promising them money and marriage. He was arrested with 14-year-old Susheela, who had eloped with him. As the tales of the girls progress, more characters enter the script. The first rapist is usually the first procurer and the first sale takes place just outside the village. "The decentralisation of prostitution along highway joints and in smaller districts has boosted the sale of the girls," says Priti Patkar of Mumbai-based NGO Prerana.

Some procurers pretend to be well-wishers of girls who fall hook, line and sinker for the promise of marriage and a comfortable life in the city. A vigilance checkpost at the Sonauli border between India and Nepal found that 80 per cent of girls who were intercepted claimed to be married to their traffickers. "The porous border with numerous unmanned entry points makes it easy for the girls to pass through unchecked," says Jata Shankar, executive director of Seva Beyond Border, a Gorakhpur-based NGO active along the Indo-Nepal border. The sale of girls into the sex trade is the most documented aspect of trafficking yet it cannot be used as a synonym for prostitution. It involves other forms of coerced sale: domestic work, agricultural and industrial labour, circus activities, organ trade, bogus marriages, begging and adoption rackets. So little is the value placed on daughters and so compelling the pangs of starvation that almost anybody can walk into many villages, pick out a poor family and buy a girl for a few thousand rupees. As one villager said, "We sold the little jewellery that we had, then the farm and the bullock. Now the only saleable thing left with us are our daughters." Even in the face of development, bonded labour still thrives in India. In Dalersinghwala village of Punjab many poor Dalit families have sold their daughters as labourers to zamindars.

In urban India, a bigger story is being scripted. Mumbai, Delhi and Kolkata serve as business hubs. Mumbai, the import-export point, is the undisputed capital of this crime. Rescued girls interviewed in Ranchi in Jharkhand, Nepal and Murshidabad repeatedly mentioned Mumbai. Tourist spots like Baina in Goa are the emerging markets. Punjab and Haryana feature on trafficking maps as states where girls are sold for domestic and agricultural labour or as "wives". Jharkhand activist Dayamani Barla, who rescued 21 girls by posing as an agent, reveals that 20,000 tribal girls are listed with unregistered agencies as potential domestic helps in Delhi. "The police and local politicians have a nexus with these gangs," she says.

Barla's accusation is not unjustified. The keepers of law are ignorant and apathetic, if not a party to the crime. Nitin Yadav, the sub-divisional magistrate who helped rescue Jamila was not even aware of the Juvenile Justice Act and the fact that a minor cannot be produced before a judicial magistrate or detained in a police station. As Circle Officer A.S. Rai posted in Gorakhpur argues, "Seldom do criminal activities thrive on such a large, organised level unless they are done hand in glove with the police." Not to mention that some policemen also violate human rights. Despite the growth in this trade, nobody seems to be doing anything about it. Andhra Pradesh, the second largest supplier of girls after West Bengal, is the only state in India with an anti-trafficking policy and is working on judicial provisions. The Immoral Trafficking Prevention Act (ITPA), amended in 1986, is a sound legal provision, but it only takes into cognisance victims of sexual exploitation, not other forms of trafficking as mentioned in the UN protocol.

In 1997, the Supreme Court ordered a national plan of action for an in-depth study and a committee to look into prostitution. "But nothing has been done," says Rishi Kant Srivastava of Faridabad-based Shakti Vahini. "Small brothels are raided and shut down only to become bigger call girl rings." As Nair points out, "About 80 per cent of the convictions under ITPA are of victims of sexual exploitation. Instead of arresting victims of sexual exploitation, traffickers should be punished."

NHRC member Justice Sujata Manohar feels the Government has to snap out of its stereotypical responses and train the police and policymakers to be more sensitive. Her argument is pertinent because though rescues take place, rehabilitation is another ballgame. There is a dearth of transit and rehabilitation homes for minors. After rescue, policemen don't know where to keep the girls. They are taken to Nari Niketans, some of which are worse than prisons. Here, in the name of counselling, girls are berated. Until counselling moves beyond hammering, welfare beyond tailoring classes, and reintegration beyond retrafficking, effective rehabilitation will be a dream. Which is why initiatives like that of Prajwala, which collaborates with companies like Amul Pizza Corner to start micro enterprises for the rescued girls, make sense. The villagers of Harra near Ranchi and former devadasis of Andhra Pradesh and Karnataka, have formed anti-trafficking lobbies. NHRC's Action Research will be a permanent programme, backed by the Ministry of Human Resources Development.

CHILD AND FEMALE FOETICIDE AND INFANTICIDE

Technologies like amniocentesis and ultrasound used in most parts of the world, largely for detecting foetal abnormalities, has been used in large parts of the Indian subcontinent for determining the sex of the foetus so that it can be aborted, if it happens to be a female. The information of the sex of the unborn was being extensively misused. To prevent female foeticide and to restrict this misuse, the Prenatal Diagnostic Techniques (Regulation and Prevention of Misuse) Act was passed on 20th September 1994. The Act forbids the communication of the sex of the foetus, but the enforcement of this act is not easy.

Medical Termination of Pregnancy Act (MTPA) 1971 allows abortion if the doctor is of the opinion that the continuance of the pregnancy would endanger the life of the pregnant woman or involve grave injury to her physical or mental health; or there is substantial risk that the child would suffer from disabling physical or mental abnormalities. The anguish caused by pregnancy as a result of rape, or as a result of failure of any device or method used by a married couple for the purpose of limiting the number of children, may be presumed to constitute a grave injury to the woman's mental health. If the pregnancy is twelve weeks old, the opinion of one registered medical practitioner is sufficient; for pregnancy of between twelve and twenty four weeks, the opinion of two registered medical practitioner is required.

The matter is thus purely between her and the medical practitioner and even the husbands' consent becomes unnecessary. In reality, however, a woman's' right to abortion is very restricted and mostly it turns out to be a family decision. Various court judgements have held that aborting a foetus without the husbands' consent would amount to cruelty under the Hindu Marriage Act and hence a ground for divorce.. The procedure gets rampantly misused with the collaboration of the medical fraternity, as an alternative in the case of couples who do not opt to practise family planning methods and who want to do away with the unwanted child.

The earliest known legislation against female infanticide was enacted by the British Government in 1870. Prior to this, there were regional regulations established by the British, such as the Bengal Regulation of XXI 1795 and Regulation III of 1807, that declared that infanticide amounted to murder. The Infanticide Regulation Act of 1870 was passed nearly a hundred years after the British discovered it officially. This Act acquired the compulsory registration of births and deaths to enable verification of female children a few years after birth. Since Independence, the Constitution of India contains certain provisions that guarantee the welfare and development of children. The Indian Penal Code also has defined infanticide as murder. While the deliberate act of causing a miscarriage or injury to the new born child, exposure of the infant and concealment of births are covered under Sections 312 to 318 of the I.P.C, the intention of preventing a child being born and causing bodily harm to the infant are covered under I.P.C Section 315. Section 317 makes the concealment of the birth and secret disposal of the dead body an offence.

Miller categorises infanticide as a fatal form of child abuse. There are more passive forms of infanticide like neglect, sustained nutritional deprivation, delayed health care for female infants or, in other words, an unequal allocation of household resources detrimental to the health of the girl child. In fact, the passive forms of infanticide remain unrecorded as infanticide by health workers and sociologists.

Female infanticide and foeticide has occurred not only in several cultures across history, but is known to occur in contemporary societies as well. Several scholars have documented female infanticide for the period of British Colonial rule. In the period since independence, the practice has been reported as occurring in many parts of the country including Tamil Nadu where the practice was not known to exist before independence. The first recorded instance in India, dates to 1789 when Jonathan Duncan, a British Resident at Benares, Uttar Pradesh State, North India, detected the practice among a Rajput clan. The British passed the Infanticide Regulation Act in 1870 and subsequently, a special Census was taken in 1881 in the Western Provinces and Oudh to detect female infanticide. Evidence from the British records and other historical sources shows that the practice was confined to Northern and Western regions of the country including present day Rajasthan, Punjab, Uttar Pradesh and Bihar. By contrast, female infanticide in Tamil Nadu is essentially a post independence phenomenon. In South India, the practise of female infanticide existed among the Toda tribe of Tamil Nadu. The only factual evidence to prove that it still exists among them, is the sex ratio data in the Nilgiri District of Tamil Nadu. The data that Chunkath and others analysed confirmed that, the practise of female infanticide is widespread in Dharmapuri, Salem and Madurai Districts. They arrived at this conclusion after preparing a table on, distribution of Blocks by number of female infanticide deaths, as per PHC records. They observed that there is a contiguous cluster of blocks where female infanticide occurs and what should be a cause for particular concern is that the phenomenon is spreading from the core area to a much wider neighbouring periphery area and beyond.

In 1986, when the practice of female infanticide in Madurai District of Tamil Nadu first received major media attention, the focus was on the caste group known as 'Piramalai Kallars' and it was held that the practice was confined to this caste. Over the past two decades, the region has attracted wide attention due to the prevalence of the practice of female infanticide in Usilampatti taluka. This region has a predominant large population of Kallars.

In 1992, when female infanticide was found to be widespread in Salem District and the Gounder community was considered to be the one practising it. In a survey done by Chunkath and Athreyai, it was found that this practice has spread to many castes. The data they collected from one district alone-Dindugal (now Mannar Tirumalai), Tamil Nadu, show occurrence of female infanticide in 35 (self ascribed) caste groups. They conclude that while the Piramalai Kallars and Gounders in their respective areas of numerical and social dominance may have initiated the practice of female infanticide, it now appears to cut across all castes. They say that, probably the practice of female infanticide by the dominant peasant/landlord caste of the local community served to legitimate and provide social sanction to the practice and contribute substantially to its spread among all castes. The value system and norms of ritual expenditure pattern of the dominant peasant/landlord caste of the region raise the perceived cost of bringing up female infants, for poorer members of the dominant caste in particular, and for all castes in general. Although this may be true in some areas, it cannot be generalised. Chunkath & Athreya in their study, also found that the practice is widespread among the scheduled castes and tribes. According to the study done by George and othersii in 1992, out of the 18 cases of female infanticide (of married mothers) that they came across, 17 were among the Gounders. The remaining one case occurred among the Arunthatis (cobblers) a scheduled caste. In Bihar, according to a study done by Adithi, a local NGO in Katihar District, of 35 Dais, this practise originally began among Rajputs but spread to many castes including the Bumihars, Brahmins, Kayasthas, Yadavas and some scheduled castes. This, they say, is similar to the case in Tamil Nadu, where it originally began with Gounder caste and has now spread to almost all castes (Times of India, 22nd April).

What makes the practice important in the contemporary society is that there are indications of its increase in occurrence. It is difficult to obtain carefully confirmed first hand data on infanticide cases and social variables related to infanticide. There is also a problem of gathering data on direct or indirect infanticide through any brief field work (George et al, 1992:1153) It makes it even more difficult to obtain data when people remain tight lipped about the situation. Now that the practice has been recognised as a crime by law and the increase in awareness among the people, they have become cautious about revealing facts to investigators.

There are few clear indicators to identify the extent of female infanticide. However it is known that in any genetic group, the proportion of males to females is fairly equal. Studies based on hospital birth records show that boys outnumber girls at birth under natural circumstances. Initially the mortality rate among boys is higher than among girls, so the ratio balances out in the long run. Hence an adverse sex ratio (number of females per thousand males) especially in the first few years of life, and gender differences in Infant Mortality Rate (IMR) are significant pointers towards the possibility of female infanticide.

Agnihotri (1995), has worked out a statistical formula for disaggregating the 'missing females' in the overall population of the country and has computed the missing females in a demographic analysis based on sex ratio. He has used the census data for this purpose. Sex ratio data would undoubtedly include those who are victims of malnutrition, delayed health care and other forms of childhood abuse, including infanticide, and in recent years foeticide. His estimation is based on the total number of females required to be added on to reach the level of the male population over a period of years. This disaggregation can be done for the whole country, for any caste, class, age, or regional sub group to show which section is contributing largely to the 'missing females' in the population.

Chunkath and others in their report say that PHC provide information on pregnancies, deliveries, births, still births, early neo natal (0-6 days) deaths, other neo natal deaths (7-27 days), and post natal (28-364 days) deaths gender-wise. The field staff of the public health network also obtains information on causes of infant deaths and one of the cause is 'death due to social causes'.

This category refers to male/female infanticide The most significant indicator would be the neo natal mortality rate (0-7 days) and it is here that the gender differences assume significance especially if the analysis is based on PHC records. What also needs to be found is the accuracy of this data. It may be possible that the registering of a neo natal death is done in the post natal period, in which case the data will be distorted. Tamil Nadu, in 1996, had decided to conduct the survey of 24 revenue districts (RDs) divided into 41 health unit districts (HUDs). The data that is easily accessible and available in Tamil Nadu, may not be in some other states. The National Family Health Survey (1995) found that the post neonatal mortality is 13% higher for females than males, and child mortality is 43% higher for female than for males. But these are all India figures, which do not convey the regional differences. What is required is data on gender-neo natal, post natal and infant mortality rates for all India, State and District level.

The experience of Chunkath and others in their survey has been that, reliable data on vital rates is available through Sample Registration Survey (SRS), but only for the State as a whole.

Hospital records are a major source by which, one can speculate that female infanticide has occurred. Negi states, in a number of cases, especially in hospitalised delivery, the female infants are sent home in good health. Subsequently, within a few hours after reaching home, the family claims that the child has died due to various causes. This leads to speculate that, a case of infanticide has occurred. Even the ritual, that is normally observed on death in the family is never followed in cases of female infanticide. There are also survey findings to prove that the babies and mothers vanish from hospitals on knowing that a girl child has been born. George and others in their study recorded nearly 600 girls born into the Kallar caste in the Usilampatti government hospital every year. Out of these an estimated 570 babies vanish from the hospital, with their mothers. Hospital sources estimate that nearly 80 per cent of these vanishing babies (more than 450) become victims of infanticide. The Registrar General of India, Mr Vijay Unnikrishnan says that each year there are 25 million births and 9 million deaths in the country, but only 40% of these events are registered. These non-registered births and deaths are untraceable by any secondary data.

The hospital records can only report the births that take place in hospitals. It is a common practice in rural India that the delivery is done by the midwives and at home. It is also known through various surveys that midwives are pressurised to kill the children. Women may migrate to their paternal home for delivery. All these factors make it difficult to record the death of female babies. The people who actually kill the child are the dais, fathers, mothers or elder female members of the family. Adithi, a local NGO in Katihar District, Bihar conducted a survey in four districts in Bihar. According to their findings, Katihar District alone accounts for over 1000 infanticides cases per year. The survey, based on interviews with the 35 midwives in the district reveals that each of them kill at least three to four babies every month. A similar situation was found in Sitamarhi, Gumla and Purnia districts. In Bihar, the new born girls are killed primarily by the dais, at the behest of the parents. They receive an amount of Rs 25 to 30/-for the deed. (Times of India, 22nd April 1995). The child is normally killed within the first three days or the first week of its birth, after which the chances of its survival increases. It is only in rare instances that the child is killed after the first week. 17 of the 19 female infanticides occurred within seven days of birth, one on the ninth day after birth, and the remaining one on the 16th day. In the entire study population, there were a total of 18 female infant deaths during the first seven days after birth.

One of the key points that emerged from the findings of Chunkath and others, is that, there is hardly any gender differential in post-natal infant death rates in most of the districts surveyed in Tamil Nadu. On the other hand, mortality rates are considerably higher for female as against male infants in the entire neo-natal phase.

This means that the babies are killed at a neo natal stage, which makes it more important to find out when the reporting of death is done in the PHCs. Modernisation has been cited by Negi as a reason for female in fanticide, as there was a shift from growing traditional crops to cash crops. Madurai District was rainfed zone and both women and men used to be jointly involved in the process of cultivation. Women had the knowledge of how to cultivate seeds in the traditional way, when to start collecting them, when to sow them and how to store them. They also had the knowledge of, what kinds of fertilisers are necessary and should be used and so on. With the construction of Vaigai dam in 1950, Madurai District came to be irrigated and with it came the introduction of cash crops. The local traditional pattern vanished and the knowledge of women were no more needed or required. The skills and resources were external. The seeds, pesticides, loans, electricity and skills of management came from outside. The men started going out to government offices to get loans, to bring seed and pesticides, to sell the crops and overlook the irrigation and started making decisions.

Over the period of time the land lost its fertility, the ground water has gone down. Women became mere liabilities with her knowledge having become redundant and men aspired to marry only those women whose family can afford to offer more dowry (Asia Pacific Hearing, 1997: 38). Sergent et al, 1996 has mentioned that, in the landless classes, the presence of sons ensures a higher labour participation and correspondingly a high financial support to the family, as a consequence, the family is likely to favour a male child, increasing the probability of female infanticide.

Modernisation has brought about changes in the traditional systems and thereby lowering the status of women in the society. Dowry, given at the time of the daughter's marriage, has influenced the status of women. The daughter is considered to be a liability as her contribution to the family is temporary upto the time she is married and sent to another family. Dowry is not the only transaction as far as the daughter's marriage is concerned. Krishnaswamy, 1988 has mentioned about a series of ceremonies in South India, Tamil Nadu, associated with the girls in the family. Gifts in cash and kind to the husband's family during ceremonies connected with pregnancy, childbirth and ceremonies for piercing the ear of the girl child and so on.

It is the inability to meet the dowry-related demands from the in-law's family, that is a major cause for female infanticide. The fear of sexual abuse of the girl child is also a cause for female infanticide. The husbands' inability to do anything against the practice of sexual abuse of his wife by his father is due to the fear that he would lose his share of the property from his father. The father-in-law due to his own child marriage loses interest in his wife and finds it more convenient to find a bride for his son and to have his "sexual fulfilment" through her. Mothers, sometimes, kill their babies as an act of 'mercy' that they may be saved from future excesses by husbands in the form of domestic violence. They feel justified in killing their girl child so that she is saved from all the suffering she may have to undergo all her life. Harris-White (1997) has cited poverty as one of the reasons for female infanticide. According to the survey done by Chunkath and others, the occurrence of female infanticide is widespread among the poorer and socially disadvantaged community including the thevars, vaniyars and scheduled castes. In contrast, Adithi & Community Services Guild (1992) has mentioned several communities, including the wealthy Gounder community, the landed caste in Salem District,

Tamil Nadu, also practice female infanticide. George and others (1992:1155) in their study point out although the Gounders, live in remote villages, they own a significant proportion of land and are in the upper social stratum of their villages, in the North and South Arcot Districts in Tamil Nadu. It has been proved through various studies that the practise cuts across all classes and caste.

Negi in her report has mentioned, the society and families having used coercive tactics to ensure that female infanticide continues, limiting the scope for outside influences in arresting the problem. Experiences of Negi, 1997 and others who have researched on this issue, is that, there is a social sanction to the deed. The familial and social situations seem to outweigh personal reactions and therefore women opt to kill their new born girl children. Indian Council for Child Welfare (ICCW), Tamil Nadu has mentioned that the feeling of guilt and trauma is almost absent in the community that perpetrates the practise, although there is grief among the mothers.

Social pressures play a vital role in bringing about changes in society for the better or worse situations. George and others have also observed maternal motivation in their study as a factor affecting infanticide. They also came across one case of male infanticide just before the beginning of their study period (Feb. 1997) where the mother lost her husband and killed the male child soon after birth, after which the mother remarried. In case of the unwed mother, she tried to abort the pregnancy, which was unsuccessful and committed infanticide when it was born. Maternal motivations for infanticide may be said, therefore, to vary on the basis of marital status.

According to one of the dai interviewed, in the survey conducted by Adithi, Bihar, "mothers are never willing, it is the men who force them" (Times of India, 22nd April 1995). The same study holds that the male mainly take the decision to carry out the killing of the newborn babies with females being reluctant participants (The Pioneer, 13th Nov. 1995). One mother justifies her action by saying that they have hardly any access to medical care.

All deliveries take place at home and often the mother is left to bleed after a particularly difficult child birth. They categorically state that they do not wish to expose their girls to such harsh conditions (Arunachalam, 1994). A question that arises with regard to female infanticide is whether birth order influences the chance of survival of the female infant. According to the study by Chunkath and Athreya in Tamil Nadu, the first female infant is, in a majority of cases, not a victim of female infanticide even in the high female infanticide Health Unit Districts (HUDs), although there are instances when it is. The second female infant has a much greater chance of escaping infanticide in Madurai HUD than she does in Periyakulam and Dharmapuri HUDs. While the third female is at much greater risk than the first in all three HUDs, both the second and third seem to be equally at risk in Periyakulam. The survey finding by George and others mentions 19 female infanticides and 18 of the victims had birth orders greater than one and one involved a first born daughter. Each of these families had at least one surviving female child at the time and usually they had two. In their study they also found that no twin died as a result of direct infanticide, however, they also say that they are subject to more neglect than a male twin and a female infant born after a set of twins is very likely to be killed. The above given studies prove that birth order does influence the chances of child's survival.

Negi after conducting interviews and discussions with people and NGOs closely working in Madurai District point out to the prevalence of a superstition that, killing a new born girl child increases the probability of a male child being born in the family. Some of the other findings in the survey conducted by George and others in 1989 is that, the villages in which female infanticide occurs tend to be even more remote and have less educated people than the villages with no cases of infanticide. Lack of scanning centres has also been cited as reason for infanticide. As people do not have this facility, they kill the child after it is born. According to Soma Wadhwa, every year 50,000 female foetuses are aborted in India. These people are not very different from those who kill the baby after she is born. The latter, she says, simply do not have enough money or facility to kill her in the womb (Times of India, 29 Dec., 1995) Observation made by Kumarbabu, 1996, is that even in the so-called remote, less-developed areas, "scanning centres exist. Although it may be true in some cases, one cannot generalise whether remoteness of the village, education of the people, or lack of scanning centres have any correlation with the occurrence of female infanticide.

Psychopathologists have also tried to analyse why people kill new born girl children. Sabu George, Rajaratnam Abel and B.D.Meller have carried out research in 12 villages of K.V.Kuppam block, North Arcot Ambedkar District in Tamil Nadu State for four years beginning in April 1987 to September 1989. After creating a good rapport with the people, the father or other family members would tell the village worker that if the current pregnancy resulted in the birth of a female, it would be killed. They found that each village had an assigned village level worker whose primary function was to provide education about child care to village mothers. The worker in all cases was a local resident of the village.

The main findings of the survey conducted by George and others, was that in the study population of 13,000 there were a total of 773 birth outcomes recorded, involving 759 live births of which 378 were male and 381 were female. Among the cohort of live births, 56 died in the period of two and a half years (from April 1, 1987 to September 30, 1989), and of these 23 were males and 33 females.

Thus the female male ratio was about 3:4. Of the 23 male deaths, there was no infanticide. Among the 33 female deaths, there were 19 infanticides. Thus more than half the female deaths in the 12 study villages were due to direct or indirect infanticide. In the six villages in which all infanticides occurred, infanticide constitute 72 per cent of female deaths (excluding the only case of the female infanticide to the unwed mother) In the 12 village study population, the overall sex ratio (female per males) at the time of the study was 977.5. In the village where female infanticide was practised, the sex ratio was 939.8, while in the other villages, it was 1018.6.

Child Marriage

A girl child is twice vulnerable for being a child and a girl. Discrimination against them begins even before their birth and continues as they grow. Their psychological, physical and economic dependence on the family makes them vulnerable to violence and child abuse within or outside the family.

Since 1872, the following efforts have been made to legalise the minimum age of marriage. The Civil Marriage Act of 1872 was passed as a result of the efforts made by Raja Ram Mohan Roy, before which, a provision of the Indian Penal Code rendered the consummation of marriage before the girl attained the age of 10, punishable with life imprisonment. Social reformers of 19th and 20th century tried to counteract child marriage as they felt it was marring child's educational, physical and economic progress. Noted social reformer Har Bilas Sarda, from Ajmer District, Rajasthan authored and piloted a Bill in British Legislature to stop child marriage, which, in course of time became law. The Child Marriage Restrain Act of 1929 (popularly known as Sarda Act) which fixed the minimum age for boys at 18 and girls at 15, extended only to British India. The Act did not prohibit marriages nor did it declare these marriages invalid or illegal (Saxena, 1999). With the codification of the Hindu Law, the Hindu Marriage Act passed in 1955 made the minimum age of marriage for girls at 15. In 1978, a further revision was made in the minimum legal age. With this last amendment, the law was finally brought nearer in line with the accumulated scientific medical evidence showing that the adolescent girl is at grave risk of her health, as also that of her children, until she has reached the age of 18 at least. Alongside, the minimum age of marriage for boys also underwent an upward revision to 21 years.

However, it did not empower the police to prevent the marriage by arresting a person without warrant or magisterial order. Under the amended provision of this Act the jurisdiction was given to metropolitan magistrates or to judicial magistrates. They have been empowered to try any case related to child marriage. Anybody including social organisations, the police or the any person can make a complaint to the police or to the magistrate directly. Acting on a complaint, any court can itself make inquiries. However in practice this whole process is so complicated and so time consuming that by the time these authorities are in a position to take preventive action the marriage is already over and all proof of such a ceremony obliterated. Further, Section 12 of the amended Child Marriage Restraint Act empower the magistrate to issue injunctions prohibiting marriages in contravention of this Act, but before issuing injunction the affected parties have to be given a notice to enable them to present defence. An injunction issued without this notice is not valid. This procedure is so time-consuming that marriages in contravention of this Act are completed before the court can pass an order preventing them. The court cannot even issue a general direction that marriage of a child shall not be solemnised within some particular time limit, say eight months or two years. The punishment under the amended Child Marriage Restraint Act remains mild, i.e. only simple imprisonment extended to three months and a fine of Rs 1000. According to the provisions of Section 5 of the Act whoever performs, conduct or direct child marriages shall be punishable (Saxena, 1999).

Ancient Hindu religious manuals like the Manu Smriti and Grihayastra set the age of life partners at 13 for girls and 16 for boys. In the Vedic period early marriage of girls began to gain approval and it became obligatory to have a girl married before she attained puberty. The age was lowered still further in the Brahminical period, resulting in the abuse of children (The Statesman, 1998). In India, 37.48 per cent of the total districts have a mean age of marriage below the legal age of 18. The phenomenon of child marriage prevails all over the country. According to Chattopadhyay, 1986, the phenomenon of marrying off minors persists in almost every caste and community of Rajasthan. This practice prevails in Gaduliya Lohars of Central, Western and South Eastern Rajasthan. It also exists among the Muslim converts and among higher castes of Pushkaran Brahmins. According to Saxena, 1999, during the Akha Teej or Akshaya Trithiya, the most auspicious day for marriages, practically everywhere in Western Rajasthan-Bikaner, Tonk, Jhalwar, Jodhpur and Jaisalmer, marriages are performed en masse. Every street, house, tractor and even buses seem to reverberate with music and marriage guests. But in all marriages the bride and the groom are children, some just two or three years old and some babies barely able to walk. These brides and grooms are carried by their parents or are perched on a thaliv and taken around the holy fire for performing the most important ceremony of their life (Saxena, 1999).

In communities like Dakot, Dhobi, Jatava, Kasai, girls are married between the age group of 11 to 13, and in case of boys it ranges from 14 to 16 years of age. The number of minor children married in a mass marriage, in Rajasthan was reported to be 25000 in 1984 and 30,000 in 1983, 40,000 in 1985 and unofficial sources confirmed no decline in 1986 (Chattopadhyay, 1986). On 29th April, 1998 the day of Akshay Trithiya, National Human Rights Commission (NHRC) deputed a senior officer to Bikaner and Jodhpur to report on the actual state of affairs. According to a Senior Superintendent of Police (SSP) from the Commissioner's Investigation Division, who was witness to the event, says several marriages were solemnised with great celebration and gaiety and without any obstruction from the authorities or members of the public. (Hindu, 19th Aug. 1998). Nair sites an example of Dumma Village in Deogarh District, Uttar Pradesh where almost all girls become brides before attaining the age of 10. There is not a single girl unmarried above 12 years of age in the village (Nair, 1995). The child-brides or grooms do not understand the solemnity of these ceremonies, but for elders it is the safest and most tested way of keeping property and money within the family and innocent children become pawns in family business (Saxena, 1999).

According to Nair (1995), the phenomenon of child marriage is linked to poverty, illiteracy, dowry, landlessness and other such social evils. There are several social factors that have contributed to the prevalence of child marriage. The girl is considered to be a burden of the household and thereby she is married in an early age. Marriages between cousins is common in South India. Sometimes marriages are settled even before the birth of the child. In Rajasthan communities like Balai, Bhangi, Bolal, Chamar, Dholi, Gujars, Malis and Meenas believe, that marriage can be performed in childhood days irrespective of their age and maturity. Sometimes betrothal takes place before the pair is born, commonly known as 'kotha tharpana' (Chattopadhyay, 1986). This custom ensures that the girl is secure as she has been married within the clan.

Parents believe that, it is easy for the child-bride to adapt to a new environment as well as it is easy for others to mould the child to suit their family environment and practices. Child marriage is also done to maintain pre-marriage chastity among the girls. Sex within or outside families, as a result of a chance encounter-willing or otherwise-happens oftener than one can predict. After having spoken to a number of parents of such girls, Kuala is convinced that this apprehension of their unmarried daughters getting pregnant is the single largest cause of parents being so eager to marry off their girls at a young age-'lest they bring shame and scandal to the family' (Kaul, 1996). According to Ahuja's (1998: 42) findingsvi, among the 94 rape victims he studied, unmarried girls constituted 63 percent, married girls 33 percent and widows 4 percent. Some parents believe that, it is easier to impose their will on their children while they are still infants. They believe that, once married, boys do not flirt around with village girls and the girls learn to take responsibilities. There is also a conviction that it is easier for the couple to adapt themselves to each other as the children stay with each other since childhood. Despite growing up together, the boys are not completely connected or committed to their wives and some even seek relationships outside marriage (Saxena, 1999).

The girl is considered to be an additional labour as she is involved in unpaid jobs within or outside the house in the rural as well as urban scenario. This is another reason why the parents are worried about the girl's chastity before marriage. There are various economic factors that lead to the prevalence of child marriage. In some parts of rural India, mass marriages are conducted and the marriage celebrations become less expensive if the girls are married on this occasion. Elders are convinced that child marriages, since they are solemnised in groups are cheaper and easier to perform (Saxena, 1999) In the month of April, Rajasthan celebrates the Akha Teej festival, the day of Akshay Trithiya, by solemnising thousands of child marriages (Nair, 1995). The prevalent ritual of the childhood ceremony in Rajasthan, according to Kabra, is based on social financial considerations. Firstly, there is no system of dowry in this agreement. Secondly, since the marriages are conducted for a number of children in the family simultaneously, it works out as group marriage, thereby cutting down the expenditure drastically. Finally, its seasonal, one time community occurrence operates as very convenient social logistics for the rural folk (Kabra, 1997).

The main arguments of the parents are that if a girl is married off early they will have to pay only Rs 500 or less as dowry. After girls attain puberty, the cost of marriage could go upto Rs 15,000 (Chattopadhyay: 1986). However, a large amount is paid when the girl is sent to the groom's house. According to Nair (1995), elders hold their poverty responsible for the prevalence of this phenomenon. In case of those who have landed property, irrespective of any caste, the preference to marry the son/daughter to the brother's/sister's children or maternal uncle was largely based on the economic principle that, the landed property would remain undivided and would not go out of the clan. To save the cost incurred, marriages are conducted at times when there is finance available with the people. It is also conducted jointly with other events which require feast to be given to all relatives.

On the eldest daughter reaching puberty, all the daughters are married at a time, regardless of their age. In the event of a death in the family, marriage of the girl, regardless of her age, is performed, so that the feast to be given during the marriage can be jointly given. Marriages are also conducted immediately after the harvesting since the finances would be available with the farmer. In case of the joint families, the parents would want to perform the marriage of their daughter before the division of the property among the sons. Marriages within the clan is also arranged as the monetary adjustments are easier within the clan than an outside alliance where else, the socio, psychological and economic security is unpredictable.

The impact of child marriage over the young bride's future is enforced widowhood, inadequate socialisation, education deprivation, lack of independence to select the life partner, lack of economic independence, psychological as well as marital adjustment, low health/Nutritional status as a result of early/ frequent pregnancies in an unprepared psychological state of the young bride. Thousands of adolescent girls are at risk from child marriage and the implications are not only on their health but also on the right to fulfil their human potential unhampered by the premature assumption of adult roles and responsibilities (Joseph, 1996). Boys suffer less in this male dominated society. Most grooms, once educated and grown up, migrate to urban areas and get better jobs. Many abandon their village brides for city women. Some continue to keep two wives. In some cases the grown up boys, don't even bother to acknowledge their child marriage and the brides are forced to go back to their parent's house (Saxena, 1999). The argument that it is easier for the couple to adapt themselves to each other may not always be true in reality.

In case the husband dies before even the consummation of the marriage, these child brides are treated like widows and cannot remarry. The deserted and widows are invariably given in nata to some widower in the family. Nata is an obnoxious custom. Officially, the child is the wife of some widower but in fact she becomes the common property of all the male members of the family (Saxena, 1999). Roopa Shaha, who has stopped several child marriages says that child marriages are the root cause for many personality disorders and sexual problems later in life. Girls get a mental shock when their husbands force them to have sex and they develop a feeling of hatred because they cannot emotionally understand the changes in their body and feelings during pregnancy (Kapoor, 1996).

There have been arguments that child marriage does not lead to early pregnancies and child abuse. It has been argued that, the girl does not go to the in law's house immediately after marriage and she is sent only after she attains puberty. On the other hand there have been arguments that the norms and customs are highly flexible. According to Singh, since women work outside the home, the girl is an economic asset, and therefore her parental family tries to keep her with them for as long as possible (1994: 1378). According to Kabra, the ceremony practised in the rural areas of India is only for social authentication of an agreement between two families to marry their wards at an opportune age much later. He adds that, child marriages do not result in early pregnancies or more children as child bride never goes to the husband's house after the marriage. The real age at which the marriage is consummated is 17 to 19 years (Kabra,, 1997). While there is a widespread recognition that girls should begin regular cohabitation only after they attained puberty, the custom was customarily violated. Once the marriage had been performed, a lot of domestic, especially feminine pressures pull the wife into the husbands family much earlier than puberty.

In many cases, gaunavii is also done before the permitted age. The girl becomes a mother early. Herself a child, she is unable to look after another child. She is pressurised with multiple responsibilities of being a wife, mother and daughter-in-law (Saxena, 1999) After marriage, in case of there being no daughter in the in-laws house, she is taken there to work, or to facilitate the work during the harvest season. Early child bearing that is, under the age of 20 years has serious consequences on the health of both mothers and children. Age differentials of risk are further sharpened in a society with poor health, low income, inadequate medical care and nutrition. Ravindran, 1995 says child marriage is one of the indirect causes of infant and maternal mortality. An adolescent conceiving and giving birth to a child when her body is not fully developed and that too without adequate prenatal care, puts the lives of her child and herself in jeopardy. A study conducted by Family Planning Foundation, 1991, reported that mortality rates were higher among babies born to women under 18 and the rate two to three times higher among women suffering from malnutrition. The study covered 800 villages of 33 districts in Uttar Pradesh, Madhya Pradesh, Orissa, Karnataka and Maharashtra. According to the study, nearly 29 to 58 percent girls from poorer sections married under age and also became mothers.

There are other socio-economic factors that determine absolute levels of risk at any age, but it is the biological processes that determine the age pattern of risks. Medical research from all over the world shows that maternal age has an independent influence on relative risks and that childbirth is much more hazardous for mothers under 20 years than for those in their twenties. In addition to those who die, many women suffer from serious illnesses related to pregnancy, abortion or childbirth. Maternal age also influences infant mortality.

Almost everyone is equally guilty, whether it is local MLA or the school teacher. They have either themselves married their children very young or have enthusiastically participated in such marriages. Besides administrative laxity, it is the rigidity and callousness of the local people, which has led to widespread and open practise of child marriages. Despite the administration being fully aware of the custom, and sometimes even having advance knowledge about it, the crime against innocent children continues. As the administration has turned a blind eye to the problem, local people have no fear for law. Caste affinity and social pressure is so great that no one reports such cases or comes forward to give evidence. Past experiences have taught a lesson to many, that authorities don't respond in time of such crisis. Bhanwari Devi, a Saathin of the Women's Development Programme in rural Rajasthan, was gang raped as a punishment for her efforts to prevent child marriages in her village in 1992. Joseph writes, "all she got for trying to implement the existing laws was harassment, humiliation and violation, not only from hostile sections of the local community but also, subsequently, from members of the official law enforcing agencies, including the police and the judiciary" (Joseph, 1996).

A few years ago a cop who tried to stop a child marriage in Bharatpur, Rajasthan, was murdered and his body tossed into a nearby well (The Statesman, 1998) Of course, every year routine appeals for not performing child marriages are issued by the government and non-government organisations. Sathins, anganwadi workers, social organisations and the police are alerted and asked to take preventive measures. Yet the baraatviii with the baby groom arrives for the toddler bride. Festivities take place in the open. The tractor trolleys with the festive people even drive past the local police station but no action is taken by anyone. How can any person of the community or authority raise the issue, when everyone is guilty? (Saxena, 1999).

Child Sexual Abuse

Sexual abuse is defined as "all sexually oriented conduct, commentary or gestures, intentional and repeated, not desired or accepted freely by their object, for whom it is an imposition, a humiliation or attack on their dignity". (Diaz, 1996) (Adriana Gomez, 1996) The term abuse includes physical as well as non-physical acts. There is enough evidence to suggest that it often receives wider familial sanction. It is institutionalised in various forms, ranging from long hours of labour, often within and outside the home, denial of food, neglect of ailments and verbal abuse to physical violence by the husband and sometimes other family members. Far more difficult to acknowledge are problems caused by the narrow definition of sexuality as a means of perpetuating control over their minds and bodies in a conjugal relationship. (Fourth World Conference on Women, Beijing, 1995)

Legally child sexual abuse is interpreted as 'rape' of a child who is below 16 years of age and rape as defined in Indian Penal Code is penetration without her consent. However, in Indian law has interpreted and defined rape as penile-vaginal penetration. This definition is inadequate as in most of the child sexual abuse cases, Sakshi has worked with, there has been no sexual penetration (Sakshi is an NGO working in Delhi). Child sexual abuse is the physical or mental violation of a child with sexual intent. Thus Narang, 1998 defines child sexual abuse as follows:

- An adult exposing his/her genitals to a child or persuading the child to do the same.
- Adult touching a child's genitals or making the child touch the adult's genitalia
- An adult involving a child in pornography which includes exposing a child to pornographic material.
- An adult having oral, vaginal or anal intercourse with a child
- Any verbal or other sexual suggestion made to a child by an adult
- An adult persuading children to engage in sexual activity.

According to Kemps sexual abuse is defined as "the involvement of dependent, developmentally immature children and adolescents in sexual activities they do not really comprehend, to which they are unable to give informed consent, or that violate the social taboos of family roles.

According to Schmit (1980), Sexual abuse is defined as any sexual misuse of the child by a care-taking adult. Sexual abuse includes incest, oral-genital contact; sodomy, molestation, digital manipulation and so on. RAHI (an NGO based in Delhi) includes exploitative sexual activity, whether or not they involve physical contact, between a child and another person, who by virtue of his power over the child due to age, strength, position, or relationship uses the child to meet his or her own sexual and emotional needs to the definition of child sexual abuse. The act though sexual in nature is also about the abuse of power and the betrayal of trust. A child's dependency needs for nurturance, touch, caring, caressing, and the like are not the same as adult sexual desires. The adult or older person completely disregards the child's own developmental immaturity and inability to understand sexual behaviours. The act, therefore, is not only a gross violation of the child's body but also of the trust implicit in a care giving relationship. Child sexual abuse, according to the report is any sexual contact between a child and an adult. The contact covers a wide range of behaviours. It may or may not involve physical contact, force or violence, but always involves coercion.

It can also include fondling of the breast or genitals, rape, oral sex, and/or sodomy. It can also include an adult demanding that a child touch his/her genitals either directly or through clothing. Non-physical sexual contact also includes exhibitionism, obscene talk or pornography.

Child sexual abuse takes place in all cultures, races and in every strata of the society. Both males and females are sexually abused. Girls however, are abused more frequently and over a longer period of time. Findings based on research done at Sakshi as well as international statistics on child sexual abuse indicate that at least 2 out of 4 girls and 1 out of 6 boys are victims of sexual abuse. A study carried out by a Bangalore based NGO, Samvada, in 1994 of 348 girls from Karnataka, revealed that 83% of the respondents had experienced some form of child sexual abuse. The preliminary report of an ongoing survey of Sakshi with about 650 girl students (as of December, 1997) indicates that about 60% of the girls had experienced some form of abuse till the age of 15 years. Out of these 60%, about 20% had suffered abuse by close relatives. DCP (Northeast Delhi) S.B.K.Singh reported in a daily newspaper, 'The Pioneer', that 85% of the rape cases registered in the District during 1997, involved persons known to the victims. According to the World Health Organisation, one in every ten child is sexually abused.

In a 1980 study of 1000 victims of child abuse, A.B.Dave, et al found that 81 per cent could be classified as victims of physical abuse, 7 per cent of what the authors call neglect, 9.3 per cent of sexual abuse and 2.7 per cent of emotional abuse. None of these categories can be treated as exclusive and it is important to note that studies of this kind are extremely difficult to undertake. This particularly so in the area of sexual relations where the overall attitude of secrecy and suppression which governs any discussion or reference to sex making it difficult to come to any definite conclusion on the extent of sexual abuse of children. Yet of available figures, of almost 10,000 reported rapes in 1990, an alarming 25 per cent are of girl children below the age of 16 and about a fifth are those under ten. A recent analysis done by the Crimes Against Women Cell, Delhi Police, points out that of the 143 rape cases registered between January and June 1992, 107 or almost 75 per cent were in the age range 7-18 years. Forty of the rapists were immediate neighbours and seven were relatives. Conversations with those in charge of the cell indicate that such cases are on the increase.

According to a survey done by Sakshi, sixty per cent of 650 school girls questioned in a survey said they had suffered abuse, close relatives having abused twenty per cent of them (Reporter, The Asian Age 1998). The word perpetrator is used in relation to the person or people who are directly abusing a child or children. Although this can be applied to the person responsible for any other form of mistreatment, it tends to relate to those committing child sexual abuse. It is not used to refer to other adults who may have played a role but were not directly involved, such as a non-abusing parent who might have been aware of the abuse but unable to intervene.

In most cases, the abuser is known to the child family friend, sibling, relative, servant, teacher and so on. There have also been cases where the abusers have been very close relatives-father, grandfather, brother and uncle. The abuser is usually an older person who is in some position of trust and/or power vis-avis the child. Even though both men and women can sexually abuse a child, most abusers are male. The abuser violates a relationship of trust with the child.

They may use tricks or threats to persuade the child to take part in a sexual activity. The abuse generally takes place in the child's home or the abuser's home. Given that the abuser is often known to the child and usually has both access to as well as authority over the child, the abuse does not commonly involve physical violence and generally continues over a long period of time. The abuser uses threats or blackmail to warn the child against telling any one about the abuse. This may be the primary cause for the child's silence. Child sexual abuse is on the increase because of the responses to it and towards the victims. One of the response being denial of its existence and disbelief: Many people with whom Sakshi has interacted, deny any existence of child sexual abuse especially within a family. The concept of Indian families is perhaps the most sensitive and revered. Therefore, it is difficult to believe that sexual abuse in the families really happens. For them, if at all the concept of child sexual abuse exists, it is limited to a particular class. The popular belief is that it is very rare and happens only in low class families (slums). Even if some people believe that child sexual abuse exists, there is denial publicly as it is difficult for them to deal with the fact that it is prevalent in our traditional Indian families.

Due to ignorance, denial of its existence, and inability of adults to deal with the subject, the child is met with disbelief when he/she finally summons up the courage to confide in someone about the experience and trauma of being sexually abused. Thus the child is forced to suffer in silence giving the abuser greater power over the child. Sexual abuse is shrouded in shame and secrecy. Sexual organs or any reference to sex is considered to be shameful. Children are not given proper answers when they ask questions about sexual organs. They get the messages that certain body parts are dirty and they should never be talked about. So, when a child is abused, there is total silence. The child knows that there is something wrong going on, yet the child does not have the language or the words to express it. There is loneliness because the child cannot talk about it to anybody and does not know whom to approach. This hampers disclosure and thus the abuse continues.

In families where parents/relatives accept and realise that a child has suffered sexual abuse, the child is forced into silence given the culture of privacy, family prestige and family unity. The child generally does not receive much support from the family as they do not want the matter to be disclosed and the family name exposed. Thus the abuser is not confronted and the child is encouraged to 'forget' the traumatic experience. The child and her future are sacrificed for the image of the family.

A healthy environment is a family situation where family communication is clear, direct and specific and rules are flexible.

Children can freely approach elders or adults with questions or concerns about sexual experiences in the full knowledge that the adults concerned will address these issues with the child's welfare in mind. In this situation no trusted older individual violates the child's person and the child feels the freedom to say no to potential abusers and report the incident with full confidence that he or she will be protected. Families in which incest occurs often appear to be like any other family. However, they are riddled with secrets and psychological stress. Incestuous families tend to be closed, inward families lacking in any real emotional connection to people outside the family. These families often have a history of problems for several generations, which increase the potential for incest. Frequently the mothers of abused children were themselves molested as children. Many victims assume that being dominated and treated poorly by the offender is just a fact of life and not something to be challenged. However it is vital to note that, while family influences may contribute to incest, the dysfunction itself cannot cause an individual to become sexually abusive. However, the situation makes it easier for the symptoms to play themselves out. The offender is the sole person responsible for the abuse.

In some cases, the mothers do not want to take action against the abused as they are constrained by the status of the abuser within the family, for example; a father. Economic dependence, low self esteem, lack of power within the family, incapacity to accept the responsibility of single parent and moral shame of the act keep the mother quite Members of voluntary organisations says that a mother would often suppress and wish away the event, not only because of a sense of shame and outrage, but also out of fear of reprisals from her husband, son, or other relatives. According to Wadhwa 1993, in 1992-93, there were eight cases of rape and molestation reported by mothers to Crime Against Women Cell in Delhi. Officials at the cell pointed out that this was a significant development as hardly any such instances were reported earlier. At the same time, wives expected the police to merely caution their husbands; filing a case against them would be unheard of.

Society constantly judges women including young girls and children. They are made to feel responsible, guilty or persecuted.

Girls are very scared of this judgement, and of being exposed, which forces them into silence. Abusers are aware of this societal attitude towards women and this becomes their power. Society's attitude enables them to go scott-free. Child sexual abuse is usually dismissed because in most cases it is not 'rape' as defined by law. It is met with disbelief and girls are accused of being destructive when the complaint is against a family member. In cases where there is no penile penetration or when rape cannot be proved due to inadequate evidence, the accused is charged for 'outraging the modesty of a woman' where they may be sentenced only for a period of six months of two years. In most cases, the accused are acquitted in absence of adequate laws on child sexual abuse and inadequate interpretation of existing laws. The court room environment is hostile and girls are humiliated over and over again. This poses to be a major obstacle for girls who want to file a complaint against their abuser. The effects of child abuse are long lasting and are carried into adulthood leaving deep scars on the personality of the abused. Healing is an important process and must begin as early as possible.

Singh (1997) has pointed out that child sexual abuse triggers a host of complexities in the child's psyche. Periodic bouts of low self esteem, sexual dysfunctioning, guilt are some of the problems that arise out of child sexual abuse and which continue to haunt the individual well into adulthood (Singh Dhiraj, 1997).

Sexual abuse is not the only childhood experience that causes difficulty for people as they mature. Long term effects are often identical to those of other early developmental setbacks. The difference however is that most of them can be talked about freely and without involving embarrassment. The person who is sexually abused in childhood is faced with the taboo of talking about it. Most former victims keep their experiences a secret for many years. Consequently their emotions are likely to run very deep and when they eventually surface the effects can be devastating. The abuser conveys the message that the abuser's needs come first and so it destroys the basis for child-adult trust. Victims of sexual abuse grow up without a sense of protection and security, something that is essential for them to build inner strength and venture into new experiences. As a result, they also have difficulty in trusting others and forming relationships. Survivor's sexual activity as children were dominated by perpetrators emotional needs and selfish orientation towards sexuality. Tension, fear, betrayal, pain and mistrust coloured the victim's sexual awakening. Consequently, as adults, the sexual behaviour of survivors is severely impacted. They face issues such as sexual maladjustment, abstaining from sex or compulsively seeking it out. Adult women victimised as children are also more likely to manifest depression, self destructive behaviour, anxiety, feelings of isolation, low self esteem, a tendency towards substance abuse, over-eating and various other addictions.

The most disturbing effect of child sexual abuse is that the worst scars are on the emotional and mental health, which may show up as unidentifiable symptoms. Children are prone to a variety of psychological and behavioural disturbances caused by the trauma of abuse. These include bed wetting, nightmares, sleep disorders, depression, anxiety, running away from home, multiple personality disorders, low self esteem caused by guilt and shame. Many children also develop a negative attitude towards their body as they blame themselves for the abuse. Renu, victim of sexual abuse began hating herself and her body. She started eating constantly, as she wanted to look ugly and so that she would not fall prey to abuse again. Thus it can lead to disturbing the child's relationship with her sexual identity/sexuality and she can fall anywhere in the spectrum, which extends from promiscuity to frigid. It effects her self worth and the future interactions that she will have, especially with men.

Shobha Srinath NIMHANS, points out to a fact that a young child below ten may not always be aware that her sexual violation is in fact qualitatively different from thrashing and abuse; it is only with the onset of puberty that she becomes aware of her sexuality. In fact in an environment where physical contact, both affectionate and abusive, by relatives of both sexes is not uncommon, child rape needs to be viewed a little differently from the rape of a post-pubertal girl. Not unexpectedly, the families rarely talk about the rape of their young daughter: when the rapist is a father or brother, the chances of reporting is even lower.

According to Prasad (1998), a victim of incest may attempt suicide, may have bouts of panic attack and depression. The child may not even confide in the parents. He adds that, the wide prevalence of the crime can be gauged by the fact that according to a study, 16 per cent of the patients being treated for genito-urinary symptoms in the dermatology and sexually transmitted diseases department of a public hospital in New Delhi, were below 14 years of age.

The child feels three Ds according to him-dirty, damaged and different. There is a lot of anger, shame and guilt involved. There are suicidal tendencies, drug addiction and alcoholism. They also exhibit self-mutilating behaviour and have panic attacks and depression. According to Dr. Khetrapal, at times the impact plays itself out in certain compulsive behaviour like over-eating, bulimia, anorexia nervosa (repulsion to food) generally seen in abused girls. According to Ms Seema Prakash a counsellor at RAHI, there would be a slump in academic performance, increased temper tantrums, "different" conduct with some members (offenders), exhibition of sexual awareness in crude manner which are indicators of abuse (Prasad, 1998).

According to Singh Dhiraj, most often children do not have the language to describe sexual activity. It is difficult for a child to articulate his or her experience. Moreover, they are extremely traumatised as they try to make sense of what has happened to them.

Hurt and fear of disclosure or punishment are the initial responses that prevent a child from speaking out. Hence it is very important to cultivate openness within the immediate family where the children can confide in their parents without the fear of ridicule or reproach. Parents can look for certain telltale signs and reactions to find out how safe their children are, says Singh, The child tries to stay away from friends and people he was close to earlier. This could be due to guilt that has flooded his little conscience. He or she may seem depressed. Depression itself may not be easy to gauge in children but it is translated into more expressible emotions such as being irritable, withdrawn and listless. The child may resume bed-wetting if he or she has stopped it. Sometimes he or she can get incontinent while awake.

Child Prostitution and Trafficking

The UN Special Rapporteur on the sale of Children, Child Prostitution and Child Pornography defines Child Prostitution as the sexual exploitation of a child for remuneration in cash or in kind, usually but not always organised by an intermediary (parent, family member, procurer, teacher, etc.) (Bruce, 1996: 9). Thus the violence against the girl child acquires a new dimension in the sale of young girls below the age of 18 for prostitution and trafficking. To curb this, the Suppression of Immoral Trafficking Act, later modified to the Prevention of Immoral Trafficking Act has been passed.

Prostitution in India is a Rs 40,000 crore annual business. It has been estimated that 30% of the sex workers are children, who earn Rs.11,000 crore. This has been reported by a study by the Centre of Concern for Child Labour (CCL). (The Times of India, 10 Nov 1998). At present the number of child prostitutes in India is between 270,000 and 400,000, with the number of children in "commercial prostitution" increasing at the rate of 8-10% per annum. The practice of child prostitution is in blatant contravention of the UN Declaration on the Rights of the Child, endorsed by the "National Policy for Children" of the Ministry of Social Welfare, Government of India. Principle 9 of the Declaration states: The child shall be protected against all forms of neglect, cruelty and exploitation. These shall not be the subject of traffic in any form."(Rozario, 1988:57).

Poverty and deprivation, coupled with a low status in society for girls is a primary factor for child prostitution. It is well known that prostitution exists in the Third World because of poverty (Grant,1996). According to a UNICEF Report, children are often required to work to supplement their meagre incomes. (Hindustan Times, 28 Oct 1996). Thus in a country like India, child prostitution in most cases stems from child labour. Prostitution is often viewed as an avenue providing easy money, which seems attractive for families steeped in poverty. Dr. K.K.Mukhpadhyay from Delhi School of Social Work, University of Delhi, in his presentation based on surveys he conducted for the Government of India, said that young girls in India were taken away from their parents in poor backward and drought affected districts of the country for purposes of trafficking.

These were also states with gender inequality and low literacy rates. The trafficking network was well organised in these areas. He found in his survey that about eighty per cent of the girls who were in this profession entered it as children and due to difficult circumstances, such as poverty, illiteracy, ignorance, and deception.

The increasingly consumerist society only further complicated the situation. Children are often hired out or sold by their families to agents who may or may not reveal the true nature of the work offered. The agent may promise a job as a domestic servant or factory worker at a wage many times higher than is customary in rural areas. A sum which is large in the eyes of the family, may be handed over to them, and the child is obligated to work to pay off the debt. Some young girls are deceived by young urban boys who go to villages. The biys conduct fake marriages with these girls, bring them to the cities and sell them to the brothels (Mukhopadhyay, 1995:7).

On the economic front, it must be noted that development policies and patterns of development promoting tourism, industrialisation, rural to urban migration particularly of males generate a demand for commercial sex. In such a situation, the developing countries bear the brunt of the problem. Economic disparities within countries, and between countries and regions fuels the demand for trafficking from low income to high income areas. In addition, population mobility has been facilitated by globalization and liberalization as they have opened borders and relaxed controls. (Trade in Human Misery,1998) Such a scenario gives a spurt to tourism which leads to 'sex tourists' from the West journeying East with the purpose of exploiting children. Goa has become one such haven for paedophiles and people indulging in child prostitution. According to unofficial estimates, there are at least 400 minors in the locality involved in the trade.

Further, there is no respite in the situation as the existence of minors is often hidden on receiving a tip off about the raids. There are also instances of the arrest of 25 odd girls and their being summarily released subsequently, once their ages have been found to be above 18 (Menon, 1997.) The exploitation is shown in the fact that a girl below the age of 16 is available for Rs 300-Rs 500, justifying for Goa the name of 'India's

Bangkok' (Rai, 1997). Men who travel to the Third World for 'sex with children', argue that there is nothing new in going abroad to escape the moral strictures at home (Grant, 1996). This phenomenon is further enhanced by the growing demand for very young girls with a premium on virgins. According to Ms. Prasanna, a research scholar with the Department of Criminology at Madras University, the fear of AIDS often makes the Western 'sex tourist' to seek virgins. Such a demand is catered to by large markets in Bombay and Hyderabad also (The Hindustan Times, 5 Oct 1994).

Child prostitution in India is further aggravated by the presence of social conventions and myths prevailing in society. It is popularly believed that sex with a virgin is a cure for venereal and other diseases. Moreover, a reason for the rise in child trafficking can be attributed to the myth that having sexual intercourse with a child would protect the client from AIDS. This was stated at a workshop organised by UNICEF on "The Rights of the Child" (The Hindustan Times, 28 Aug 1997). With the low levels of education and literacy, such myths are only perpetuated.

It is well known that the female sex is further disadvantaged due to the inadequate educational and employment opportunities, gender disparities in access to opportunities and the lack of social safety nets (Trade in Human Misery, 1998). Social conventions play an important role in the continuance of the phenomenon of child prostitution. These include child marriages, polygamy, dowry and social stigma against single, unwed, divorced women and girls who have been sexually abused (Trade in Human Misery,1998).

Children, especially young girls, in these circumstances are especially vulnerable to the prostitution racket. There have been instances of girls being driven into the sex trade following traumatic sexual experiences during childhood, including rape. If, in the case of Shahida of Kozhikode, it was the violence inflicted by her father's younger brother followed by molestation by her cousin and then rape (The Hindustan Times, 2 Oct 1998), Lakshmi's tale of woe began when she was raped by her step father at age 8 and her further sexual exploitation for food when she left home (Uniyal,1998). Prostitution thus becomes a viable option for children who have been abandoned, for those from disrupted families and for those who are financially supporting their families.

The prevalence of traditional and religious practices in some communities that consist of dedicating girls to gods and goddesses serve to encourage child prostitution (Trade in Human Misery, 1998). The evolution of the Devadasi cult can be traced to a period earlier than the entry of Aryans in India. The cult appears to be a relic of the Dravidian matriarchal society. It exists today in India with many regional variations. This social convention condemns nearly 5 to 10 thousand girls every year to a life of sexual servitude (concubinage) and subsequently into prostitution. The devadasi girls form 15% of the total women in prostitution in India.

In the border districts of Maharashtra and Karnataka states, their percentage in prostitution is nearly 80%. The striking fact is that all of them have entered prostitution in an extremely organised manner. This process involves first making the girl a devadasi and then legitimising her entry into prostitution with the help of 'religion'. The practice receives sanction from mythology and was once supported by feudal land owning systems. Social backwardness is the most closely linked factors to both devadasis and prostitutes. It is known that ethnic minority, "scheduled castes" and "other backward classes", indigenous people, hill tribes, refugees and illegal immigrants are particularly susceptible to the racket (Trade in Human Misery, 1998). Interestingly, the "signs" used to identify the chosen child (who is then dedicated to the goddess Yellamma) are those of ill health-white patches of eczema, leprosy and even mental retardation. Researchers now speculate whether prostitution was one lucrative way of making use of such otherwise "worthless children" (Aiyar, 1997).

Among those involved in child prostitution, it is the street children who are most vulnerable to it. According to Dr. A.B.Bose, advisor in the Planning Commission, the problem of street children is primarily the outcome of four circumstances-poverty, nonexistence of a supportive social and economic structure, rapid urbanisation leading to chronic housing shortage and the growth of slums and an oppressive home environment (Kanth, 1994). The prevailing situation is aggravated by the lack of awareness of legal rights, the exploited situation of the victims and the absence of a channel for seeking redress. In the presence of the growth of trans-national crime and expansion of drug trafficking networks, weak law enforcement mechanisms, exploitation by corrupt law enforcers and officials are the order of the day (Trade in Human Misery, 1998). On paper, prostitution per se is not illegal and hence there are loopholes in the law that ensure a person goes scot-free even if he sells a minor girl to a brothel, provided there is a stamped receipt.

The erosion of traditional family systems and values and the pursuit of consumerism encourages sale of children (Trade in Human Misery, 1998). The National Commission for Women identifies sexual glorification by the electronic media as one of the prime reasons for minors in prostitution (Prabhudesai, 1997). In 1991, the Central Social Welfare Board conducted a study on Child Prostitution. Among the causes of entry to prostitution, economic distress accounted for 41%; desertion by spouse = 24.5 %; deception = 11.9%; social customs = 5.35%; family tradition = 5%; kidnapping and abduction = 2.25%. The study also indicates that many of the young girls join, emulating the example of girls who have joined the trade and as a consequence are living well.

It has also been shown that most prostitutes are forced to remain in their professions due to police highhandedness and the clout of local henchmen (Jha, 1998). This makes chances of rescue and rehabilitation very slight. It has been found in 1994 that India has four lakh child prostitutes. According to Mr. K.T. Suresh of the Bangalore based NGO "Equations", about 20% of India's 2 million prostitutes are below the age of 15. Bombay city alone is believed to have 40,000 child prostitutes. The flesh trade in India is liberally replenished from Nepal, which is believed to contribute an estimated 20,000 young girls every year (The Hindustan Times, 5 Oct 1994). The survey conducted by the Central Social Welfare Board in 1991-92 in the cities of Bombay, Calcutta, Delhi, Madras, Hyderabad and Bangalore shows that 15% are below the age of 15 at the time of entry and 25% are minors in the age group of 16-18 years (Pioneer, 8 June 1994).

However, among the various studies conducted, there does appear to be some discrepancy in their findings. A study on prostitution in Delhi has challenged the findings of a report by the National Commission for Women on child prostitution. While the NCW says that children form 60% of the prostitutes in the Capital's main sex market at G.B. Road, the study by Jan Shakti Vahini figures it as low as 7% (Indian Express, 20 Dec 1998). On a similar note, very few cases of child sex workers have been reported in the state of Kerala. However, according to the study conducted by Loyola College of Social Sciences on "Girl Children in Prostitution", this does not imply their total absence; it merely indicates that locating them is difficult (Chadha, 1998).

Violence against prostitutes is of two kinds, argued Mr Dasgupta, and relates to violence at the workplace. Girls are sold by their parents or procured by abductors. A good number, about 25% to 30% are known as chukris in Calcutta. These women who are sold by their parents or husbands are severely beaten and tortured into submission. As a rule they have to pass on all their earnings to the keepers and any deviation from this norm is also countered with violence. Lack of space accounts for the presence of keepers in a big way. However those with a place of their own face yet another problem: Goondas (toughs) forcefully seek entry into the women's houses and assume the role of the pimps.

They live off their earnings and, in case of resistance, get violent. Data revealed that clients were the least prone to use violence. Mr Dasgupta's study showed that 75% of women in the prostitution industry are from West Bengal, of whom a third are from Murshidabad, Birbhum and Burdwan or the Radh area. The Radh are a has traditionally sent girls to Calcutta for prostitution. What is important here is the prevalence of child marriage and child widows. When they returned to their parent's home, as they were considered burdens, they were sent off to Calcutta to work as housemaids or prostitutes. Earlier, these women came from Kulin Brahmin and Kayastha families, nowadays they are from all castes.

Micro studies conducted by Prerana, Mumbai, conducted 10 focus group interviews of five children in each group reveals that the age of becoming a prostitute was under 18 for 90.3 per cent of the girls, the average age being 16 years (Prerana, 1995; 10). When dealing with child prostitution, the best possible available indicator as to its prevalence is the incidence of AIDS and sexually transmitted diseases in the age group below 18. According to UNAID, one in every two women in Mumbai's brothels was infected by 1993 and one in every three attend STD clinics. Nationally, it estimates that the incidence of HIV was 25% among women in prostitution and 10% among clients (D'Monte,1996).

Sudden increases in the number of kidnappings and abduction of young girls and their subsequent adoptions could possibly be indicators of the practice of child prostitution. The National Crime Records Bureau reported a 100% increase in kidnappings in the last two years. Often, young girls are kidnapped from their homes. 60% of these children are forcibly "married", and then hidden by the brothel owner until they reach the "profitable" ages of 9-13 years (Aiyar, 1997).

3

Problems of Women

WOMEN ARE IN POOR HEALTH

Surviving through a normal life cycle is a resource-poor woman's greatest challenge. "The practice of breast-feeding female children for shorter periods of time reflects the strong desire for sons. If women are particularly anxious to have a male child, they may deliberately try to become pregnant again as soon as possible after a female is born. Conversely, women may consciously seek to avoid another pregnancy after the birth of a male child in order to give maximum attention to the new son."

A primary way that parents discriminate against their girl children is through neglect during illness. When sick, little girls are not taken to the doctor as frequently as are their brothers. A study in Punjab shows that medical expenditures for boys are 2.3 times higher than for girls. As adults, women get less health care than men.

They tend to be less likely to admit that they are sick and they'll wait until their sickness has progressed before they seek help or help is sought for them. Studies on attendance at rural primary health centres reveal that more males than females are treated in almost all parts of the country, with differences greater in northern hospitals than southern ones, pointing to regional differences in the value placed on women. Women's socialization to tolerate suffering and their reluctance to be examined by male personnel are additional constraints in their getting adequate health care.

MATERNAL MORTALITY

India's maternal mortality rates in rural areas are among the highest in the world. A factor that contributes to India's high maternal mortality rate is the reluctance to seek medical care for pregnancy-it is viewed as a temporary condition that will disappear. The estimates nationwide are that only 40-50 percent of women receive any antenatal care. Evidence from the states of Bihar, Rajasthan, Orissa, Uttar Pradesh, Maharashtra and Gujarat find registration for maternal and child health services to be as low as 5-22 percent in rural areas and 21-51 percent in urban areas.

Even a woman who has had difficulties with previous pregnancies is usually treated with home remedies only for three reasons: the decision that a pregnant woman seek help rests with the mother-in-law and husband; financial considerations; and fear that the treatment may be more harmful than the malady. It is estimated that pregnancy-related deaths account for one-quarter of all fatalities among women aged 15 to 29, with well over two-thirds of them considered preventable. For every maternal death in India, an estimated 20 more women suffer from impaired health. One village-level study of rural women in Maharashtra determined on the basis of physical examinations that some 92 percent suffered from one or more gynecological disorder.

CONTRACEPTION USE

Women's health is harmed by lack of access to and the poor quality of reproductive services. "About 24.6 million couples, representing roughly 18 percent of all married women, want no more children but are not using contraception. (Operations Research Group, 1990). The causes of this unmet need remain poorly understood, but a qualitative study in Tamil Nadu suggests that women's lack of decision-making power in the family, opportunity costs involved in seeking contraception, fear of child death, and poor quality of contraceptive service all play an important role." (Ravindran 1993).

Some estimates suggest that some 5 million abortions are performed annually in India, with the large majority being illegal. As a result, abortion-related mortality is high. Although abortion has been legal since 1972 in India, "studies suggest that although official policy seeks to make pregnancy-termination services widely available, in practice guidelines on abortion limit access to services, particularly in rural areas. In 1981, of the 6,200 physicians trained to perform abortions, only 1,600 were working in rural areas."

JOB IMPACT ON MATERNAL HEALTH

Working conditions result in premature and stillbirths. The tasks performed by women are usually those that require them to be in one position for long periods of time, which can adversely affect their reproductive health. A study in a rice-growing belt of coastal Maharashtra found that 40 percent of all infant deaths occurred in the months of July to October. The study also found that a majority of births were either premature or stillbirths. The study attributed this to the squatting position that had to be assumed during July and August, the rice transplanting months.

Impact of Pollution on Women

Women's health is further harmed by air and water pollution and lack of sanitation. The impact of pollution and industrial wastes on health is considerable. In Environment, Development and the Gender Gap, Sandhya Venkateswaran asserts that "the high incidence of malnutrition present amongst women and their low metabolism and other health problems affect their capacity to deal with chemical stress. The smoke from household biomass (made up of wood, dung and crop residues) stoves within a three-hour period is equivalent to smoking 20 packs of cigarettes. For women who spend at least three hours per day cooking, often in a poorly ventilated area, the impact includes eye problems, respiratory problems, chronic bronchitis and lung cancer. One study quoted by WHO in 1991 found that pregnant women cooking over open biomass stoves had almost a 50 percent higher chance of stillbirth.

Anaemia makes a person more susceptible to carbon monoxide toxicity, which is one of the main pollutants in the biomass smoke. Given the number of Indian women who are anaemic-25 to 30 percent in the reproductive age group and almost 50 percent in the third trimester-this adds to their vulnerability to carbon monoxide toxicity. Additionally, with an increasing population, diseases caused by waste disposal, such as hookworm, are rampant. People who work barefooted are particularly susceptible, and it has been found that hookworm is directly responsible for the high percentage of anaemia among rural women.

WOMEN ARE UNEDUCATED

Women and girls receive far less education than men, due both to social norms and fears of violence. India has the largest population of non-school-going working girls. India's constitution guarantees free primary school education for both boys and girls up to age 14. This goal has been repeatedly reconfirmed, but primary education in India is not universal. Overall, the literacy rate for women is 39 percent versus 64 percent for men. The rate for women in the four large northern states-Bihar, Uttar Pradesh, Rajasthan and Madhya Pradesh-is lower than the national average: it was 25 percent in 1991. Attendance rates from the 1981 census suggest that no more than 1/3 of all girls (and a lower proportion of rural girls) aged 5-14 are attending school.

Although substantial progress has been achieved since India won its independence in 1947, when less than 8 percent of females were literate, the gains have not been rapid enough to keep pace with population growth: there were 16 million more illiterate females in 1991 than in 1981.

Sonalde Desai in Gender Inequalities and Demographic Behaviour asserts that "parents' reluctance to educate daughters has its roots in the situation of women. Parents have several incentives for not educating their daughters. Foremost is the view that education of girls brings no returns to parents and that their future roles, being mainly reproductive and perhaps including agricultural labour, require no formal education. As more and more boys are engaged in education, there is a growing reliance on the labour of girls. Girls are increasingly replacing their brothers on the farm while carrying on their usual responsibilities in housework. A large proportion of the roughly 40 million "nonworking" girls who are not in school are kept at home because of responsibilities in housework."

The role of parents is to deliver a chaste daughter to her husband's family. Sonalde Desai goes on to point out that "another disincentive for sending daughters to school is a concern for the protection of their virginity. When schools are located at a distance, when teachers are male, and when girls are expected to study along with boys, parents are often unwilling to expose their daughters to the potential assault on their virginity." There is little response to counter these obstacles: school hours remain inflexible to the labour demands of girls; many villages do not have a school; and fewer than 1/3 of India's primary and middle-school teachers are women.

According to Mapping Progress, "educational funds were cut by 801.3 million rupees in the 1991-92 budget. Funds for the mass literacy movement, in which women participate enthusiastically, have been reduced by 5 percent from the previous year. Budgetary provisions for non-formal education have been cut by 17 percent, leading to closure of many night schools and adult education programs in which working-class women participate. Reduction in government expenditures on higher education and encouragement to private colleges will reduce women's opportunities for higher education since privatization in education promotes only male-dominated professional and technical courses, as they are lucrative."

WOMEN ARE OVERWORKED

Women work longer hours and their work is more arduous than men's. Still, men report that "women, like children, eat and do nothing."

Hours Worked

Women work roughly twice as many as many hours as men. Women's contribution to agriculture-whether it be subsistence farming or commercial agriculture-when measured in terms of the number of tasks performed and time spent, is greater than men. "The extent of women's contribution is aptly highlighted by a micro study conducted in the Indian Himalayas which found that on a one-hectare farm, a pair of bullocks works 1,064 hours, a man 1,212 hours and a woman 3,485 hours in a year."

In Andhra Pradesh, (Mies 1986) found that the work day of an woman agricultural labourer during the agricultural season lasts for 15 hours, from 4 am to 8 pm, with an hour's rest in between. Her male counterpart works for seven to eight hours, from 5 am to 10 am or 11 am and from 3 pm to 5 pm. Another study on time and energy spent by men and women on agricultural work (Batliwala 1982) found that 53 percent of the total human hours per household are contributed by women as compared to 31 percent by men. The remaining contribution comes from children.

The linking of agricultural activities to male dominance is described by Roy Burman (in Menon 1991): The anxiety of man to monopolize his skill in plough culture is reflected in the taboo that is observed almost all over India, against the women's handling the plough. In many societies, she is not even allowed to touch it.

Mies further observed that "whereas operations performed by men were those that entailed the use of machinery and draught animals, thereby using animal, hydraulic, mechanical or electrical energy, women almost always relied on manual labour, using only their own energy." Rice transplantations, the most arduous and labour intensive task in rice cultivation, is carried out entirely by women without the help of any tools. "Girls learn to assist their mothers in almost all tasks, and from the age of 10 years participate fully in the agricultural work done by women. Mies cites the case of Laxmi, a three-year-old infant who, along with her mother, pulled seedlings for transplanting. Boys on the other hand were seldom seen transplanting or weeding though they did help out in ploughing or watering the fields."

"Not only do women perform more tasks, their work is also more arduous than that undertaken by men. Both transplantation and weeding require women to spend the whole day and work in muddy soil with their hands. Moreover, they work the entire day under the intensely hot sun while men's work, such as ploughing and watering the fields, is invariably carried out early in the morning before the sun gets too hot. Mies argues that because women's work, unlike men's, does not involve implements and is based largely on human energy, it is considered unskilled and hence less productive. On this basis, women are invariably paid lower wages, despite the fact that they work harder and for longer hours than do men." In contrast, a study in Uttar Pradesh reports that men "only reluctantly conceded that their womenfolk really work. The researchers in this area were repeatedly told that women, like children, simply eat food and do nothing."

The Invisibility of Women's Work

Women's work is rarely recognized. Many maintain that women's economic dependence on men impacts their power within the family. With increased participation in income-earning activities, not only will there be more income for the family, but gender inequality should be reduced. This issue is particularly salient in India because studies show a very low level of female participation in the labour force. This under-reporting is attributed to the frequently held view that women's work is not economically productive.

In a report of the National Commission on Self-Employed Women and Women in the Informal Sector, the director of social welfare in one state said, "There are no women in any unorganized sector in our state." When the Commission probed and asked, "Are there any women who go to the forest to collect firewood? Do any of the women in rural areas have cattle?" the director responded with, "Of course, there are many women doing that type of work." Working women are invisible to most of the population. If all activities-including maintenance of kitchen gardens and poultry, grinding food grains, collecting water and firewood, etc.-are taken into account, then 88 percent of rural housewives and 66 percent of urban housewives can be considered as economically productive.

Women's employment in family farms or businesses is rarely recognized as economically productive, either by men or women. And, any income generated from this work is generally controlled by the men. Such work is unlikely to increase women's participation in allocating family finances. In a 1992 study of family-based texile workers, male children who helped in a home-based handloom mill were given pocket money, but the adult women and girls were not.

The Impact of Technology on Women

The shift from subsistence to a market economy has a dramatic negative impact on women. According to Sandhya Venkateswaran, citing Shiva, the Green Revolution, which focused on increasing yields of rice and wheat, entailed a shift in inputs from human to technical. Women's participation, knowledge and inputs were marginalized, and their role shift from being "primary producers to subsidiary workers."

Where technology has been introduced in areas where women worked, women labourers have often been displaced by men. Threshing of grain was almost exclusively a female task, and with the introduction of automatic grain threshers-which are only operated by men-women have lost an important source of income. Combine harvesters leave virtually no residue. This means that this source of fodder is no longer available to women, which has a dramatic impact on women's workload. So too, as cattle dung is being used as fertilizer, there is less available for fuel for cooking.

"Commercialization and the consequent focus on cash crops has led to a situation where food is lifted straight from the farm to the market. The income accrued is controlled by men. Earlier, most of the produce was brought home and stored, and the women exchanged it for other commodities. Such a system vested more control with the women."

WOMEN ARE UNSKILLED

Women have unequal access to resources. Extension services tend to reach only men, which perpetuates the existing division of labour in the agricultural sector, with women continuing to perform unskilled tasks. A World Bank study in 1991 reveals that the assumption made by extension workers is that information within a family will be transmitted to the women by the men, which in actual practice seldom happens. "The male dominated extension system tends to overlook women's role in agriculture and proves ineffective in providing technical information to women farmers."

Mapping Progress, states, "in the farm sector, the process of mechanization of agricultural activities has brought in tendencies for gender discrimination by replacing men for a number of activities performed by women and also by displacing the labour of women from subsistence and marginal households. Women are employed only when there is absolute shortage of labour and for specific operations like cotton-picking.

"To supply food-processing industries being set up with foreign collaboration, there has already been a major shift from subsistence farming method of rice, millet, corn and wheat to cash-crop production of fruit, mushrooms, flowers and vegetables. This shift has led to women being the first to lose jobs." A number of factors perpetuate women's limited job skills: if training women for economic activities requires them to leave their village, this is usually a problem for them. Unequal access to education restricts women's abilities to learn skills that require even functional levels of literacy. In terms of skill development, women are impeded by their lack of mobility, low literacy levels and prejudiced attitudes toward women. When women negotiate with banks and government officials, they are often ostracized by other men and women in their community for being 'too forward.' Government and bank officials have preconceived ideas of what women are capable of, and stereotypes of what is considered women's work.

WOMEN ARE MISTREATED

Violence against women and girls is the most pervasive human rights violation in the world today. Opening the door on the subject of violence against the world's females is like standing at the threshold of an immense dark chamber vibrating with collective anguish, but with the sounds of protest throttled back to a murmur. Where there should be outrage aimed at an intolerable status quo there is instead denial, and the largely passive acceptance of 'the way things are.'

Male violence against women is a worldwide phenomenon. Although not every woman has experienced it, and many expect not to, fear of violence is an important factor in the lives of most women. It determines what they do, when they do it, where they do it, and with whom. Fear of violence is a cause of women's lack of participation in activities beyond the home, as well as inside it. Within the home, women and girls may be subjected to physical and sexual abuse as punishment or as culturally justified assaults. These acts shape their attitude to life, and their expectations of themselves.

The insecurity outside the household is today the greatest obstacle in the path of women. Conscious that, compared to the atrocities outside the house, atrocities within the house are endurable, women not only continued to accept their inferiority in the house and society, but even called it sweet. In recent years, there has been an alarming rise in atrocities against women in India. Every 26 minutes a woman is molested. Every 34 minutes a rape takes place. Every 42 minutes a sexual harassment incident occurs. Every 43 minutes a woman is kidnapped. And every 93 minutes a woman is burnt to death over dowry. One-quarter of the reported rapes involve girls under the age of 16 but the vast majority are never reported. Although the penalty is severe, convictions are rare.

Selective Abortions

The most extreme expression of the preference for sons is female infanticide and sex-selective abortion. A study of amniocentesis in a Bombay hospital found that 96 percent of female fetuses were aborted, compared with only a small percentage of male fetuses.

"Government officials event suspect that the disproportionate abortion of female fetuses may be a major underlying cause of the recent decline in the nation's sex ratio. In 1971 there were 930 females for every 1,000 males. A decade later this figure had increased to 934, but by 1991, instead of continuing to rise, the ratio dropped to 927, lower than the 1971 figure. This sex ratio is one of the lowest in the world." Sonalda Desai reports that there are posters in Bombay advertising sex-determination tests that read, "It is better to pay 500 Rs. now than 50,000 Rs. (in dowry) later."

Government has passed legislation to curb the misuse of amniocentesis for sex selection and abortion of female fetuses. Women activists have been critical of this act because of its provision that calls for punishing the women who seek the procedure. These women may be under pressure to bear a male child.

WOMEN ARE POWERLESS

Legal protection of women's rights have little effect in the face of prevailing patriarchal traditions.

Marriage: Women are subordinate in most marriages. Exposure to and interactions with the outside world are instrumental in determining the possibilities available to women in their daily lives. The situation of women is affected by the degree of their autonomy or capacity to make decisions both inside and outside their own household. "The position of women in northern India is notably poor. Traditional Hindu society in northern rural areas is hierarchical and dominated by men, as evidenced by marriage customs. North Indian Hindus are expected to marry within prescribed boundaries: the bride and groom must not be related, they have no say in the matter, and the man must live outside the woman's natal village. "Wife givers" are socially and ritually inferior to "wife takers", thus necessitating the provision of a dowry. After marriage, the bride moves in with her husband's family. Such a bride is "a stranger in a strange place." They are controlled by the older females in the household, and their Behaviour reflects on the honour of their husbands. Because emotional ties between spouses are considered a potential threat to the solidarity of the patrilineal group, the northern system tends to segregate the sexes and limit communication between spouses-a circumstance that has direct consequences for family planning and similar "modern" Behaviours that affect health. A young Indian bride is brought up to believe that her own wishes and interests are subordinate to those of her husband and his family.

The primary duty of a newly married young woman, and virtually her only means of improving her position in the hierarchy of her husband's household, is to bear sons." Sonalde Desai points out that the perception that sons are the major source of economic security in old age is so strong in the north that "many parents, while visiting their married daughters, do not accept food or other hospitality from them. However, given women's low independent incomes and lack of control over their earnings, few can provide economic support to their parents even if parents were willing to accept it."

In the south, in contrast, a daughter traditionally marries her mother's brother or her mother's brother's son (her first cousin). Such an arrangement has a dramatic impact on women. "In southern India, men are likely to marry women to whom they are related, so that the strict distinction found in the north between patrilineal and marital relatives is absent. Women are likely to be married into family households near their natal homes, and are more likely to retain close relationships with their natal kin." "Over the past several decades, however, marriage patterns have changed markedly. Social, economic, and demographic developments have made marriages between close relatives less common, and the bride price has given way to a dowry system akin to that in the north. Nevertheless, as long as the underlying ethic of marriage in the south remains the reinforcement of existing kinship ties, the relatively favourable situation of southern Indian women is unlikely to be threatened."

Kinds of Violence Against Women

Domestic Violence

Violence against women in the family occurs in developed and developing countries alike. It has long been considered a private matter by bystanders--including neighbours, the community and government. But such private matters have a tendency to become public tragedies. In the United States, a woman is beaten every 18 minutes. Indeed, domestic violence is the leading cause of injury among women of reproductive age in the United States. Between 22 and 35 per cent of women who visit emergency rooms are there for that reason.

The highly publicized trial of O. J. Simpson, the retired United States football player acquitted of the murder of his former wife and a male friend of hers, helped focus international media attention on the issue of domestic violence and spousal abuse. In Peru, 70 per cent of all crimes reported to the police involve women beaten by their husbands.

In Pakistan, Prime Minister Benazir Bhutto strongly defended a 35-year-old mother of two who was severely burned by her husband in a domestic dispute. "There is no excuse for such a behaviour", the Prime Minister declared after visiting the hospitalized victim. "My presence here is to send a message to all those who violate Islamic teachings and defy laws of the land with their inhuman treatment of women. This will not be tolerated."

According to the Human Rights Commission of Pakistan, in the 400 cases of domestic violence reported in 1993 in the province of Punjab, nearly half ended with the death of the wife. According to the Special Rapporteur's report, many Governments now recognize the importance of protecting victims of domestic abuse and taking action to punish perpetrators.

The establishment of structures allowing officials to deal with cases of domestic violence and its consequences is a significant step towards the elimination of violence against women in the family.

The Special Rapporteur's report highlights the importance of adopting legislation that provides for prosecution of the offender. It also stresses the importance of specialized training for law enforcement authorities as well as medical and legal professionals, and of the establishment of community support services for victims, including access to information and shelters.

Traditional Practices

In many countries, women fall victim to traditional practices that violate their human rights. The persistence of the problem has much to do with the fact that most of these physically and psychologically harmful customs are deeply rooted in the tradition and culture of society.

Female Genital Mutilation

According to the World Health Organization, 85 million to 115 million girls and women in the population have undergone some form of female genital mutilation and suffer from its adverse health effects. Every year an estimated 2 million young girls undergo this procedure. Most live in Africa and Asia--but an increasing number can be found among immigrant and refugee families in Western Europe and North America. Indeed, the practice has been outlawed in some European countries.

In France, a Malian was convicted in a criminal court after his baby girl died of a female circumcision-related infection. The procedure had been performed on the infant at home. In Canada, fear of being forced to undergo circumcision can be grounds for asylum. A Nigerian woman was granted refugee status since she felt that she might be persecuted in her home country because of her refusal to inflict genital mutilation on her baby daughter.

There is a growing consensus that the best way to eliminate these practices is through educational campaigns that emphasize their dangerous health consequences. Several Governments have been actively promoting such campaigns in their countries.

Son Preference

Son preference affects women in many countries, particularly in Asia. Its consequences can be anything from foetal or female infanticide to neglect of the girl child over her brother in terms of such essential needs as nutrition, basic health care and education. In China and India, some women choose to terminate their pregnancies when expecting daughters but carry their pregnancies to term when expecting sons.

According to reports from India, genetic testing for sex selection has become a booming business, especially in the country's northern regions. Indian gender-detection clinics drew protests from women's groups after the appearance of advertisements suggesting that it was better to spend $38 now to terminate a female foetus than $3,800 later on her dowry. A study of amniocentesis procedures conducted in a large Bombay hospital found that 95.5 per cent of foetuses identified as female were aborted, compared with a far smaller percentage of male foetuses. The problem of son preference is present in many other countries as well. Asked how many children he had fathered, the former United States boxing champion Muhammad Ali told an interviewer: "One boy and seven mistakes."

Dowry-related Violence and Early Marriage

In some countries, weddings are preceded by the payment of an agreed-upon dowry by the bride's family. Failure to pay the dowry can lead to violence. In Bangladesh, a bride whose dowry was deemed too small was disfigured after her husband threw acid on her face. In India, an average of five women a day are burned in dowry-related disputes--and many more cases are never reported. Early marriage, especially without the consent of the girl, is another form of human rights violation. Early marriage followed by multiple pregnancies can affect the health of women for life. The report of the Special Rapporteur has documented the destructive effects of marriage of female children under 18 and has urged Governments to adopt relevant legislation.

Violence in the Community

Rape

Rape can occur anywhere, even in the family, where it can

take the form of marital rape or incest. It occurs in the community, where a woman can fall prey to any abuser. It also occurs in situations of armed conflict and in refugee camps. In the United States, national statistics indicate that a women is raped every six minutes. In 1995, the case of a Brazilian jogger raped and murdered in New York City's Central Park drew international attention once again to the problem. The incident occurred only a few years after an earlier sensational jogger-assault case in which the victim--an American assaulted in the same general area of the park--barely survived after her assailants left her for dead. Relations between residents of the Japanese island of Okinawa and American GIs were thrown into turmoil in 1995 after two marines and a sailor allegedly kidnapped and raped a 12-year-old girl.

The Special Rapporteur's report underlines the importance of education to sensitize the public about the special horrors of rape, and of sensitivity training for the police and hospital staff who work with victims.

Sexual Assault within Marriage

In many countries sexual assault by a husband on his wife is not considered to be a crime: a wife is expected to submit. It is thus very difficult in practice for a woman to prove that sexual assault has occurred unless she can demonstrate serious injury. The report of the Special Rapporteur noted that light sentences in sexual assault cases send the wrong message to perpetrators and to the public at large: that female sexual victimization is unimportant.

Sexual Harassment

Sexual harassment in the workplace is a growing concern for women. Employers abuse their authority to seek sexual favours from their female co-workers or subordinates, sometimes promising promotions or other forms of career advancement or simply creating an untenable and hostile work environment. Women who refuse to give in to such unwanted sexual advances often run the risk of anything from demotion to dismissal. But in recent years more women have been coming forward to report such practices--some taking their cases to court. In her report, the Special Rapporteur stressed that sexual harassment constitutes a form of sex discrimination. "It not only degrades the woman", the report noted, "but reinforces and reflects the idea of non-professionalism on the part of women workers, who are consequently regarded as less able to perform their duties than their male colleagues."

Prostitution and Trafficking

Many women are forced into prostitution either by their parents, husbands or boyfriends--or as a result of the difficult economic and social conditions in which they find themselves. They are also lured into prostitution, sometimes by "mail-order bride" agencies that promise to find them a husband or a job in a foreign country. As a result, they very often find themselves illegally confined in brothels in slavery-like conditions where they are physically abused and their passports withheld. Most women initially victimized by sexual traffickers have little inkling of what awaits them. They generally get a very small percentage of what the customer pays to the pimp or the brothel owner. Once they are caught up in the system there is practically no way out, and they find themselves in a very vulnerable situation.

Since prostitution is illegal in many countries, it is difficult for prostitutes to come forward and ask for protection if they become victims of rape or want to escape from brothels. Customers, on the other hand, are rarely the object of penal laws. In Thailand, prostitutes who complain to the police are often arrested and sent back to the brothels upon payment of a fine. The extent of trafficking in women and girl children has reached alarming proportions, especially in Asian countries. Many women and girl children are trafficked across borders, often with the complicity of border guards. In one incident, five young prostitutes burned to death in a brothel fire because they had been chained to their beds. At the same time, sex tours of developing countries are a well-organized industry in several European and other industrialized countries. The Special Rapporteur has called on Governments to take action to protect young girls from being recruited as prostitutes and to closely monitor recruiting agencies.

Violence against Women Migrant Workers

Female migrant workers typically leave their countries for better living conditions and better pay--but the real benefits accrue to both the host countries and the countries of origin. For home countries, money sent home by migrant workers is an important source of hard currency, while receiving countries are able to find workers for low-paying jobs that might otherwise go unfilled. But migrant workers themselves fare badly, and sometimes tragically. Many become virtual slaves, subject to abuse and rape by their employers. In the Middle East and Persian Gulf region, there are an estimated 1.2 million women, mainly Asians, who are employed as domestic servants. According to the independent human rights group Middle East Watch, female migrant workers in Kuwait often suffer beatings and sexual assaults at the hands of their employers.

The police are often of little help. In many cases, women who report being raped by their employers are sent back to the employer--or are even assaulted at the police station. Working conditions are often appalling, and employers prevent women from escaping by seizing their passports or identity papers.

The report of the Special Rapporteur draws attention to the fact that there are many international instruments that can be used to prevent abuse against migrant women and suggests some measures to protect the human rights of migrant women.

Pornography

Another concern highlighted in the Special Rapporteur's report is pornography, which represents a form of violence against women that "glamorizes the degradation and maltreatment of women and asserts their subordinate function as mere receptacles for male lust".

Violence Perpetrated or Condoned by States

Custodial Violence against Women

Violence against women by the very people who are supposed to protect them--members of the law enforcement and criminal justice systems--is widespread. Women are physically or verbally abused; they also suffer sexual and physical torture. According to Amnesty International, thousands of women held in custody are routinely raped in police detention centres worldwide. The report of the Special Rapporteur underlines the necessity for States to prosecute those accused of abusing women while in detention and to hold them accountable for their actions.

Violence against Women in Situations of Armed Conflict

Rape has been widely used as a weapon of war whenever armed conflicts arise between different parties. It has been used all over the world: in Chiapas, Mexico, in Rwanda, in Kuwait, in Haiti, in Colombia. Women and girl children are frequently victims of gang rape committed by soldiers from all sides of a conflict. Such acts are done mainly to trample the dignity of the victims. Rape has been used to reinforce the policy of ethnic cleansing in the war that has been tearing apart the former Yugoslavia. The so-called "comfort women"--young girls of colonized or occupied countries who became sexual slaves to Japanese soldiers during the Second World War--have dramatized the problem in a historical context. Many of these women are now coming forward and demanding compensation for their suffering from Japanese authorities. "Such rape is the symbolic rape of the community, the destruction of the fundamental elements of a society and culture--the ultimate humiliation of the male enemy", the report by the Special Rapporteur noted. It stressed the need to hold the perpetrators of such crimes fully accountable.

Violence Against Refugee and Displaced Women

Women and children form the great majority of refugee populations all over the world and are especially vulnerable to violence and exploitation. In refugee camps, they are raped and abused by military and immigration personnel, bandit groups, male refugees and rival ethnic groups. They are also forced into prostitution. In her report, the Special Rapporteur proposes the following measures to be taken for the protection of women and girls in refugee camps: improvement of security, deployment of trained female officers at all points of the refugees' journey, participation of women in organizational structures of the camps and prosecution of government and military personnel responsible for abuse against refugee women.

Legal Steps to Criminalize Violence against Women

In recent years some countries have taken significant steps towards improving laws relating to violence against women. For example:

- In July 1991, Mexico revised its rape law in several important ways. A provision was eliminated that allowed a man who rapes a minor to avoid prosecution if he agrees to marry her. Now judges are required to hand down a decision regarding access to an abortion within five working days.
- On 9 June 1994, the Organization of American States adopted the Inter-American Convention to Prevent, Punish and Eradicate Violence against Women (also called Convention of Belém do Parà), a new international instrument that recognizes all gender-based violence as an abuse of human rights. This Convention provides an individual right of petition and a right for non-governmental organizations to lodge complaints with the Inter-American Commission of Human Rights.
- In Australia, a National Committee on Violence against Women was established to coordinate the development of policy, legislation and law enforcement at the national level as well as community education on violence against women.
- In 1991, the Government of Canada announced a new four-year Family Violence Initiative intended to mobilize community action, strengthen Canada's legal framework, establish services on Indian reserves and in Inuit communities, develop resources to help victims and stop offenders, and provide housing for abused women and children.
- In Turkey, a Ministry of State for Women was established whose main goals are, among others, to promote women's rights and strengthen their role in economic, social, political and cultural life. Legal measures are being adopted towards the elimination of violence against women. The establishment of special courts to deal with violence is envisaged. Psychological treatment for abused women is also planned, along with the establishment of women's shelters around the country. Specially trained female police officers could provide assistance to victims of violence.
- In Burkina Faso, a strong advertising campaign by the Government as well as television and radio programmes

on the unhealthy practice of genital mutilation were launched to educate and raise public awareness about the dangerous consequences of such an "operation". A National Anti-Excision Committee was established in 1990 by the present head of State. Today, the practice of genital mutilation has been eliminated in some villages of Burkina Faso. In others, there has been an incredible drop in the number of girls excised: only 10 per cent of the girls are excised compared to 100 per cent 10 years ago.

- Some countries have introduced police units specially trained for dealing with spousal assault. In Brazil, specific police stations have been designated to deal with women's issues, including domestic violence. These police stations are staffed entirely by women.

DOWRY HARASSMENT AND WIFE MURDER

Dowry has always been part of marriage in India, but the dramatic increase in dowry-giving in the post-independence period, reflects the declining value of women in the Indian society. Though the giving and taking of dowry is a legal offense since the passage of a legislation in 1961, the custom has flourished, invading lower castes and working class communities among whom this was not a practice. Such requested products as videocassette recorders, washing machines, refrigerators, and scooters reflect the higher dowry demands asked from the girl's family. Sudha Tiwari of Shakti Shalini (a women's shelter in Delhi), blames the excessive demands by the boy's family on the western influence of capitalist materialism and the promotion of mindless consumerism by the mass media.

The first protests against dowry in the contemporary Indian women's movement were made by the "Progressive Organization of Women" in the city of Hyderabad in 1975. Though some of their demonstrations numbered as many as 2,000 people, the protests did not grow into a full-fledged campaign. The Mahila Dakshata Samiti was the first women's organization in Delhi to take up the issue of dowry and dowry harassment, but it was Stri Sangharsh whose campaign made "dowry murder" a household term. These organizations use many different methods: investigation and collection of evidence; recording witness accounts; working with specialist lawyers' collectives; using the mass media; mobilizing anti-violence women's networks; organizing local and national marches; lobbying the courts and the Government with high level of publicity; publicizing corrupt police system which colludes with the batterer and his family. If a girl's parents are not able to meet the demands, even after the marriage the violence may escalate over many years, forcing many woman to either kill themselves to escape daily torture or be killed. Madhu Kishwar and Ruth Vanita, in their book In Search of Answers: Indian Women's Voices from Manushi, tells the tragic story of Dr. Shakuntala Arora, who was a lecturer in a women's college and who died of burns. Her family and her colleagues feel that emotional and physical abuse and torture over many years drove her to kill herself.

The harassment of Dr. Shakuntala Arora started at the time of her wedding, when the bridegroom insisted on a scooter as an item in the bride's dowry. Shakuntala's parents had to comply with this demand or else the wedding would have been called off. When Shakuntala moved into her in-laws' house, she was asked to pay off wedding costs of 25,000 rupees, which she was forced to obtain from her parents. Any resistance on Shakuntala's part led to physical and emotional abuse. Shakuntala was allowed a meager pocket money from her salary as a lecturer for food and transport. At the birth of her first child, she received no help from her husband. Her husband became increasingly more violent at her second delivery; he kicked her in the stomach before taking her to the hospital. Only a few weeks after her cesarean section, Shakuntala, badly beaten and in tears, with a small baby in her arms, entered her mother's house to seek temporary respite from the tortures of her husband. She had no money to pay off the taxi. These were some of the economic, physical and emotional tortures that turned Shakuntala's life into a nightmare. Two days before her death, she was beaten up and forbidden to attend her brother's marriage ceremony, because she had failed to get money from her widowed mother.

The term dowry and "dowry deaths" has become synonymous with wife-battering and domestic violence. It has become a key issue and rallying cry in practically all movements in which women are active. However, we need to remember that dowry is only an excuse used by patriarchal families to continue to torture and kill women. The unfortunate consequence of using this term as a rallying cry is that it minimizes the regular abuse and killing of women. The result is that dowry-related wife murders and suicides are criticized, but other domestic violence may not be since it is thought that the wife could have been provoking the abuse.

Sexual Harassment at Work

According to Mac Kinnons (1979) sexual harassment of working women is primarily a problem faced by women, that men rarely face this problem and therefore it should be considered a form of sex discrimination.

Sexual harassment as defined by the court stipulates:

- Such unwelcome sexually determined behaviour (whether directly or by implication) as physical contact and advances,
- A demand or request for sexual favours, sexually coloured remarks,
- Showing pornography and any other unwelcome physical, verbal or non verbal conduct of sexual nature".

Burt (1980) says "unwanted sexual overtures", has the virtue of parsimony but necessarily concerns intentions and motivation, not just overt behaviour. Defining sexual harassment as unwanted sexual overtures has the same problem inherent in defining rape as unwanted sexual relations. In practise the woman has to prove that the sexual relations or the sexual overtures were unwanted (Sikri, 1999: 128). The male colleague will go out of the way to prove that the woman is of loose character. According to Quinn (1977) defining sexual harassment means setting boundaries on the term and differentiating sexual harassment from expressions of sexual interest. Not all expressions of sexuality in the workplace could possibly be called sexual harassment. Men and women do meet dating partners and future spouses at work. Some people may even enjoy sexual jokes and flirting that can be ego enhancing and enrich their fantasy life.

National Commission for Women has laid down the code of conduct at work place to prevent sexual harassment of women, which has been sent to all Government offices, Ministries, and Universities with the hope that employers would become more sensitive towards women. The guidelines highlight that it shall be the duty of the employer to prevent or deter the commission of any act of sexual harassment at workplace would include unwelcome sexually determined behaviour by any person either individually or in association with other persons such as eve teasing, unsavoury remarks, jokes causing embarrassment, innuendo and taunts, gender based insults or sexist remarks and unwelcome sexual overtones in any manner, touching or brushing against any part of the body, molestation or displaying pornographic or other derogatory pictures or sayings (Hindu, Sept 16, 1998). Recommendations to the National Commission for Women based on the view that the definition of sexual harassment is deficient and that "sexual favours......sought by homosexual or lesbian employers of the same sex" also be included (Hindu, April 26, 1998).

The Court places an obligation on employers in both the public and private sector to "take appropriate steps to prevent sexual harassment" and "provide appropriate penalties" against the offender. The criminal law should be resorted to where the behaviour amounts to a specific offence under the Indian Penal Code. The Court also recommends that a complaint made by the victim and that such a committee should be headed by a woman, and not less than half its members should be women (Hindu, April 26, 1998). However this guidelines does not specify any time limit for drafting the code. The Court provides that the employer is responsible for drafting codes to prevent sexual harassment in the workplace. If the power to evolve these codes is to be in the hands of the employer, then given the conservative sexual climate in which we live, what is to prevent the employer from producing a code that encourages gender segregation in the workplace. The codes could be formulated so as to discourage gender interaction in the workplace, or encourage the establishment of same sex schools and universities instead of co-educational institutions. Perhaps more specific guidelines are required which provide that such sex segregation is not an appropriate response for dealing with sexual harassment (Hindu, April 26, 1998). In many cases, it has been found that the committees within the organisations were set up only when there were serious allegations of sexual harassment. Many working women point out that, even if there is an enquiry committee, does anyone really bother to find out what happens to the victim when the enquiry is going on? She is an object of curiosity, sympathy, disdainful glances or simply isolated by her colleagues. The situation at home is worse. Instead of sympathising with her plight or standing by her, the attitude is one of distrust and suspicion or often humiliation and shame (Sikri, 1999: 40). The work environment where sexual harassment occurs has hierarchy, norms, rules and constraints that profoundly affect the way people behave in that setting. In particular, the formal rules and informal norms of managers affect both the managers and their subordinates. The top management has the power to influence the employee's work habits, style of dress, recreational interests and social behaviour. When the top management tolerates or condones sexual harassment of employees, the standard reverberates throughout the organisation.

Certain individuals use their positions of relative power to engage in sexual interactions. This type of behaviour clearly constitutes sex discrimination (Hindu, April 26, 1998). Male ego problems, sexual perversion, sexual obsession, widow-hood, pornographic materials and media portrayal is said to be some of the reasons for their harassment. Lawyers facing sexual harassment at work:

A survey conducted by Sakshi, a Delhi based NGO, in a few major cities reported that 65 per cent of women lawyers interviewed were always or often subjected to, or had observed, verbal or physical sexual harassment from other lawyers. The harassment would take various forms according to the survey. They include use of stereo-typed role characterisation, sexual innuendo, devaluation of women's work, use of obscene or vulgar language, and comments on appearances and character. The bar report narrates two incidents.

In one case, a woman lawyer was openly punched by a male colleague in the High Court premises for refusing to join him for a cup of coffee. When she tried to report the incident, a senior member of the bar dissuaded the police from registering it, on the ground that "it would tarnish the reputation of the Bar". Forty-eight per cent of the women lawyers surveyed also stated that they had heard or experienced remarks or jokes that were demeaning to women (Rameshan G, Hindu, July 19, 1998).

In a survey done by National Commission for Women of 1200 women, nearly 50 per cent complained of gender discrimination and physical and mental harassment at work. While 40 per cent of the women said they "usually ignored" such provocation, 3.54 per cent said they reported these to their supervisors, 7.8 per cent to their colleagues and 1.24 per cent to the police. About 10 per cent said that they protested against such behaviour while 9 per cent said they warned the offenders. At least 20.17 per cent of the respondents said that no investigation was done on their complaints while 1.5 per cent said police harassed them again instead of making the enquiry.

A majority of the respondents 84.97 % were not aware of the supreme court judgement given in August 1997, for specific protection of women from sexual harassment at work (Bhatnagar.R., August 19, 1998)

RELIGION AND FAMILY VIOLENCE

Sati, as the practice of self-immolation, is a long-standing tradition among upper caste Hindus. Although legitimized through myth, it is a violent practice against women. It is complicated by the fact that it is often used against women to take control of land that they might inherit as widows. Widows have very little status in Hindu India and are often seen as bad omens. Therefore, they are treated miserably. Some do commit suicide rather than be subject to daily torture and humiliation and some are killed.

There has been on an average, something like one sati a year, but the death of Roop Kanwar in September 1987 led to a massive agitation both for and against sati. Sati was most common in the state of Rajasthan, amongst the Hindu Rajput caste. The Indian feminist magazine, Manushi and Radha Kumar in her book, The History of Doing: An Illustrated Account of Movements for Women's Rights and Feminism in India, 1800-1990, describe the practice of sati and the movements against it.

The pro-sati organizations invoked a chivalric Rajput (Hindu upper caste identity) tradition in which men defended the Hindu tradition on battlefields by killing and being killed, while women defended it at home by killing themselves. One case of sati was that of Roop Kanwar. Roop Kanwar had brought a large amount of gold in her dowry and had only been married for six months before her husband, who was suffering from mental disorder, died. Roop Kanwar's in-laws decided she would become sati-and did not inform her parents.

The evidence that feminist organizations gathered pointed to murder: some of her neighbors said she had run away and tried to hide before the ceremony, but was dragged out, pumped full of drugs, dressed in bridal finery and put on her husband's funeral pyre. The feminists held counter-demonstrations along the route of the procession and were confronted by groups of hostile women, who had appropriated the language of rights, stating that they should have the right, as Hindus and as women, to commit, worship and practice sati.

The "Joint Action Committee Against Sati" formed and demanded state intervention on three levels: first, Roop Kanwar's in-laws and the doctor who drugged her should be charged with murder; second, that all those who profited financially or politically from her death should be punished; and third, that a law should be passed banning both commission and glorification of crimes against women in the name of religion. Even though the government passed a law under which sati was defined as unlawful, the first person to be punished was the woman herself, for attempting to commit suicide. In the current fundamentalist climate, sati is seen as a return to old "wonderful" and traditional values with women being the upholders of all moral traditions. In fact, careful scrutiny of the Roop Kanwar case shows that this sati was a complex mixture of misogyny, economics and fundamentalism.

Religion is also a significant factor in the multiple oppression faced by Muslim women. The Muslim community is one of the largest minority groups in India. Muslim women face violence at home and outside the home in the same way as Hindu women. One difference was that Muslim women had the right to divorce, inheritance, and maintenance. However, these rights have been eroded over time. All leaders of the women's movement have urged the restitution of these rights. Due to the passage of the Hindu Code bill in 1956, the inequality between the rights of Hindu men and women was technically eliminated.

But this was not the case with the Muslim Personal Law, which is based on religion. As a result, the inequality between Muslim women and men remained. Women's organizations started examining laws in an attempt to look at women's rights in marriage, divorce, property and maintenance and demanded secular laws which allowed universal rights for all women.

The issue of personal law became extremely controversial in the Shah Bano case between 1986-1987. After she had been thrown out of her home following fifty years of marriage, Shah Bano filed a case under a criminal law (Section 125 of the Criminal Procedure Code), asking that her husband be ordered to pay maintenance. This law granted divorced or deserted women maintenance from their husbands. Muslim feminists, women's groups, liberals and social reformers began campaigns all over India to publicize the upholding of this law and to demand improvements. Many women's organizations like the Janwadi Mahila Samiti, the Mahila Dakshata Samiti, the National Federation of Indian Women and the Dahej Virodhi (Anti-Dowry) Chetna Manch, campaigned for universal legal rights for all women. The courts granted Shah Bano maintenance from her previous husband. However, fundamentalists on both sides saw this case as a rallying point for their cause. The old scars of partition in India in 1947 were raised again and communalism saw a steep rise with severe oppression of the Muslim community and the destruction of a critical mosque-Babri Masjid. The government caved in to fundamentalist demands eroding the limited rights of Muslim women.

Most women's organizations recognize the issue of communal harmony as vital when doing anti-violence work. AWAG is one such group which not only focuses on issues surrounding violence against women but carries out extensive work around communal harmony in riot-torn areas. Sofia Khan of AWAG explains, "After the bloody riots of 1992 that followed the demolition of Babri Masjid, this issue was so emotionally charged, you could not talk about this within the Muslim communities. Women's groups now talk about equality between

Muslim women and men when they campaign for universalizing these laws so that Muslim women would have the same legal rights as Hindu women". The Indian women's movement has made many creative interventions for social change in mobilizing against violence against women. For example, AWAG, provides training for police and judiciary around gender issues and violence in order to counter their attitudes and implement law more effectively. Shakti Salini is planning a "police sensitization program," and training on reproductive health, family planning techniques, and mental health awareness.

Sofia Khan of AWAG remains optimistic about the changes happening at the grass roots level and on the governmental level. She thinks that the system of reserving spots for women on different levels of the governmental power structure will allow women access to resources. In 1990, a National Women's Commission was established to investigate the subordinate position of women in India. There were plans to establish women's commissions on the state level. Recently, due to an amendment, 33 percent of the designated posts have been reserved for women in the Village Panchayat (village council). The Panchayat controls the power structure in the village, in relation to land and access to water, mediates conflicts, and has connection to the State government. More women having access to resources could lead to improvement in the lives of women at this village level.

Like the pioneering work of Jagori, most women's anti-violence organizations work on many levels and use many methods or organizing. But regardless of their methods, their goals are the same: to change the culture of violence against women systemic in Indian society.

PROSTITUTION AS VIOLENCE AGAINST WOMEN

International policies and legislation increasingly omit prostitution per se from the category of violence against women. Various governmental and non-governmental groups make efforts to distinguish and thus to legitimize certain practices of sexual exploitation, drawing distinctions, for example, between "forced" and "free" prostitution. These efforts culminated in lobbying for what would be finally included in the Beijing Declaration and Platform for Action that emerged from the Fourth World Women's Conference in Beijing. This article addresses these efforts; the NGOs who advocate such distinctions; and the consequences of revising the harm done to women in prostitution into a consenting act. c 1998 Janice G. Raymond. Published by Elseview Science Ltd.

The Beijing Declaration and Platform for Action that emerged from the Fourth World Women's Conference in Beijing is clear in its condemnation of violence against women. It denounces the systematic rape of women in wartime and advocates prosecuting perpetrators as war criminals. It acknowledges that domestic violence is a worldwide problem and urges governmental intervention. And it condemns genital mutilation of girls and sexual harassment as human rights violations (United Nations, 1995a, pp. 51-65). What the Platform excludes as violence against women, however, is a tale of governmental stonewalling and NGO (non-governmental organization) complicity that began before Beijing

There has long been an effort on the part of many NGOs to exempt prostitution per se from the category of human rights violations. This effort culminated especially in lobbying for what would be finally included in the Platform for Action in Beijing (Centre for Women's Global leadership, 1995). Many NGOs--instead of viewing prostitution itself as violence against women, and thus a human rights violation--acted on the assumption that prostitution is a human right, a right of woman to do what she wants with her body. In this article, I want to address the role of NGOs and their position on prostitution and sex trafficking.

The philosophy that prostitution is a human right has been advanced, in international forums such as Beijing, by drawing distinctions between forced and free, adult and child, third world and first world prostitution, and between prostitution and trafficking. These distinctions are then used to make some forms of prostitution acceptable and legitimate, revising the harm that is done to women in prostitution into a consenting act and excluding prostitution from the category of violence against women. The sex industry thrives on this language and these distinctions.

When distinctions are made between forced and free prostitution, for example, it becomes almost insurmountable for many, if not most, women in prostitution to prove that they have been forced. When distinctions are made between child and adult prostitution, the age of consent in some countries is simply reduced. In practice, the age of children in prostitution is becoming lower and lower; Human Rights/Asia, in their report on the trafficking of Nepali girls and women into India, states that the average age of the thousands of Nepali girls recruited every year for prostitution in Indian brothels, has dropped from 14-16 years of age during the 1980s, to 10-14 years of age during the 1990s.

NGOs that work to abolish institutionalized trafficking and prostitution per se receive funding only if they adhere to these distinctions; only if they call prostitutes commercial sex workers; only if they refer to prostitution as "forced prostitution;" only if they separate trafficking from prostitution and focus on closed brothels where women are kept in obvious indentured conditions; and only if they work with other groups who accept these conditions and distinctions. Some governments who have vocally opposed making prostitution a violation of human rights are also funding NGOs, such as the Dutch Foundation Against Trafficking in Women (STV) and its international offshoot, the Global Alliance Against Traffic in Women (GAATW), which take similar positions. Thus governments and funding agencies are able to exert enormous influence over the agenda of what gets counted as violence against women. Increasingly, prostitution per se is declared a violence-free zone.

A lot of NGOs have the right words to say against violence against women. For example, the recent report of Human Rights Watch/Asia, referred to previously and which is entitled Rape for Profit, is a carefully researched and sensitively written report on the trafficking of Nepali Girls and Women into India's Brothels. Yet after documenting the extreme youth, the poverty, the horrendous abuse, the coercion, and outright abduction of young 10-14 year old girls into prostitution in India, the Report goes on to refer to them as "sex workers" (Human Rights Watch/Asia, 1995). In a footnote designed to show that the researchers are familiar with the controversy over this term, the report says: "...many activists in India who work with trafficking victims object to its use (i.e., the term sex worker or commercial sex worker)..." (Human Rights Watch/Asia, 1995).

However, the Human Rights Watch reporters have obviously sided with those who favor the term sex worker, and that is the term that is used throughout the Report.

What are we to make of this? If reality hangs on the thin thread of language, this debate is no mere semantic quarrel. Many claim they use the term, sex work, to dignify and professionalize the women in prostitution. "The more 'professional' the sex worker, the more care she takes of herself. The more 'legal' or 'legitimate' she feels,... the more she will... be able to develop a degree of professionalism in her work. Is this not an argument in favour of recognition of prostitution as a form of legitimate work?" (Foundation Against Trafficking in Women, 1995, p. 3). But the term, "sex work," doesn't dignify the worker; all it dignifies is the sex industry--the pimps, procurers and traffickers. And coming from human rights activists and feminists, it gives the sex industry more dignity than it has ever had, or could get anyplace else. The term "sex work" doesn't convey the exploitation of trafficking and prostitution. It ratifies prostitution as simply another form of work, something that has become a way of making a living. But for most of the women and children in prostitution, it's not living; it's barely surviving.

WHISPER, a Minneapolis-based organization of women who have both survived and who are coming out of prostitution, and who are committed to ending prostitution as a form of violence against women, found it difficult to identify job skills gained in prostitution which would advance anyone's career (Gamache, 1991). They found that the "skills" of prostitution are: performing sex acts, feigning sexual enjoyment, enduring all kinds of bodily violation, and allowing your body to be used in any imaginable way by another person (Giobbe, 1990). What young girl would we encourage to develop these "skills?" Yet there are now "courses" to teach would-be "sex workers," as they are called, the sexual techniques of prostitution and everything they need to know to become "skilled" in the trade.

What prostituted women must endure in their "employment" is, what in other contexts, would be the accepted definition of sexual harassment and sexual abuse in the workplace-- "employer" Behaviour that is unwanted and insulting, and unwelcome sexual attention, violence, and conduct that is offensive and threatening. What then happens to women in prostitution whose very "job"--if we term it "commercial sex work"--constitutes, what in any other "workplace," would be defined as sexual harassment and abuse? It is the exchange of money in prostitution that serves to transform what is actually sexual harassment, sexual abuse, and sexual violence into a "job" known as "commercial sex work," a "job" performed primarily by racially and economically disadvantaged women in the so-called first and third worlds, and by overwhelming numbers of women and children who have been the victims of childhood sexual abuse.

Another term that misrepresents the exploitation of prostitution, and the harm that it does to women, is the term "forced prostitution." What does this term mean? It means we are encouraged to distinguish forced prostitution from free prostitution? The Human Rights Watch Report not only consistently uses "forced prostitution" throughout, but also the term "forced trafficking"(Human Rights Watch/Asia, 1995). Are we to assume, then, that there is "free trafficking?" Building on the shaky foundation of consensual prostitution, do we now have "consensual trafficking" where some women and children freely choose to be trafficked from one place to another? Few human rights activists and people of conscience would use the term "forced slavery" or "forced apartheid" but so glibly slip into the language of forced prostitution and, now, forced trafficking.

The sex industry makes no distinctions between forced and free prostitution while encouraging others to do so. The industry is linked financially and politically with groups like COYOTE in the United States to promote prostitution as a woman's personal choice, proclaiming that the worst thing about prostitution is that the women are stigmatized. But the worst thing about prostitution is its violation of and violence against women and children. Although claiming to be a prostitutes rights organization, COYOTE works more for the rights of the customers and the industry, rather than for the rights of women to leave prostitution. The former director of COYOTE, Margo St. James, served as a witness for the defence at the pimping trial of well-known U.S. pornographers, and works to abolish U.S. laws against pimping and soliciting women for the purpose of prostitution. It is doubtful that COYOTE's membership even includes many women in prostitution. For example, Priscilla Alexander, one of COYOTE's founders, equates prostitution with her own promiscuous dating experiences at Bennington College in Vermont. Referring to this time, Alexander writes: "I never have literally worked as a prostitute...although I was stigmatized as a whore at one time" (Alexander, 1987). Yet Alexander worked in the leadership of COYOTE for years building a career for herself as a prostitutes rights spokeswoman, even to the extent of being employed by the WHO (World Health Organization) as a consultant on AIDS/HIV) and prostitution. To all appearances, she has been accepted as speaking on behalf of women in prostitution because she has been there--but she was never in prostitution. The same is true for Margo St. James, another founder of COYOTE who recently ran for an elected seat on the San Francisco City Council.

Furthermore, COYOTE does not reveal its membership or the percentage of its members who are prostitutes, thus making it seem as if COYOTE is an organization of women in prostitution. Even researchers who write in praise of COYOTE and agree with its positions have alluded to the "institutionalizing [of] an organizational myth" upon which COYOTE is built. For example, author Valerie Jenness states that "Contrary to COYOTE's public image, only a small percentage of its members have worked as prostitutes, and an even smaller percentage are active prostitutes who are also active in the organization. On occasion, St. James has admitted that COYOTE is not an organization of and for prostitutes" (Jenness, 1993). COYOTE capitalizes on this lie with its spokeswomen promoting the image of COYOTE as an organization by and for prostitutes (Jenness, 1993).

Meanwhile, groups who truly represent prostituted women--groups such as WHISPER and the Council for Prostitution Alternatives in the United States--are composed of many women who are survivors of prostitution, or women currently in prostitution trying to leave. Whenever I speak in the United States on the topic of prostitution, the question inevitably arises who represents the concerns of women in prostitution. Most of the audience has heard of COYOTE and immediately assumes that COYOTE speaks for all women in prostitution.

Very few know about the work of WHISPER in Minneapolis; the Council for Prostitution Alternatives in Portland; PROMISE is San Francisco; Genesis House in Chicago; RESPECT in Madison; and SAGE in San Francisco. These are several of the groups advocating for women in prostitution--who are composed of many survivors of prostitution, who oppose prostitution per se as a human rights violation, who are not linked with the sex industry, and who work primarily to help women out of prostitution and create sustainable alternatives to prostitution in women's lives. Because such groups are not supported financially and politically by the sex industry, and thus do not have the resources to publicize their policies and positions, they do not receive the same public attention and prominence as the pro-prostitution industry groups.

A lot of NGOs are now working for women's rights to better their conditions in prostitution instead of helping them out of prostitution. Annabel Fan, a US lawyer, spoke of her impressions after completing a research trip to Thailand. "A lot of the NGOs whom I met with talked about ending the exploitation of women. Nowhere did I get the impression that prostitution itself is being targeted, to stop the practice. Definitely, what NGOs are concerned about is women's rights to determine how they work as prostitutes...Also, my sense is that there is not a lot of alternatives being offered by NGOs, but rather that the work done tends to maintain the system. The empowerment of women seems to be in the context of prostitution...It is empowerment in prostitution and not separate from prostitution...a lot of organizations I talked to do not want the criminalization of anybody, not clients, not pimps, no one, because they say, if you penalize the clients and pimps, then you disadvantage the women in the way they operate...Brothels are everywhere in Thailand...There are more brothels than schools" (Fan, 1995). Such NGO groups talk about women's empowerment in prostitution and primarily teach women how to perform better as prostitutes, how to negotiate with customers, and how to get men to use condoms and make it part of the sex, but they don't offer women a way out. Why? Because it's easier to believe that prostitution is a choice for these women. And talking about women's empowerment in prostitution means you don't have to confront the controversial issue of the customer.

In fact, the silent participant who is actually a silent perpetrator of prostitution, is the customer. He is often depicted, like the woman in prostitution, as a victim too, but this sentimentalizes his reality as opposed to hers. Surely, the question is not why do women choose to enter prostitution, but why do so many men choose to buy women and children in prostitution? If the issue of choice must be raised, let it be raised in the context of the men who buy the sex of prostitution. Why do men choose to buy the bodies of millions of women and children, call it sex, and seemingly get tremendous pleasure literally over their bought bodies?

Confronting the issue of the male customer also means, for many non-governmental organizations, confronting the fact that many of their own members are part of the clientele that buy women for the sex of prostitution. I was in Sweden in May, 1995, shortly after the Social Summit had taken place in Copenhagen. I spoke with an advocate who works with Danish women in prostitution, and she told me that many human rights activists attending the Social Summit, as well as United Nations staff and personnel, had avidly visited the brothels of Copenhagen. She related that this NGO and governmental stampede for commercial sex made the pages of several Danish newspapers who noted the irony of a Summit focused on economic development providing Denmark's sex industry with the greatest economic development it had experienced in a long time. Opponents of making prostitution a human rights violation argue that past attempts to abolish prostitution have been repressive and worked against women. This is true, but only because such legislation has punished the women in prostitution and not the pimps, procurers and customers. To argue that prostitution and trafficking are violations of a person's human rights means that we cannot regulate prostitution into categories of good and bad prostitution. We cannot create a zone of brothels or "eros centres," the usual approach to regulating prostitution, within which anything goes. Germany, for example, restricts prostitution activity to specific "eros centres," or large prostitution buildings--a type of barracks mentality--which are the designated sex zones in cities with populations over 20,000, the cities in Germany where prostitution is legal. "Red-light" districts, or zoned areas in which brothels, as well as other forms of sex "entertainment," may function are found in many countries as diverse as Turkey, Tunisia, Holland, Belgium, and South Korea. The U.S. version of zoned prostitution is Nevada where regulated prostitution functions throughout the state except in Reno and Las Vegas. Brothels, such as the infamous Mustang Ranch on the outskirts of Reno, were located outside the city limits, so as not to violate the law.

"The normalization of prostitution in European regulationist countries has actually promoted trafficking in women to the Netherlands. Neo-regulation relaxes the policing of prostitution, making it easier for traffickers to move in and out of the country. Trafficking from the Philippines, Latin America, and Eastern Europe has expanded in the Netherlands as it did a few decades earlier when Germany legalized prostitution" (Barry, 1995, pp.234-35). In fact, the case can be made that when a country regulates prostitution, the number of unregistered and unregulated women in prostitution increases simply because women are pressured into identifying as prostitutes, paying taxes on paltry earnings, and undergoing non-elective and often demeaning health screening and testing. "The regulations governing prostitution (medical, check-ups, card and brothels) were historically one of the main causes of the prostitution of women, and still are, because they do not allow them to abandon this activity and return to their social group. Because of the regulations, they come to form a separate category of women living on the fringes of society, who are vulnerable and 'marked for life' " (UNESCO, 1986).

The reality is that during the 1980s as the sex industry in several European countries underwent notable development, commercialization, and legitimation through regulationist legislation, it also became an international business. "In certain parts of the world...prostitution is...a 'planned' and 'institutionalized' part of it [the national income]...in South-East Asia and Europe, the existence of mass prostitution and the structure of the market, which makes use of the media, airlines, hotel chains, international communication and the banks, mean that it could neither exist nor develop without the tacit or implicit agreement of the institutions" (UNESCO, 1986). This kind of trafficking in women for prostitution is linked with economic development policies of so-called "promotional states" which directly or indirectly foster sex tourism for the remission of foreign currency. Additionally, Asian women bear the brunt of migration policies which channel them into gendered jobs, such as domestic labour and "entertainment" that often become sexually exploitative. The internationalization of the labour markets, and free trade, has also meant the internationalization of women's bodies for sex (de Dios, 1993). Migration, turned into migrant trafficking, has also become a bonanza for organized crime. Large numbers of women from developing countries and, with the end of the cold war, from Russia and eastern Europe are illegally brought into western European countries for sex. Major John Alleart of the Belgian national police states that these international crime syndicates are "...very sophisticated, far-flung networks with acccess to high-tech communications equipment and the best legal advice money can buy" (Hood, 1995).

Women became goods and services in an industry without national borders. The sex industry treats women as moveable property, passing them from one club to another, from one district to another, and from one country to another. The presence of legalized or regulated brothels, eros zones, sex clubs, and recruitment agencies made all this possible--ready made and legitimate locations for the flesh handlers and trade. It was regulation that, in large part, made possible increased trafficking in women from developing countries into Europe. Sex businesses had to cut costs to compete in the sexual marketplace for cheaper and more exotic male tastes and demands so they imported women from developing countries to meet the demand (De Stoop, 1992). It has been estimated that there are between 200,000 and 400,000 prostitutes in Germany, 60 per cent of whom are foreigners, and most who work illegally within the regulated eros zones (De Stoop, 1992). The Netherlands, which has a specific policy against trafficking in women but at the same time regulates prostitution, has an active and thriving sex industry that promotes demand for cheaper and more exotic women from developing countries.

"The Netherlands differentiated between Dutch women...and Third World women...Making the distinction between 'free' and 'forced' prostitution, their economic interests are apparent. Third World and Eastern European immigrant women in the Netherlands, Germany, and other regulationist countries lower the prostitution market value of local Dutch and German women. The price of immigrant prostitution is so low that local women's prices go down, reducing the pimps' and brothels' cuts. The result: a movement against 'trafficking in women' that promotes local prostitution on the basis of an erroneous distinction between 'free' and 'forced' prostitution to protect market prices" (Barry, 1995). A large number of Dutch towns and villages have their sex clubs or their sex farms offering women deemed to be "exotic" and mostly from developing countries (De Stoop, 1992). Rife with contradictions, the anti-trafficking policy of the Netherlands makes it easier for traffickers to move in and out of the country because of the ready-made set up for prostitution and the relaxing of policing.

What kind of public policy and legislation do we need? For one thing, we need to encourage more countries to ratify the 1949 Convention for the Suppression of the Traffic in Persons and of the Exploitation of the Prostitution of Others, and to add a new protocol to the Convention whereby countries that have ratified it are made accountable for enforcing its provisions.

Most importantly, we need to reinforce and expand the 1949 Convention with a new Convention Against All Forms of Sexual Exploitation that, among other things, makes all prostitution and trafficking violations of a person's human rights; that de-criminalizes the women in prostitution; and that punishes pimps, procurers and customers. This new Convention also addresses the social services, educational opportunities and economic alternatives necessary for survivors of sexual exploitation.

Any feminist or human rights activist knows that legislation alone is not the answer. But legislation that punishes the perpetrators and not the victims of the crime of prostitution is necessary; together with political activism, education, economic alternatives and social services aimed at helping women in prostitution.

4

Laws of Women and Child

INTERNATIONAL LEGAL RESPONSES

Substantive Law

One response has been to call municipal and international legal systems into play, which in turn raises the questions of the adequacy of legal norms and the effectiveness of their implementation. A number of substantive international legal regimes are currently applicable. States are liable for harm done to individuals which constitutes violation of the laws and customs of war by troops under their authority and command, for violations of internationally guaranteed human rights, including genocide and torture, and for wrongdoing to aliens under the normal principles of State responsibility. These different legal regimes allow for analysis of rape through different lenses: violations of the laws of war, violence against women as a violation of women's human rights, and protection of ethnic groups against genocide. In addition to State responsibility there is individual criminal responsibility for the commission of war crimes and crimes against humanity. The plea of superior orders is not available as a defence to such actions.

Meron has demonstrated that rape has long been prohibited by the laws of war and has been incorporated into various modern Codes of Military Conduct. The currently applicable laws of war are contained within the 1949 Geneva Conventions, the 1977 supplementary Protocols, and in the body of law arising from the judgment of the Nuremberg Tribunal and the

Military Tribunal for the Far East. Unfortunately, in these documents the position with respect to rape is ambiguous. Rape was not included in the listed war crimes in Article 6 of the Nuremberg Charter, although the list was specifically stated not to be exhaustive. The Fourth Geneva Convention provides protection for civilians in international armed conflict and specifically provides that women should be protected against rape. This provision is almost exactly reiterated in Protocol I.

It is noticeable that these provisions do not impose a blanket prohibition against sexual abuse, but rather oblige States to offer women protection against attacks on their honour and to accord them special respect. Article 4 of the Fourth Geneva Convention applies to those `who at a given moment and in any manner whatsoever find themselves, in case of a conflict or occupation, in the hands of a Party to the conflict or Occupying Power of which they are not nationals'. Article 76 of Protocol I enhances this protection by extending its scope to all women in the power of a Party to the conflict including a Party's own nationals. In non-international armed conflict, Article 3 to the Geneva Conventions provides a minimum standard of behaviour that applies both to government and non-government forces. Prohibited actions include violence to life and the person, cruel treatment and torture, and humiliating and degrading treatment. It is easy to interpret these Articles so as to include rape, but it is nevertheless unfortunate that it is not spelled out as an explicit prohibition. For this reason the affirmation by the World Conference on Human Rights in Vienna in 1993 that `violations of the human rights of women in situations of armed conflict [with no distinction drawn between international and non-international armed conflict] are violations of the humanitarian principles of international human rights and humanitarian law' is to be welcomed. The Declaration and Programme of Action continues that violations, including systematic rape and sexual slavery `require a particularly effective response'.

The same is true of the enforcement provisions. States are under an obligation to make grave breaches of the Geneva Conventions and Protocols subject to the jurisdiction of their own courts and punishable by severe penalties. Rape is not however explicitly listed as a grave breach of the Convention, although acts wilfully committed and causing great suffering or causing injury to body or health do constitute grave breaches. Protocol I includes among its list of grave breaches `degrading practices involving outrages upon personal dignity based upon racial discrimination' but makes no reference to gender discrimination.

War crimes, that is violations of the laws or customs of war, are not the only possible legal regime for the prosecution of rape committed during international armed conflict. There is also the concept of a crime against humanity and, it has been argued in the context of the former Yugoslavia, genocide. A crime against humanity was defined in the Nuremberg Charter as: murder, extermination, enslavement, deportation, and other inhumane acts committed against any civilian population before or during the war, or persecutions on political, racial, or religious grounds in execution of or in connection with any crime within the jurisdiction of the Tribunal whether or not in violation of the domestic law of the country where perpetrated.

A number of points require special mention. First, although crimes against humanity were established as a separate category from war crimes, the crimes in question were inevitably associated with the occurrence of the Second World War. This association between armed conflict and crimes against humanity has been continued in the case of the former Yugoslavia. Second, despite the enormous incidence of rape of civilian populations during the Second World War, prosecutions of crimes against humanity were limited to persecutions on racial, political or religious grounds, in accordance with the wording of Article 6.

These words import a requirement of discriminatory behaviour into the concept of crimes against humanity, which is equally well provided by the gender discrimination inherent in violent crimes against women. Thirdly, for actions to come within the category of crimes against humanity they had to be committed against a civilian population, not against individual civilians. Fourthly, in contrast to war crimes, it has been necessary to establish systematic government planning for crimes against humanity. Crimes against humanity are not easily established in light of these restrictive requirements. Nevertheless, when the four occupying powers in Germany adopted Control Council Law No. 10 they departed from the

Nuremberg precedent and incorporated rape as a crime against humanity.

Genocide is defined in Article II of the Genocide Convention. There must be an intention to destroy, in whole or in part, a national, ethnic, racial or religious group through the commission of such acts as killing or causing serious bodily or mental harm to members of the group; deliberately inflicting on the group conditions of life calculated to bring about its physical destruction in whole or in part; imposing measures to prevent births within the group; or forcibly transferring children of the group to another group. At first sight rape does not appear to fall within this definition, but it has been forcefully argued that where it has been carried out on a massive and systematic basis for the purposes of producing babies of the ethnic class of the rapists, of destroying the family life of the victims and of cleansing the surrounding area of all other ethnic groups rape becomes genocidal. This categorization has been further supported by allegations that impregnated women were forcibly detained until it was too late to abort.

Despite this impressive body of formal prohibition, the incidence of rape in armed conflict has been widely ignored, underplayed or tolerated. Rape is too frequently regarded as an unfortunate but inevitable side-effect of conflict, or as an anticipated bonus for soldiers on all sides. Rape did not figure prominently at Nuremberg, `not because the Germans were not guilty of rape, but because the allied forces, especially the Russians and the Moroccan forces under French control, were also guilty of many rapes'. Rape was also largely invisible in the trials of the Japanese war criminals.

This silence by international law enforcement agencies denotes a double irony for women. Feminist writers have argued that the distinction drawn in international law between public acts of the State and private actions has been an important factor in its failure to address denial of human rights to women. Violence against women for example has not been readily viewed as torture, or as being imputable to the State, because of its widespread commission by private actors within the private arena of the home. Yet rape in international armed conflict, which is largely committed by military agents of the State under public authority, has also been ignored.

Law Enforcement

However, in the context of the former Yugoslavia there has been widespread pressure to ensure that this long silence is broken. The substantive law on rape in armed conflict has now become entangled with the question of arenas for its application. Condemnation of violations and calls for compliance have been made within international political fora, notably the Security Council, the Human Rights Commission, the Commission on the Status of Women, and the Committee on the Elimination of Discrimination Against Women. Proceedings have been commenced against Yugoslavia (Serbia-Montenegro) in the International Court of Justice by Bosnia-Herzegovina. Yugoslavia (Serbia-Montenegro) has counter-claimed in similar terms. Since under Article 34 of the Statute of the Court only States can be parties before it, this litigation will deal with the question of the responsibility of the State under the relevant treaties and customary international law. The options for the prosecution of individuals alleged to have committed such crimes are the domestic courts of any State, or an international war crimes tribunal on the precedent of Nuremberg.

Criminal proceedings have been commenced in domestic courts, for example in Germany, France and by a Bosnian military tribunal in Sarajevo. In the United States civil proceedings have been commenced under the Alien Torts Claims Act and the Torture Victim Protection Act against Radovan Karadzic, who has command authority over the Bosnian-Serb military forces. These claims rely upon the jurisprudence following the case of Filartiga v. Pena-Irala.

There Judge Kaufman accepted civil jurisdiction within the United States for offences violating the law of nations, in that instance torture, irrespective of where the offence had been committed and the nationalities of the accused and victim. While there may be concerns about the extension of United States' extra-territorial jurisdiction, there are advantages for the plaintiffs in such civil actions.

Jurisdiction can be established for the violation of international law provided personal service can be achieved. Amicus briefs from interested third parties, including non-governmental organizations, which set out many aspects of the issue can be admitted. A default judgment may be entered against an absent defendant on the basis of the burden of proof appropriate in civil cases. While it is highly unlikely that any award of damages would ever be forthcoming, the proceedings prevent free access to the United States for the defendant and allow a domestic court to assert its understanding of customary international law.

In Resolutions 808 and 827 the Security Council, acting under Chapter VII of the United Nations Charter, established an International Criminal Tribunal for the prosecution of persons responsible for serious violations of international humanitarian law committed in the territory of the former Yugoslavia since 1991. The Tribunal has been accorded jurisdiction over war crimes, genocide and crimes against humanity. Since a prevailing principle is that of nullum crimen sine lege, the definition of each offence relies upon pre-existing customary and conventional humanitarian law. In addition, all the parties to the conflict have largely accepted the application of the Geneva Conventions and Protocols to it.

Thus the Tribunal can determine whether grave breaches of the Geneva Conventions have been committed. As already stated these do not explicitly include rape, although as a matter of interpretation it can be readily included. The Tribunal also has jurisdiction over violations of the laws or customs of war. These include `employment of... weapons calculated to cause unnecessary suffering'. If rape is correctly regarded as a weapon of war in the way described above, it can readily be brought within this prohibition. The definition of crimes against humanity follows that of the Control Council Law No. 10 and therefore includes rape. The Secretary-General's report makes it clear that to constitute a crime against humanity the acts must be of a very serious nature and be committed as part of a widespread or systematic attack against any civilian population.

The purpose of the International Tribunal is to put an end to the commission of war crimes in the former Yugoslavia and to provide effective measures for bringing to justice those responsible for them. In accordance with the requirements for Chapter VII action, the Security Council has stated that the establishment of the International Tribunal will help to restore and maintain international peace in the area. There are enormous legal and practical questions relating, inter alia, to the identification, arrest and detention of accused persons, the collection and presentation of evidence, and the rules of evidence and procedure to be followed, which will have to be resolved for the Tribunal to become effective. While the practical and deterrent effect of such a Tribunal may be questioned, the importance of an authoritative public articulation of the relevant norms of international law cannot be understated. In a decentralized legal system where principles of customary international law are generated through State practice and opinio juris, the conclusions of the Tribunal resting upon the authority of the Security Council will inevitably have normative and educative effect. It is for this reason that it is essential that rape is considered separately from the other charges and is explicitly condemned. It is not sufficient for it to be regarded as an add-on to other offences.

International Legal Remedies: An Adequate Response to Rape?

Despite the importance of an affirmation of the illegality of rape in armed conflict, some reservations about the role of the Tribunal from the perspective of the survivors of rape must be expressed. Some of these can be addressed by sensitivity towards the process and procedures of the Tribunal, while others go directly to the inadequacies of international legal remedies in the case of rape.

The focus of the Tribunal is on punishing the wrongdoers, not on providing compensation and support to those who have suffered the harms described above. Admittedly this is a defect shared by municipal criminal legal systems, but these may be backed up by other domestic support services. A war crimes tribunal must be supplemented by long-term practical assistance from governments, such as medical care, shelter, support and counselling. Survivors of rape must be provided the space to specify their own needs within their own communities. Appropriate support must be made available to all concerned within the community to enable survivors to regain control of their own lives. The health and emotional needs of those who were not themselves raped must also be given consideration.

Indeed it has been argued that to concentrate only upon the survivors of rape can be `counter-productive by possibly stigmatizing and further traumatizing' those women. It cannot be assumed that all women will share the same needs. For example, some who feel that crimes committed against them have been disregarded may feel a sense of empowerment in the establishment of the Tribunal, while others may consider this a further intrusion into their lives, or fear the consequences of proceedings. Responses must take into account both individual preferences and the needs of the harmed society. The traditional exclusion of women from decision-making with respect to the use of force must not be here continued.

Those performing these tasks must receive adequate and relevant training, including psychological counselling. The international community must ensure that survivors do not become victims of, or become manipulated by, a well-meaning international reaction to the offences committed against them which fails to take account of their own concerns. It is important that fact-finding missions report their findings accurately and objectively and that research into the conflict reflects the complexities of its historical and ethnic origins. The fears of the Zagreb-based Centre for Women War Victims need to be taken seriously and responded to:

... we fear that the process of helping raped women is turning in a strange direction, being taken over by governmental institutions... and male gynaecologists in particular. We fear that the raped women could be used in political propaganda with the aim of spreading hatred and revenge, thus leading to further violence against women and to further victimization of survivors.

The pain of women raped and abused in armed conflict has often been appropriated by males for propaganda purposes. Suzanne Gibson discusses the examples of how rape of women in France during World War One became `transformed into a representation of France as an innocent female nation assaulted by a barbaric and brutishly male Germany' and British military conscriptors used the image of `the Hun' violating their sisters. She concludes with a warning that must be borne in mind throughout any criminal proceedings:... rape has not throughout most of recorded history, been a crime against women. It has significantly however been a heinous crime against men: a humiliation inflicted upon a nation, an affront to a man's pride as guardian of his women.

It is essential that prosecutions are brought against accused people from all sides. While the International Tribunal is unique in that it was established during the continuation of the conflict and is therefore untainted by notions of `victor's justice', it must not be used to prosecute offenders from only one side. Prosecutions must be brought against the alleged perpetrators and those higher up in the chain of command. It is essential that the message is made clear that rape of women is illegal and will be punished whoever is responsible for the commission of the offence.

There are various aspects of the Tribunal's composition and procedure that must be considered. Only two women judges have been nominated to it. While this is an advance on the composition of the International Court of Justice which has never had an elected woman judge, it is still far from the goal of 50% female judges sought by women's groups. Attention must be paid to gender distribution of all other personnel of the Tribunal, including prosecutors and investigators. Women may be fearful of retribution and publicity and thus be reluctant to testify before the Tribunal. The Special Rapporteur has pointed out that there are many reasons why survivors may be reluctant to testify as to their experiences. These include `severe traumatization, feelings of shame, lack of trust, fear of awakening bad memories as well as fear of reprisals against themselves and their families'.

A balance will have to be drawn between the rights of the accused to due process and the needs of the survivors. There has long been criticism in domestic criminal proceedings of the ways in which women in rape and other sexual abuse cases have been subject to intense and distressing personal questioning by investigators and defence lawyers. Procedural reforms have been introduced in some countries. The international tribunal should draw upon these experiences in determining its procedures. As a minimum, all people involved in the work of the tribunal, and especially those involved in judicial, investigatory or prosecutorial work should receive gender sensitivity training.

There are other still more fundamental questions that need to be addressed. The jurisdiction of the Tribunal is limited to offences in the former Yugoslavia; it will not assist women who have been raped or will in the future be raped in other conflicts all around the world, although its effectiveness is likely to impact upon its future precedential value.

Further, rape and sexual violence against women occurs along a continuum of seriousness. The widespread and systematic nature of the offences committed in the former Yugoslavia place these offences at the far end of the spectrum, as is recognized by their inclusion as crimes against humanity in the Statute of the Tribunal. The focus on these rapes and the failure to make explicit that any rape committed in armed conflict is a war crime entails the risk of creating the assumption that `lesser' rapes may still be committed with impunity.

DOWRY LAW IN INDIA

Payment of a dowry, gift — often financial, has a long history in many parts of the world. In India, the payment of a dowry was prohibited in 1961 under Indian civil law and subsequently by Sections 304B and 498a of the Indian Penal Code were enacted to make it easier for the wife to seek redress from potential harassment by the husband's family. Dowry laws has come under criticism that they are misused by women and their families.

Dowries

Gifts given by the parents of the bride are considered "stri-dhan", i.e. property of the woman, traditionally representing her share of her parent's wealth.

The 1961 Dowry Prohibition Act

This act prohibits the request, payment or acceptance of a dowry, "as consideration for the marriage". where "dowry" is defined as a gift demanded or given as a precondition for a marriage. Gifts given without a precondition are not considered dowry, and are legal. Asking or giving of dowry can be punished by an imprisonment of up to six months, or a fine of up to Rs. 5000. It replaced several pieces of anti-dowry legislation that had been enacted by various Indian states.

IPC Section 304B

This Section of the Indian Penal Code was inserted by a 1986 amendment. The Dowry deaths law defines a 'dowry death' as the death of a woman caused by any burns or bodily injury or which does not occur under normal circumstances within seven years of her marriage. For a woman's death to be a dowry death, it must also be shown that soon before her death she was subjected to cruelty or harassment by her husband or any relative of her husband for, or in connection with, any demand for dowry. If this is proved, the woman's husband or relative is required to be deemed to have caused her death. Whoever commits dowry death is required to be punished with imprisonment for a term which shall not be less than seven years but which may extend to imprisonment for life.

IPC Section 498A

Section 498A was inserted into the penal code in 1983 it reads: Whoever, being the husband or the relative of the husband of a woman, subjects such woman to cruelty shall be punished with imprisonment for a term which may extend to three years and shall also be liable to fine.

In practice, cruelty is taken to include the demanding of a dowry. This section is non-bailable, non-compoundable (i.e. it cannot be privately resolved between the parties concerned) and cognizable (i.e. the police can arrest the accused without investigation or warrants) on a report from a woman or close relative. Another examples of a cognizable law in India was the Prevention of Terrorist Activities Act.

Police often file charges against the husband, his parents and other relatives (whoever being named on the complaint by the wife or her close relatives) and put them in jail. There is no penalty (even a fine) for filing a false case. Many individuals have claimed this is being abused by the wife or her close relatives.

In urban India, the majority of families have adequate knowledge regarding section 498A of the Indian Penal Code, 1860. The Malimath committee in 2003 proposed making amendments to this section although such amendments have been opposed by women's groups. The Centre for Social Research India has released a research report opposing amendments to section 498A. According to this report, in the studied cases there were no convictions based solely on section 498A. Although the report states that 60.5 percent of the studied cases were falsified. They also state that many people believe the law has been abused by "educated and independent minded women." A police official asserted that in his district one-third of dowry murder cases were found totally false by the police. However, on December 17, 2003, the then Minister of State for Home Affairs, Mr. I.D Swami said: "There is no information available with the Government to come to the conclusion that many families in India are suffering due to exaggerated allegations of harassment and dowry cases made by women against their husbands and other family members involving them in criminal misappropriation and cruelty."

On 20 July 2005, Justices Arijit Pasayat and H.K. Seema of the Indian Supreme Court declared Section 498A to be constitutional."The object is to strike at the root of dowry menace. But by misuse of the provision a new legal terrorism can be unleashed. The provision is intended to be used as a shield and not an assassin's weapon. If [the] cry of "wolf" is made too often as a prank, assistance and protection may not be available when the actual wolf appears," the Bench said.

Several reports of the abuse of Section 498A have involved couples based outside India especially in the US. The United States Department of State has published the following travel warning: A number of U.S. citizen men who have come to India to marry Indian nationals have been arrested and charged with crimes related to dowry extraction. Many of the charges stem from the U.S. citizen's inability to provide an immigrant visa for his prospective spouse to travel immediately to the United States.

The courts sometimes order the U.S. citizen to pay large sums of money to his spouse in exchange for the dismissal of charges. The courts normally confiscate the American's passport, and he must remain in India until the case has been settled.

In a well publicized case, Dr. Balamurali Ambati, who earned his MD at age 17, and his family were detained in India for over 3 years in a suit related to alleged dowry demands by the family for his brother's wife Archana, which delayed Dr.

Ambati's entry to the ophthalmology program for 2 years, leaving him to begin his residency in 1998. All charges against him were dismissed in October of 1996 and all his family members were acquitted in June 1999. During the course of the trial the Ambatis produced a tape in which the father of Archana, demanded US $500,000 to drop all the charges although the details of this particular case are still debated in India. Section 498A in itself is, however, not meant to deal specifically with dowry — it is commonly considered to be a 'dowry law' because domestic violence against a wife related to dowry demands is considered to be within the scope of 'cruelty' envisaged by the Section.

DIVORCE IN INDIA

The Law

All major religions have their own laws which govern divorces within their own community, and separate regulations exist regarding divorce in interfaith marriages. Hindus, including Buddhists, Sikhs and Jains, are governed by the Hindu Marriage Act, 1955; Christians by the Indian Divorce Act, 1869; Parsis by the Parsi Marriage and Divorce Act, 1936; and Muslims by the Dissolution of Muslim Marriages Act, 1939, which provides the grounds on which women can obtain a divorce, and the uncodified civil law. Civil marriages and inter-community marriages and divorces are governed by the Special Marriage Act, 1956 (Kapur and Cossman 101).

Other community specific legislation includes the Native Converts' Marriage Dissolution Act, 1866 that allows a Hindu to appeal for a divorce if a spouse converts to Christianity (Virdi 36-37).

Grounds for Divorce

In most Western nations, there are approximately 16 distinct reasons for which divorces are granted. In India, however, only five main reasons are generally accepted as sufficient grounds for divorce (Choudhary 90).

Adultery. While no formal definition of adultery exists, it does have "a fairly established meaning in matrimonial law" (Diwan 171), namely "the voluntary sexual intercourse of a married man or woman with a person other than the offender's wife or husband" (Choudhary 91). While the law considers it valid grounds for either sex, adulterous women are "judged more harshly" than men (Kapur and Cossman 102). The various religious regulations a e not unanimous on this issue. The law regarding Hindus allows divorce to be granted on the grounds of infidelity of either husband or wife.

The Christian law, however, would traditionally not have granted a divorce to a woman solely on the grounds of adultery. She would have had to prove another violation, such as cruelty (Kapur and Cossman 102-4). A recent Bombay High Court decision "recognised cruelty and desertion as independent grounds for the dissolution of a Christian marriage," striking down a section of the law that allowed for an unconstitutional distinction between the sexes (Raiker-Mhatre 1).

Desertion. The three main components of desertion are the "disruption of cohabitation, absence of just or reasonable cause and their combination throughout three years" before the abandoned spouse may petition for a divorce (Virdi 71). There also must be an obvious intent on the part of the offending spouse to remain permanently apart from the other. This statute also applies to cases in which a spouse has been heard from for at least seven years (Choudhary 91).

Cruelty. As with adultery, "the definition of the type of Behaviour that constitutes cruelty varies according to the gender of the petitioner" of the divorce. "Despite the fact that cruelty is often equally available to husbands and wives, the way in which the law is interpreted and applied suggests that women and men are evaluated by rather different standards" (Kapur and Cossman 105). This category includes both physical and mental abuse and neglect (Choudhary 91). A court decision made in early May 1997 made cruelty sufficient grounds for a Christian woman to obtain a; previously, the law required both adultery and cruelty to be proven. The national Indian Christian community seems to have embraced this judgment (Raikar-Mhatre 1-2.

Impotency. This refers to the physical inability of the couple to consummate the marriage (Choudhary 91) or the refusal by one spouse to do so (Diwan 136). Some cases have established that sterility can be construed to mean non-consummation if the other partner is not aware of the condition before the marriage (Diwan 139).

Chronic Disease. Both mental and physical illnesses are included in this category, as well as sexually transmitted diseases (Choudhary 92). Not all religions recognize identical diseases as grounds for divorce. Christians and Parsis do not allow divorce for a sexually transmitted disease or leprosy while the other communities do (Diwan 204-5).

Consequences of Divorce

Economic. There is great disparity between the economic ramifications of divorce between men and women. Men remain relatively unaffected while women, especially those with children, have difficulty "providing food, clothing and shelter for themselves and their children." The government in urban areas usually provides some form of public assistance to single mothers, but this service is not fully taken advantage of because most do not know of its existence (Amato 210). Often a woman is not able to rely on her family for support because many parents "feel they have discharged their obligations to a daughter by arranging her marriage and providing a dowry." Dowries are not returned after a divorce. Also, due to the social stigma of divorce, women find it difficult to remarry and usually attempt to establish an independent household (Amato 211).

Social. While India feels that one should have the right to divorce, it is still a highly stigmatizing action. Women are looked upon more harshly than men in this regard. There continue to be segments of Indian society that feel divorce is never an option, regardless of how abusive or adulterous the husband may be which adds to the greater disapproval for women. A divorced woman often will return to her family, but may not be wholeheartedly welcomed. She puts, especially if she has children, an economic burden on her family and is often given lowly household tasks to perform. There is also the risk that a divorced woman's presence would ward off possible marriages for other daughters within the household. Unavoidably, the overall status of the family and household are lowered by having a divorcee living with amongst them. A woman's class and caste are a major factor in her acceptance back into society. Women from higher classes tend to have an easier time than middle or lower class women in returning to the social order after a divorce. An exception to this model is the extreme bottom of the society who have experienced little rebuff from peers after a divorce. This results from their already atypical status in society (Amato 212-4).

Divorce in The God of Small Things

In Arundhati Roy's The God of Small Things, the marriage and quick divorce of Ammu has devastating consequences, reflecting the social and cultural stigma of divorce in India:

> *"...Ammu left her husband and returned, unwelcomed, to her parents in Ayemenem. To everything she had fled from only a few years ago. Excpet now she had two children. And no more dreams" (42).*
>
> *"Baby Kochamma resented Ammu, because she saw her quarreling with a fate that she, Baby Kochamma herself, felt she had graciously accepted. The fate of the wretched Man-less woman" (44-5).*
>
> *"...the commonly held view that a married daughter had no position in her parents' home. As for a divorced daughteræaccording to Baby Kochamma, she had no position anywhere at all" (45).*
>
> *Chacko "said that Ammu and Estha and Rahel were millstones around his neck" (82).*
>
> *"Die-vorced?" His voice rose in such a high register that it cracked on the question mark. He even pronounced the word as though it was a form of death" (124).*
>
> *"She was [Estha and Rahel's] Ammu and their Baba and she had loved them Double" (155).*

Women's Rights and Wrongs

The All India Muslim Personal Law Board proclaims that triple talaq is a social evil, but it is equally assertive that this social evil should not be removed by legislative reform. There is no question of banning the practice. Maulana Sayed Rabey Al-Hasani Naqvi, the Board president, says: "Our laws are based on divine inspiration and triple talaq comes from the same inspiration, that is, Shariat. We have no powers to amend or abolish it. So the triple talaq is irrevocable." It is difficult to understand how what is divine can at the same time be evil.

The Hindu religion has also been replete with many social evils that Hindu women had to face. The practice of sati which forceda Hindu woman to sit on the funeral pyre of her husband was abolished by the Sati Regulation Act, 1829, itself the result of a social reform movement launched by Raja Rammohun Roy. The reform was taken to its logical conclusion with the Widows Remarriage Act of 1856.

Among Hindus, polygamy too was rampant. Yet it was abolished first in Bombay State by the Bombay Prevention of Hindu Bigamous Marriages Act, 1946. Later, the Hindu Marriage Act, 1955, put an end to polygamy throughout the country. Marriage among Hindus had been held to be sacrosanct, something that could not be dissolved — yet the Hindu Marriage Act, 1955, provides for dissolution of marriage both by husband and wife on the grounds stated in the Hindu Marriage Act. The Indian Divorce Act has also been recently amended to do away with inequality between women and men in matters of divorce among Christians. Untouchability, yet another social evil, was outlawed by Article 17 of our Constitution.

Social and legal reforms must move together to ensure that all social evils are banished. It is often said that personal laws are outside the purview of challenge under Article 13 of the Constitution of India. But this has no constitutional or legal basis. The fact is that what is inhuman is both unconstitutional and illegal. A very interesting answer to the argument of the Muslim Personal Law Board lies in the fact that in several Muslim countries triple talaq has been banned or restricted. There are several countries where there is a uniform law of divorce, for all citizens irrespective of their religion. The power to legislate on marriage and divorce is specifically conferred in entry 5, List III, Schedule VII of our Constitution.

In legal awareness camps for Muslim women which I attend and help organise regularly, women of all ages, young and old, ask me one question again and again: How can a Muslim marry four times when Hindu, Christian or Parsi men can marry only once? How is that there is a right of triple talaq for men and no right of divorce for us? I ask them to raise their voice against triple talaq, for a model Nikahnama that will secure them their rights.

Discrimination against women regardless of their religion is a matter of grave concern. The days of patriarchy are at an end. Today women are taking their rightful place in all walks of life. After the Second World War, we made a transition to a world of human rights. The United Nations Charter proclaims that all human beings are born free and equal. Contrast this with the American constitution, which proclaimed that all men are born free and equal. The Beijing Declaration also proclaims women's rights as human rights.

We cannot continue to dither on the enforcement of basic fundamental rights of women. The sooner the evil of polygamy and triple talaq in our country are banned and banished the better.

The Women's Reservation Bill has still to be passed. In the Hindi belt of our country, Hindu women have been deprived of the right of inheritance and partition in a joint Hindu family. A daughter just cannot be a coparcener like a son. This discrimination has been removed in Kerala, Tamil Nadu, Karnataka, Maharashtra and Gujarat. The Law Commission report recommending equal rights to daughters and sons in HUF property is gathering dust.

The community and the state must work together to ensure that our sisters enjoy full rights equal to men. The Constitution is supreme. Liberty and equality are the pillars of our Constitution. Let us make India a country of equal rights and dignity for women and men.

IPC-Indian Penal Code

IT(P) Act-Immoral Traffic (Prevention) Act, 1986.

AGES FOR LEGAL PURPOSES

Age of Simple Majority

The legal age of majority is eighteen (18) years for male and female persons.

Age of Consent for Sexual Activity

The legal age at which a person is currently competent to consent to sexual intercourse is currently eighteen (18) years.

Age of Consent for Marriage

The legal age of consent for marriage is eighteen (18) years for male persons and twenty-one (21) years for female persons.

RAPE

Section 376(1) of the Indian Penal Code

'Whoever, except in the cases provided for by subsection (2), commits rape shall be punished with imprisonment of either description for a term which shall not be less than seven years but which may be for life or for a term which may extend to ten years and shall also be liable to fine unless the woman raped is his own wife and is not under twelve (12) years of age, in which case, he shall be punished with imprisonment of either description for a term which may extend to two years or with fine or with both;

Provided that the Court may, for adequate and special reasons to be mentioned in the judgement, impose a sentence of imprisonment for a term of less than seven years.

(2) Whoever-

(a)-(e) (...)

(f) commits rape on a woman when she is under twelve (12) years of age; or

(g) (...),

-shall be punished with rigorous imprisonment for a term which shall not be less than ten years but which may be for life and shall also be liable to fine;

Provided that the Court may, for adequate and special reasons to be mentioned in the judgement, impose a sentence of imprisonment of either description for a term of less than ten years.'

RAPE LAWS IN INDIA

"The law of rape is not just a few sentences. It is a whole book, which has clearly demarcated chapters and cannot be read selectively. We cannot read the preamble and suddenly reach the last chapter and claim to have understood and applied it." Kiran Bedi., Joint Commissioner, Special Branch. In the Mathura rape case, wherein Mathura-a sixteen year old tribal girl was raped by two policemen in the compound of Desai Ganj Police station in Chandrapur district of Maharashtra.

Her relatives, who had come to register a complaint, were patiently waiting outside even as the heinous act was being committed in the police station. When her relatives and the assembled crowd threatened to burn down the police chowky, the two guilty policemen, Ganpat and Tukaram, reluctantly agreed to file a panchnama. The case came for hearing on 1st June, 1974 in the sessions court. The judgment however turned out to be in favour of the accused. Mathura was accused of being a liar. It was stated that since she was 'habituated to sexual intercourse' her consent was voluntary; under the circumstances only sexual intercourse could be proved and not rape.

On appeal the Nagpur bench of the Bombay High Court set aside the judgment of the Sessions Court, and sentenced the accused namely Tukaram and Ganpat to one and five years of rigorous imprisonment respectively. The Court held that passive submission due to fear induced by serious threats could not be construed as consent or willing sexual intercourse.

However, the Supreme Court again acquitted the accused policemen. The Supreme Court held that Mathura had raised no alarm; and also that there were no visible marks of injury on her person thereby negating the struggle by her.

The Court in this case failed to comprehend that a helpless resignation in the face of inevitable compulsion or the passive giving in is no consent. However, the Criminal Law Amendment Act, 1983 has made a statutory provision in the face of Section.114 (A) of the Evidence Act, which states that if the victim girl says that she did no consent to the sexual intercourse, the Court shall presume that she did not consent.

In Mohd.Habib Vs State, the Delhi High Court allowed a rapist to go scot-free merely because there were no marks of injury on his penis-which the High Court presumed was a indication of no resistance. The most important facts such as the age of the victim (being seven years) and that she had suffered a ruptured hymen and the bite marks on her body were not considered by the High Court. Even the eye-witnesses who witnessed this ghastly act, could not sway the High Court's judgment. Another classic example of the judicial pronouncements in rape cases is the case of Bhanwari Devi, wherein a judge remarked that the victim could not have been raped since she was a dalit while the accused hailed from an upper caste-who would not stoop to sexual relations with a dalit.

In another instance of conscience stirring cases, Sakina-a poor sixteen year old girl from Kerala, who was lured to Ernakulam with the promise of finding her a good job, where she was sold and forced into prostitution. There for eighteen long months she was held captive and raped by clients. Finally she was rescued by the police-acting on a complaint filed by her neighbour.

With the help of her parents and an Advocate, Sakina filed a suit in the High Court-giving the names of the upper echelons of the bureaucracy and society of Kerala. The suit was squashed by the High Court, while observing that ' it is improbable to believe that a man who desired sex on payment would go to a reluctant woman; and that the version of the victim was not so sacrosanct as to be taken for granted.'

Whereas, in State of Punjab Vs. Gurmit Singh, the Supreme Court has advised the lower judiciary, that even if the victim girl is shown to be habituated to sex, the Court should not describe her to be of loose character. The Supreme Court has in the case of State of Maharashtra Vs. Madhukar N. Mardikar, held that "the unchastity of a woman does not make her open to any and every person to violate her person as and when he wishes. She is entitled to protect her person if there is an attempt to violate her person against her wish. She is equally entitled to the protection of law. Therefore merely because she is of easy virtue, her evidence cannot be thrown overboard."

Also the Bandit Queen case, which depicts the tragic story of a village girl. Phoolan Devi-who was exposed from an early age to the lust and brutality of some men. She was married to a man old enough to be her father. She was beaten and raped by him. She was later thrown out of the village-accused of luring boys of the upper caste. She was arrested by the police and subjected to indignation and humiliation. Was also kidnapped and raped by the leader of dacoits and later by the leader of a gang of Thakurs-who striped her naked and paraded her in front of the entire village. This is truly one story that shows the apathy of the existing society.

In Chairman, Railway Board Vs. Chandrima Das, a practicing Advocate of the Calcutta High Court filed a petition under Article.226 of the Constitution of India against the various railway authorities of the eastern railway claiming compensation for the victim (Smt. Hanufa Khatoon)-a Bangladesh national-who was raped at the Howrah Station, by the railway security men. The High Court awarded Rs.10 lacs as compensation. An appeal was preferred and it was contended by the state that:

a) The railway was not liable to pay the compensation to the victim for she was a foreigner.

b) That the remedy for compensation lies in the domain of private law and not public law. i.e. that the victim should have approached the Civil Court for seeking damages; and should have not come to the High Court under Article.226.

Considering the above said contentions, the Supreme Court observed:

> *"Where public functionaries are involved and the matter relates to the violation of fundamental rights or the enforcement of public duties, the remedy would be avoidable under public law. It was more so, when it was not a mere violation of any ordinary right, but the violation of fundamental rights was involved-as the petitioner was a victim of rape, which a violation of fundamental right of every person guaranteed under Article.21 of the Constitution."*

The Supreme Court also held that the relief can be granted to the victim for two reasons-firstly, on the ground of domestic jurisprudence based on the Constitutional provisions; and secondly, on the ground of Human Rights Jurisprudence based on the Universal Declaration of Human Rights, 1948 which has international recognition as the 'Moral Code of Conduct'-adopted by the General Assembly of the United Nation.

After having studied the case laws, it is necessary to also study the definition of Rape as given in the Indian Penal Code, 1860. As per Section.375 of IPC a man is said to commit the offence of rape with a woman under the following six circumstances:

1. Sexual intercourse against the victims will,
2. Without the victims consent,
3. With her consent, when her consent has been obtained by putting her or any person that she may be interested in fear of death or hurt,
4. With her consent, when the man knows that he is not her husband,
5. With her consent, when at the time of giving such consent she was intoxicated, or is suffering from unsoundness of mind and does not understand the nature and consequences of that to which she gives consent,
6. With or without her consent when she is under sixteen years of age.

Further explanation provided to the section states that penetration is sufficient to constitute the sexual intercourse necessary to constitute the offence of rape, whereas the exception leaves out marital rape altogether if the wife is not under fifteen years of age.

Marital Exception

In R Vs. R12, the House of Lords widened the scope of criminal liability by declaring that the husband could be charged as a principal offender in the rape of his wife. This decision seems to have obliterated the protection of the husband from such prosecution under the doctrine of marital exemption. This exemption was based upon the belief under which the wife was regarded as the husbands' chattel. She was supposed to have given a general consent to her husband as a natural implication of the marriage. This has now become an outdated view of marriage in England. However, the above decision of the House of Lords has not been followed in India-where marital exemption to the husband 'still exists'.

Section. 375 therefore requires:

a) Sexual intercourse by a man with a woman;
b) The sexual intercourse must be under any of the six circumstances given in the section.

Criminal Law Amendment Act, 1983

The Criminal Law Amendment Act has substantially changed Sections.375 and 376 of the IPC. Several new sections have been introduced therein-viz. Sections. 376(A), 376(B), 501 (c) 3 376(D) of the IPC.

Section. 376(A) punishes sexual intercourse with wife without her consent by a judicially separated husband.

Section. 376(B) punishes for sexual intercourse by a public servant with a woman in custody.

Section. 376(C) punishes sexual intercourse by superintendent of jail, remand house, etc. whereas,

Section. 376(D) punishes sexual intercourse by any member of the management or staff of a hospital with any woman in that hospital.

These new sections have been introduced with a view to stop sexual abuse of women in custody, care and control by various persons-which though not amounting to rape were nevertheless considered highly reprehensible.

Attempt to Rape

In cases where an indecent assault is made upon the person of a woman, but where rape is not committed-the culprit is charged with Section.354 of IPC, because unless the Court is satisfied that there was determination in the accused to gratify his passion at any cost, and inspite of all resistance, such person is not charged with rape. Section.354 of the IPC prescribes punishment for anyone who assaults or uses criminal force to any woman with an intent to outrage her modesty.

An indecent assault upon a woman is punishable under this section. Rape is punished under Section.376; but the offence under this Section is of less gravity than rape. And also because a person who is guilty of attempting rape cannot be allowed to escape with the lesser penalty of this section.

An indecent assault, i.e., an assault which right minded persons would consider as indecent-accordingly any evidence explaining the defendants conduct, or whether any admission by him or otherwise is admissible to establish whether he intended to commit an indecent assault, as is stated under Section.21 sub clause (2) of the Evidence Act, which reads:

Section.21 (2): An admission may be proved by or on behalf of the person making it, when it consists of statements of the existence of any state of mind or body, relevant or in issue, made at or about the time when such state of mind or body existed, and is accompanied by conduct rendering its falsehood improbable.

Impediments to Justice

In the present circumstances when offences against women are on the rise-when young girls are raped by their doctors, by presidential guards in broad daylight, the definition of rape to be of any deterrence-falls extremely inadequate. It does not address forced penetration of objects and parts of the body into the vagina and anus; and forced oral or anal intercourse.

It also does not recognize other forms of sexual assaults-like protracted sexual assault by relatives, marital rape etc. as aggravated forms of rape. This causes grave injustice to many victims. In many cases of child rape, the child has been penetrated through fingers or by objects or been force to perform oral or anal sex; yet this is not considered rape by the Courts.

Adding to this is Section. 155(4) of the Evidence Act, which allows the victim to be questioned of her past sexual history-which the defence uses to humiliate the victim in the Courtroom.

One of the major obstacles in delivering justice in rape cases is the poor quality of investigations. The reason behind this ranges from gender bias and corruption to the general inefficiency of the police. In many cases the police have even refused to lodge the FIR or have lodged incomplete FIR.

The victims are not taken for prompt medical examination, because in cases of rape, or attempt to rape-medical examination of the victim and of the accused soon after the incident often yields a wealth of corroborative evidence. Therefore, such an opportunity should not be lost by the police.

The manner in which some courts have interpreted the law or assessed the evidence has often proved to be an obstacle also. Inspite of Supreme Court judgments to the contrary, lower court judges often insist on evidence of physical resistance or marks of injuries to hold that a woman has not consented. A woman's evidence without corroboration is not considered sufficient.

The long time that is taken to complete a rape trial often by allowing senseless adjournments; and the giving of evidence by the victim in the presence of the accused and the harsh cross examination in the Court are some other major obstacles.

As observed by Krishna Iyer, J. in Rafique's case,

> *"When a woman is ravished, what is inflicted is not mere physical injury but the deep sense of some deathless shame... judicial response to Human Rights cannot be blunted by legal bigotry."*

Therefore rape laws in order to be of great deterrence, must have a cooperative victim, professional investigation, diligent prosecution; and an expeditious trial. For otherwise it shall not be the law, that fails, but the applicants, the process and application. Failure of law reflects the failure of the society to protect and serve humanity. In view of the above, the Supreme Court has laid down the following guidelines for the trial of rape cases:

1. The complaints of sexual assault cases should be provided with legal representation. Such a person should be well acquainted. The Advocates role should not merely be of explaining to the victim the nature of the proceedings, to prepare for the case and assist her, but to provide her with guidance as to how she might obtain help of a different nature from other agencies-for e.g. psychiatric consultation or medical assistance.
2. Legal assistance should be provided at the police Station, since the victim may be in a distressed state. Guidance and support of a lawyer at this stage would be of great help.
3. The police should be under a duty to inform the victim of her right to a counsel before being interrogated.
4. A list of lawyers willing to act in these cases should be kept at the police station.
5. Advocates shall be appointed by the Court on an application by the police at the earliest, but in order that the victim is not questioned without one, the Advocate shall be authorized to act at the police Station before leave of the Court is sought or obtained.

6. In all rape trials, anonymity of the victim must be maintained
7. It is necessary to setup Criminal Injuries Compensation Board with regard to the Directive Principles contained under Article. 38(1) of the Constitution of India. As some victims also incur Substantial losses.
8. Compensation for the victims shall be awarded by the Court on the conviction of the offender and by the Criminal Injuries Compensation Board-whether or not a conviction has taken place. The Board will take into account pain, suffering, shock as well as loss of earnings due to pregnancy and child birth if this accrued as a result of rape.

The National Commission for Women be asked to frame schemes for compensation and rehabilitation to ensure justice to the victims of such crimes. As observed by Justice Saghir Ahmad," Unfortunately *a woman in our country belongs to a class or group of society who are in an disadvantaged position on account of several social barriers and impediments and have therefore, been victims of tyranny at the hands of men with whom they, unfortunately, under the Constitution enjoy equal status."*

LAWS AGAINST DOMESTIC VIOLENCE AND ABUSE

In 1983, domestic violence was recognised as a specific criminal offence by the introduction of section 498-A into the Indian Penal Code. This section deals with cruelty by a husband or his family towards a married woman. Four types of cruelty are dealt with by this law:

- conduct that is likely to drive a woman to suicide,
- conduct which is likely to cause grave injury to the life, limb or health of the woman,
- harassment with the purpose of forcing the woman or her relatives to give some property, or
- harassment because the woman or her relatives is unable to yield to demands for more money or does not give some property.

The punishment is imprisonment for upto three years and a fine. The complaint against cruelty need not be lodged by the person herself. Any relative may also make the complaint on her behalf.

What are the forms of "cruelty" recognised by the Courts?

- Persistent denial of food,
- Insisting on perverse sexual conduct,
- Constantly locking a woman out of the house,
- Denying the woman access to children, thereby causing mental torture,
- Physical violence,
- Taunting, demoralising and putting down the woman with the intention of causing mental torture,
- Confining the woman at home and not allowing her normal social intercourse,
- Abusing children in their mother's presence with the intention of causing her mental torture,
- Denying the paternity of the children with the intention of inflicing mental pain upon the mother, and
- Threatening divorce unless dowry is given.

What is a "matrimonial home"? What rights do women have in their matrimonial home?

The matrimonial home is the household a woman shares with her husband; whether it is rented, officially provided, or owned by the husband or his relatives. A woman has the right to remain in the matrimonial home along with her husband as long as she is married, though there is no definite law regarding this right. If a woman is being pressurised to leave the matrimonial home, she can ask the Court for an injunction or "restraining order" protecting her from being thrown out. This can usually be obtained quite easily. It is generally advisable not to leave the matrimonial home; it is easier to get a court order preventing a woman being thrown out than to get an order enforcing her right to return to it once she has left or been thrown out.

What is an 'Injunction' and how does it apply to domestic violence cases?

An injunction is a court order directing a person to do or not to do something. A woman has a lot of flexibility regarding what she can request the Court to order. For instance, if she is being stalked by somebody (including her husband), she can obtain injunctions against the person coming near her home or place of work, or even telephoning her.

What can be done in the case of dowry-related harassment or dowry death?

Section 498-A of the Indian Penal Code covers dowry-related harassment. As with other provisions of criminal law, a woman can use the threat of going to court to deter this kind of harassment. The Indian Penal Code also addresses dowry deaths in section 304-B. If a woman dies of "unnatural causes" within seven years of marriage and has been harassed for dowry before her death, the Courts will assume that it is a case of dowry death. The husband or in-laws will then have to prove that their harassment was not the cause of her death. A dowry death is punishable by imprisonment of at least seven years. When filing an FIR (First Hand Report), in a case where a woman is suspected to have been murdered after a history of torture due to dowry demands, the complaint should be filed under section 304-B rather than under section 306, which deals with abetment to suicide. Section 306 should be invoked when a woman commits suicide because of dowry-related harassment.

Can you refuse to have sex with your husband? Is there a law on marital rape?

Since India does not have a law on marital rape, even if a woman's husband has sexual intercourse with her without her consent, he cannot be prosecuted for rape. However, excessive and unreasonable demands for sex, or demands for unnatural sex have been considered forms of cruelty and may entitle a woman to a divorce. If a woman is judicially separated, her husband cannot have sexual intercourse with her without her consent. If he does, he can be prosecuted under section 376-A of the IPC. Note that consent under pressure (e.g. because of threats to injure or to stop paying maintenance) is not considered valid.

What can a woman do to prevent domestic violence?

One option is to get the woman's husband to execute a "bond to keep peace", or a "bond of good behaviour" through the Executive, Magistrate who can order the husband to put a stop to domestic violence. The husband can also be asked to deposit securities (i.e. money or property) that will be forfeited if he continues to act violently.

Distinction between Civil and Criminal Law

The distinction between civil and criminal law is a basic part of the Indian legal system. Civil laws deal with the rights and obligations of people and what is needed to protect them, while criminal law deals with offences and their punishment. In a criminal offence, the State takes upon itself the responsibility to investigate and collect evidence (through the police), to fight the case in court (through a public prosecutor) and enforce the punishment. Robbery, murder and kidnapping are examples of criminal offences. Criminal offences are dealt with by the Indian Penal Code (IPC).

The procedure by which a criminal trial is conducted is quite different from the processes involved in a civil trial. An important difference is that the "standard of proof" required in criminal cases is much higher than in civil cases. Since criminal law is centrally linked with issues of punishment, allegations and facts must be proved "beyond reasonable doubt", so that innocent people are not punished. In civil cases, the courts scrutinise the "balance of probabilities" before deciding in whose favour to make a judgement. However, there are some situations in which both civil and criminal law apply. Inflicting physical violence on a wife or daughter-in-law as well as subjecting her to cruelty-physical, mental or emotional-in a marriage is not only a civil offence and provides ground for divorce (a "matrimonial offence"), but is also a criminal offence under the Indian Penal Code, for which a person can be imprisoned. The laws dealing with marital abuse have been made very stringent through amendments in the Indian Penal Code and the Evidence Act.

DOWRY VICTIMS

Dowry deaths are the deaths of young women who are murdered or driven to suicide by continuous harassment and torture by husbands and in-laws in an effort to extort an increased dowry. Dowry deaths are reported in various South Asian countries such as India, Pakistan, and Bangladesh. Dowry death is considered one of the many categories of violence against women in South Asia.

Most dowry deaths occur when the young woman, unable to bear the harassment and torture, commits suicide. Most of these suicides are by hanging, poisoning or by fire. Sometimes the woman is killed by setting her on fire; this is known as "bride burning", and sometimes disguised as suicide or accident. According to Indian police, every year it receives over 2,500 reports of bride-burning, while human rights organisations in Pakistan report over 300 deaths per year. The Indian National Crime Records Bureau (NCRB) reports that there were about 6787 dowry death cases registered in India in 2005. Incidents of dowry deaths during the year 2005 (6,787) have increased significantly by 46.0 per cent over 1995 level (4,648).

'The 1961 Dowry Prohibition Act' prohibits the request, payment or acceptance of a dowry, "as consideration for the marriage", where "dowry" is defined as a gift demanded or given as a precondition for a marriage. Gifts given without a precondition are not considered dowry, and are legal. Asking or giving of dowry can be punished by an imprisonment of up to six months, or a fine of up to Rs. 5000. It replaced several pieces of anti-dowry legislation that had been enacted by various Indian states. Indian women's rights activists campaigned for more than 40 years to contain dowry deaths without much success. The Dowry Prohibition Act 1961 and the more stringent Section 498a of IPC (enacted in 1983) did not achieve the desired result. Using the Protection of Women from Domestic Violence Act 2005 (PWDVA) implemented in 2006, a woman can put a stop to the dowry harassment by approaching a domestic violence protection officer. Due to demands by women's rights activists, the Indian government has modified property inheritance laws and permitted daughters to claim equal rights to their parental property. Some religious groups have urged the people to curb the extravagant spendings during the marriages.

OTHER FORMS OF CHILD SEX ABUSE

Section 90 of the Indian Penal Code

'A consent is not such a consent as is intended by any section of this Code, *if the consent is given by a person under fear of injury, or under a misconception of fact, and if the person doing the act knows, or has reason to believe, that the consent was given in consequent of such fear or misconception; or*

if the consent is given by a person who, from unsoundness of mind, or intoxication, is unable to understand the nature and consequent of that to which he gives his consent; or

unless the contrary appears from the context, if the consent is given by a person who is under twelve (12) years of age.'

Misconception of fact-Consent given under a misconception is invalid if the person to whom the consent is given is aware of its existence. A consent given on the misrepresentation of fact is one given under a misconception of fact within the meaning of this section. An honest misconception by both the parties, however, does not invalidate the consent.

Section 377 of the Indian Penal Code

'Whoever voluntarily has carnal intercourse against the order of nature with any man, woman or animal, shall be punished with imprisonment for life, or with imprisonment of either description for a term which may extend to ten years, and shall also be liable to fine.'

Explanation: Penetration is sufficient to constitute the carnal intercourse necessary to the offence described in this section. Sex with a female under fifteen (15) years of age is considered rape, even if wedded.

Section 376B of the Indian Penal Code

'Whoever, being a public servant, takes advantage of his official position and induces or seduces, any women, who is in his custody as such public servant or in the custody of a public servant subordinate to him, to have sexual intercourse with him, such sexual intercourse not amounting to the offence of rape, shall be punished with imprisonment of either description for a term which may extend to five years and shall also be liable to fine.'

Section 376C of the Indian Penal Code

'Whoever, being the superintendent or manager of a jail, remand home or other place of custody established by or under

any law for the time being in force or of a women's or children's institution takes advantage of his official position and induces or seduces any female inmate of such jail, remand home, place or institution to have sexual intercourse with him, such sexual intercourse not amounting to the offence of rape, shall be punished with imprisonment of either description for a term which may extend to five years and shall also be liable to fine.'

Section 376D of the Indian Penal Code

'Whoever, being on the management of a hospital or being on the staff of a hospital takes advantage of his position and has sexual intercourse with any women in that hospital, such sexual intercourse not amounting to the offence of rape, shall be punished with imprisonment of either description for a term which may extend to five years and shall also be liable to fine.'

'Seduction of a person in custody', Section 9 of The Immoral Traffic Prevention Act, 1986

'Any person who, having the custody, charge or care of, or position of authority over, any person causes or aids or abets the seduction for prostitution of that person shall be punishable on conviction with imprisonment of either description for a term which shall not be less than seven years but which may be for life or for a term which may extend to ten years and shall also be liable to fine;

Provided that the court may, for adequate and special reasons to be mentioned in the judgement, impose a sentence of imprisonment for a term of less than seven years.'

There is no specific provision in the Indian law as regards to sexual abuse of children by parents or teachers. Such acts are covered by the general provisions relating to sexual abuse of children by their custodian, in whatever capacity they may be.

CHILD PROSTITUTION

Sections 366A and 366B are intended to punish the export and import of girls for prostitution. Section 366A deals with Procuration of minor girls from one part of India to another. Section 366B makes it an offence to import into India from any country outside India girls below the age of twenty-one (21) years for the purpose of prostitution.

Section 366A of the Indian Penal Code

'Whoever, by any means whatsoever, induces any minor girl under the age of eighteen (18) years to go from one place or to do any act with intent that such girl may be, or knowing that it is likely that she will be, forced or seduced to illicit intercourse with another person shall be punishable with imprisonment which may extend to ten years, and shall also be liable to fine.'

Explanation : This section required two things: (1) inducing a girl under eighteen (18) years to go from any place or to do an act, and (2) intention or knowledge that such girl will be forced or seduced to illicit intercourse with a person.

Where a woman, even if she has not attained the age of eighteen (18) years, follows the profession of a prostitute, and in following that profession she is encouraged or assisted by someone, no offence under this section is committed by such person, for it cannot be said that the person who assists a girl accustomed to indulge in promiscuous intercourse for money in carrying on her profession acts with intent or knowledge that she will be forced or seduced tc illicit intercourse.

The word 'seduced' is used in the ordinary sense of enticing or tempting irrespective of whether the minor girl has been previously compelled or has submitted to illicit intercourse.

Section 366B of the Indian Penal Code

'Whoever imports into India from any country outside India or from the State of Jammu and Kashmir any girl under the age of twenty-one (21) years with intent that she may be, or knowing it to be likely that she will be, forced or seduced to illicit intercourse with another person, shall be punishable with imprisonment which may extend to ten years and shall also be liable to fine.'

Section 367 of the Indian Penal Code

'Whoever kidnaps or abducts any person in order that such person may be subjected, or may be so disposed of as to be put in danger of being subjected to grievous hurt, or slavery, or to the unnatural lust of any person, or knowing it to be likely that such person will be so subjected or disposed of, shall be punished with imprisonment of either description for a term which may extend to ten years, and shall also be liable to fine.'

Section 372 of the Indian Penal Code

'Whoever sells, lets to hire, or otherwise disposes of any person under the age of eighteen (18) years with intent that such person shall at any age be employed or used for the purpose of prostitution or illicit intercourse with any person or for any unlawful and immoral purpose, or knowing it to be likely that such person will at any age be employed or used for any such purpose, shall be punished with imprisonment of either description for a term which may extend to ten years, and shall also be liable to fine.'

For the purpose of this section 'illicit intercourse' means sexual intercourse between persons not united by marriage, or by any union or tie which, though not amounting to a marriage, is recognised by the personal law or custom of the community to which they belong or, where they belong to different communities, of both such communities, as constituting between them a quasi marital relation.

This section applies to males or females under the age of eighteen (18) years.

It applies to a married or an unmarried female even where such female prior to sale or purchase, was leading an immoral life. It also applies where the girl is a member of the dancing girl caste.

Section 373 of the Indian Penal Code

'Whoever buys, hires or otherwise obtains possession of any person under the age of eighteen (18) years with intent that such person shall at any age be employed or used for the purpose of prostitution or illicit intercourse with any person or for any unlawful and immoral purpose, or knowing it to be likely that such person will at any age be employed or used for any such purposes, shall be punished with imprisonment of either description for a term which may extend to ten years, and shall also be liable to fine.'

This section and section 372 conjointly punish both the giver as well as the receiver of a person under eighteen (18) years for an immoral purpose. Both the sections relate to the same subject master.

The Immoral Traffic Prevention Act, 1986 (IT(P) Act).

Section 5, Paragraph 1 IT(P) Act, 1986

'Procuring, inducing or taking persons for the purpose of prostitution:

(l) Any person who-

(a) procures or attempts to procure a person whether with or without his consent, for the purpose of prostitution; or

(b) induces a person to go from one place, with the intent that he may, for the purpose of prostitution, become the inmate of, or frequent a brothel; or

(c) takes or attempts to take a person or cause a person to be taken away from one place to another with a view to his carrying on, or being brought up to carry on prostitution; or

(d) causes or induces a person to carry on prostitution,-shall be punishable on conviction with rigorous imprisonment for a term of not less than three years and not more than seven years and also with fine which may extend to two thousand rupees, and if any offence under this subsection is committed against the will of any person, the punishment of imprisonment for a term of seven years shall extend to imprisonment for a term of fourteen years;

Provided that if the person in respect of whom an offence committed under this subsection:

(i) is a child, the punishment provided under this subsection shall extend to rigorous imprisonment for a term of not less than seven years but may extend to life; and

(ii) is a minor, the punishment provided under this subsection shall extend to rigorous imprisonment for a term of not less than seven years and not more than fourteen years.'

'Detaining a person in premises where prostitution is carried out', Section 6 IT(P) Act, 1986

'(1) Any person who detains any other person, with or without his consent,

(a) in any brothel; or

(b) in or upon any premises with intent that such person may have sexual intercourse with a person who is not the spouse of such person,-shall be punishable on conviction, with imprisonment of either description for a term which shall not

be less than seven years but which may be for life or for a term which may extend to ten years and shall also be liable to fine;

Provided that the court may, for adequate and special reasons to be mentioned in the judgement, impose a sentence of imprisonment for a term of less than seven years.

(2) Where any person is found with a child in a brothel, it shall be presumed, unless the contrary is proved, that he has committed an offence under subsection (1).

(2A) Where a child or minor found in a brothel, is, on medical examination, detected to have been sexually assaulted, it shall be presumed, unless the contrary is proved, that the child or minor has been detained for purpose of prostitution or, as the case may tee, has been sexually exploited for commercial purposes.

(3) A person shall be presumed to detain a woman or girl in a brothel or in or upon any premises for the purpose of sexual intercourse with a man other than her lawful husband, if such person, with intent to compel or induce her to remain there-

(a) withholds from her any jewellery, wearing apparel, money or other property belonging to her; or

(b) threatens her with legal proceedings if she takes away with her any jewellery, wearing apparel, money or other property tent or supplied to her by or by the direction of such person.

(4) Notwithstanding any law to the contrary, no suit, prosecution or other legal proceeding shall lie against such woman or girl at the instance of the person by whom she has been detained, for the recovery of any jewellery, wearing apparel or other property alleged to have been lent or supplied to or for such woman or girl, or to have been pledged by such woman or girl for the recovery of any money alleged to be payable by such woman or girl.'

CHILD PORNOGRAPHY

Section 292 of the Indian Penal Code

'(1) For the purposes of subsection (2), a book, pamphlet, paper, writing, drawing, painting, representation, figure or any other object, shall be deemed to be obscene if it is lascivious or appeals to the prurient interest or if its effect, or (where it comprises two or more distinct items) the effect of any one of

its items, is if taken as a whole, such as to tend to deprave and corrupt persons who are likely, having regard to all relevant circumstances, to read, see or hear the master contained or embodied in it;

(2) Whoever-

(a) sells, lets to hire, distributes, publicly exhibits or in any manner puts into circulation, or for purposes of sale, hire, distribution, public exhibition or circulation, makes, produces or has in his possession any obscene book, pamphlet, paper, drawing, painting, representation or figure or any other obscene object whatsoever; or

(b) imports, export or conveys any obscene object for any of the purposes aforesaid, or knowing or having reason to believe that such object will be sold, let to hire, distributed or publicly exhibited or in any manner put into circulation; or

(c) takes part in or receives profits from any business in the course of which he knows or has reason to believe that any such obscene objects are, for any of the purposes aforesaid, made, produced, purchased, kept, imported, exported, conveyed, publicly exhibited or in any manner put into circulation; or

(d) advertises or makes known by any means whatsoever that any person is engaged or is ready to engage in any act which is an offence under this section, or that any such obscene object can be produced from or through any person; or

(e) offers or attempts to do any act which is an offence under this section,-shall be punished on first conviction with imprisonment of either description for a term which may extend to two years, and with fine which may extend to two thousand rupees, and, in the event of a second or subsequent conviction, with imprisonment of either description for a term which may extend to five years, and also with fine which may extend to five thousand rupees.

Exception:

This section does not extend to-

(a) any book, pamphlet, paper, writing, drawing, painting, representation or figure:

(i) the publication of which is proved to be justified as being for the public good on the ground that such book, pamphlet,

paper, writing, drawing, painting, representation or figure is in the interest of science, literature, art or learning or other objects of general concern; or

(ii) which is kept or used bona fide for religious purposes;

(b) any representation sculptured, engraved, painted or otherwise represented on or in:

(i) any ancient monument within the meaning of the Ancient Monuments and Archaeological Sites and Remains Act, 1958 (24 of 1958); or

(ii) any temple, or on any car used for the conveyance of idols, or kept or used for any religious purpose.'

Section 293 of the Indian Penal Code

'Whoever sells, lets to hire, distributes, exhibits or circulates to any person under the age of twenty (20) years any such obscene object as is referred to in the last preceding section, or offers or attempts to do so, shall be punished on first conviction with imprisonment of either description for a term which may extend to three years, and with fine which may extend to two thousand rupees and, in the event of a second or subsequent conviction, with imprisonment of either description for a term which may extend to seven years, and also with fine which may extend to five thousand rupees.'

In Support A Review Of The Protection Of Women From Domestic Violence Act, 2005

Save Indian Family

Action Alert Action Alert Action Alert

Sign–On

TO SUPPORT AND FAVOUR THE MOVE OF THE MINISTRY OF WOMEN AND CHILD DEVELOPMENT TO REVIEW THE NEWLY ENACTED AND ENFORCED ACT ON DOMESTIC VIOLENCE.

It is appropriate for the Ministry of Women and Child Development (MWCD) at the centre to set up a panel of lawyers to review several laws, namely

i. The Dowry Prohibition Act, 1961

ii. The Immoral Traffic (Prevention) Act, 1956

iii. The Indecent Representation of Women (Prohibition) Act, 1986

iv. The Commission of Sati (Prevention) Act, 1987

v. The National Commission for Women Act, 1990

vi. The Protection of Women from Domestic Violence Act, 2005

We support an in-depth review by the panel of lawyers that should also look into the complaints regarding the misuse of these laws. Groups such as Save Indian Family that are protesting about the misuse of such laws should also be interviewed by the inter-ministerial committee set up by the Ministry of Human Resource Development to review legislation that impact on women rights and to monitor the harmful side-effects of the implementation of the recommendations made by the National Commission for Women (NCW) and the Task Force on Women and Children. In addition, the core group appointed by the MWCD to prepare a revised plan of action on the National Policy for the Empowerment of Women 2001 should also ensure that all laws are made gender neutral.

All laws that affect families should also take into account that mothers and sisters are women too, and "it takes two to tango". The Immoral Traffic (Prevention) Act, 1956 etc., which has already been reviewed by statutory bodies including the Parliamentary Standing Committee should be re-looked at. Amendments to the Dowry Prohibition Act, 1961 and the National Commission for Women Act, 1990 have been finalized and forwarded to the MWCD should also take into account the various reports that this law is being misused and the suggestions regarding how to curtail the misuse. The Commission of Sati (Prevention) Act, 1987 has already been reviewed and amendments to the Indecent Representation of Women (Prohibition) Act, 1986 have been proposed and the NCW has been requested to hold consultations regarding the same The Protection of Woman from Domestic Violence Act, 2005 is not the only significant genderbiased law that should be reviewed by the proposed panel.

It was only last year in October 2006 that the women groups around the country joined together to celebrate yet another weapon for the bad women to misuse in India when the Govt of India had brought the PWDVA into force. Further, to mark the first anniversary of the PWDVA a national conference was organized by the Lawyers Collective (that is composed mainly of women who are against the institution of marriage) in collaboration with the Ministry of Women and Child Development (MWCD) and the National Commission for Women (NCW) recently on the 26th and 27th of October 2007 where the first Monitoring and Evaluation Report on the PWDVA, 2005 was released. They made it obvious that the husband and his family have no rights when faced with an abusive woman.

We are aware that there are several women's groups (including the so-called Lawyer's collective, which is in actual fact the anti-family women's collective) who have sent up blogs and websites campaigning against the review of the PWDVA In that context we apprehend that the Ministry is succumbing to pressure from vocal groups of abusive women, who believe in lawlessness and denial of rights to husbands and their families.

Every family has a right to live free from abuse, and that is not what the PVDWA guarantees. Denial of the right to reside in their own home for senior citizens is one of the most extreme forms of abuse, rendering the parents and grandparents homeless and insecure. There are concerted efforts among women's groups to abuse these badly drafted gender baised laws.

The Hon'ble Supreme Court in Batra v Batra rightly decided that the right should only available to a woman in a household owned by the husband and not in the household owned by the in laws, even though it may have been been the shared household. In a country where the joint family pattern of residence is then norm, any other judgment virtually gives a license to women to throw out senior citizens from the own home with the help of a bad law. It is the PWDVA that needs to be reviewed, not the judgment.

The Act itself had been brought in force in 2006 and has had barely one year to function but already it is obvious that it is being misused on a large scale (as are the other gender biased laws). At a recently concluded conference to monitor and evaluate the functioning of the law, it was unanimously agreed by the participants that the Act should not be implemented in its current form since it is liable to be grossly misused. In this context, we think that the move to set up a Panel to review the PWDVA is right and is being opposed by vested interests trying to undermine the rights of senior citizens. Pursuant to a commitment made by the UPA government (that succumbed to pressure from those with vested interest in its common minimum program), this ill-conceived Act has given the anti-family groups yet another easy to misuse law, which is in violation of the fundamental rights of senior citizens and families to live a life free from abuse.

WOMEN'S RIGHTS

The term women's rights refers to freedoms and entitlements of women and girls of all ages. These rights may or may not be institutionalized, ignored or suppressed by law, local custom, and behaviour in a particular society. These liberties are grouped together and differentiated from broader notions of human rights because they often differ from the freedoms inherently possessed by or recognized for men and boys, and because activists for this issue claim an inherent historical and traditional bias against the exercise of rights by women and girls.

Issues commonly associated with notions of women's rights include, though are not limited to, the right: to bodily integrity and autonomy; to vote (suffrage); to hold public office; to work; to fair wages or equal pay; to own property; to education; to serve in the military or be conscripted; to enter into legal contracts; and to have marital, parental and religious rights. Women and their supporters have campaigned and in some places continue to campaign for the same rights as men.

HISTORY

According to Dr. Jamal A. Badawin "the status which women reached during the present era was not achieved due to the kindness of men or due to natural progress. It was rather achieved through a long struggle and sacrifice on woman's part and only when society needed her contribution and work, more especial!; during the two world wars, and due to the escalation of technological change."

Ancient Civilisations

In ancient India, women are believed to have enjoyed equal status with men in all fields of life. Ancient Hindu scriptures describe a good wife as follows "a woman whose mind, speech and body are kept in subjection, acquires high renown in this world, and, in the next, the same abode with her husband." In ancient Athens women were always minors and subject to a male, such as their father, brother or some other male kin. A women's consent in marriage was not generally thought to be necessary and women were obliged to submit to the wishes of her parents or husband. Ancient Rome subject all legitimate children, regardless of age or sex to the authority of their Pater Familias while he lived, and they would only acquire any legal independence when he died. The Pater Familias could grant any of his children or slaves a Peculium, but that belonged to him and they were merely allowed to use it. All transactions made by a child in power regardless of age or sex had to be directly approved of by their Pater Familias. All children inherited equally from their Pater Familias regardless of age or sex, by the Imperial Period of Roman history even bastards were included as intestate heirs. Early in the Republic women were subject to Manus Marriage, but the custom died out by the Late Republic in favour of marriage without Manus which did not grant the husband any rights over his wife. When married without Manus a woman was not only free of her husbands legal authority, but could divorce him as she pleased without any reason required. Women in Ancient Rome when no longer under the control of their Pater Familias could and did contract, work for wages (usually without many other options), own property, and perform some (but not all) legal functions.

Early Reforms Under Islam

Efforts to improve the status of women in Islam occurred during the early reforms under Islam between 610 and 661, when Arab women were given greater rights in marriage, divorce and inheritance. In 622 the Constitution of Medina was drafted by the Islamic prophet Muhammad, outlining many of Muhammad's early reforms under Islam, including an improved legal status for women in Islam, who were generally given greater rights than women in pre-Islamic Arabia and medieval Europe. Women were not accorded with such legal status in other cultures until centuries later. Indeed according to Professor William Montgomery Watt, when seen in such historical context, Muhammad "can be seen as a figure who testified on behalf of women's rights." The general improvement of the status of Arab women included prohibition of female infanticide and recognizing women's full personhood. "The dowry, previously regarded as a bride-price paid to the father, became a nuptial gift retained by the wife as part of her personal property." Under Islamic law, marriage was no longer viewed as a "status" but rather as a "contract", in which the woman's consent was imperative. "Women were given inheritance rights in a patriarchal society that had previously restricted inheritance to male relatives." Annemarie Schimmel states that "compared to the pre-Islamic position of women, Islamic legislation meant an enormous progress; the woman has the right, at least according to the letter of the law, to administer the wealth she has brought into the family or has earned by her own work."

The Middle Ages

According to English Common Law, which developed from the 12th Century onward all property which a wife held at the time of a marriage became a possession of her husband. Eventually English courts forbid a husband's transferring property without the consent of his wife, but he still retained the right to manage it and to receive the money which it produced. "French married women suffered from restrictions on their legal capacity which were removed only in 1965." In the 16th century, the Reformation in Europe allowed more women to add their voices, including the English writers Jane Anger, Aemilia Lanyer, and the prophetess Anna Trapnell. Despite relatively greater freedom for Anglo-Saxon women, until the mid-nineteenth century, writers largely assumed that a patriarchal order was a natural order that had existed. This perception was not seriously challenged until the eighteenth century when Jesuit missionaries found matrilineality in native North American peoples.

The Enlightenment

In the late 18th Century the question of women's rights

became central to political debates in both France and Britain. At the time some of the greatest thinkers of the Enlightenment, who defended democratic principles of equality and challenged notions that a privileged few should rule over the vast majority of the population, believed that these principles should be applied only to their own gender and their own race. The philosopher Jean Jacques Rousseau for example thought that it was the order of nature for woman to obey men. He wrote "Women do wrong to complain of the inequality of man-made laws" and claimed that "when she tries to usurp our rights, she is our inferior".

In 1791 the French playwright and political activist Olympe de Gouges published the *Declaration of the Rights of Woman and the Female Citizen*, modelled on the Declaration of the Rights of Man and of the Citizen of 1789. The Declaration is ironic in formulation and exposes the failure of the French Revolution, which had been devoted to equality. It states that: "This revolution will only take effect when all women become fully aware of their deplorable condition, and of the rights they have lost in society". The Declaration of the Rights of Woman and the Female Citizen follows the seventeen articles of the Declaration of the Rights of Man and of the Citizen point for point and has been described by Camille Naish as "almost a parody... of the original document". The first article of the Declaration of the Rights of Man and of the Citizen proclaims that "Men are born and remain free and equal in rights. Social distinctions may be based only on common utility." The first article of Declaration of the Rights of Woman and the Female Citizen replied: "Woman is born free and remains equal to man in rights. Social distinctions may only be based on common utility". De Gouges expands the sixth article of the Declaration of the Rights of Man and of the Citizen, which declared the rights of citizens to take part in the formation of law, to:

> *"All citizens including women are equally admissible to all public dignities, offices and employments, according to their capacity, and with no other distinction than that of their virtues and talents".*

De Gouges also draws attention to the fact that under French law women were fully punishable, yet denied equal rights. Mary Wollstonecraft, a British writer and philosopher, published *A Vindication of the Rights of Woman* in 1792, arguing that it was the education and upbringing of women that created limited expectations. Wollstonecraft attacked gender oppression, pressing for equal educational opportunities, and demanded "justice!" and "rights to humanity" for all.

The 19th Century

In his 1869 essay The Subjection of Women the English philosopher and political theorist John Stuart Mill described the situation for women in Britain as follows:

> *"We are continually told that civilization and Christianity have restored to the woman her just rights. Meanwhile the wife is the actual bondservant of her husband; no less so, as far as the legal obligation goes, than slaves commonly so called."*

During the 1800s women in the United States and Britain began to challenge laws that denied them the right to their property once they married. Under the common law doctrine of *coverture* husbands gained control of their wives' real estate and wages. Beginning in the 1840s, state legislatures in the United States and the British Parliament began passing statutes that protected women's property from their husbands and their husbands' creditors. These laws were known as the Married Women's Property Acts. Courts in the nineteenth-century United States also continued to require privy examinations of married women who sold their property. A privy examination was a practice in which a married woman who wished to sell her property had to be separately examined by a judge or justice of the peace outside of the presence of her husband and asked if her husband was pressuring her into signing the document.

SUFFRAGE, THE RIGHT TO VOTE

During the 19th Century women began to agitate for the right to vote and participate in government and law making. The ideals of women's suffrage developed alongside that of universal suffrage and today women's suffrage is considered a right (under the Convention on the Elimination of All Forms of Discrimination Against Women). During the 19th Century the right to vote was gradually extended in many countries and women started to campaign for their right to vote. In 1893 New Zealand became the first country to give women the right to vote on a national level. Australia gave women the right to vote in 1902, while the USA, Britain and Canada gave women the vote after the First World War. Sweden would also be a contestant as the first independent nation to grant women the right to vote. Conditional female suffrage was granted in Sweden during the age of liberty (1718–1771)

In Britain women's suffrage gained attention when John Stuart Mill called for the inclusion of women's suffrage in the Reform Act of 1867 in a petition that he presented to Parliament. Initially only one of several women's rights campaign, suffrage became the primary cause of the British women's movement at the beginning of the 20th Century. At the time the ability to vote was restricted to wealthy property owners within British jurisdictions. This arrangement implicitly excluded women as property law and marriage law gave men ownership rights at marriage or inheritance until the 19th century. Although male suffrage broadened during the century, women were explicitly prohibited from voting nationally and locally in the 1830s by a Reform Act and the Municipal Corporations Act. Throughout the 19th century women had organised through various groups until, by 1903, the National Union of Women's Suffrage Societies and the Women's Social and Political Union had emerged. Leaders in the struggle were Millicent Fawcett and Emmeline Pankhurst with her daughter Christabel. In 1918 the British Parliament passed a bill allowing women over the age of 30 to vote, and the voting age for women was lowered to 21 in 1928.

The Seneca Falls Convention of 1848 formulated the demand for women's suffrage in the United States of America and after the American Civil War (1861–1865) agitation for the cause became more prominent. In 1869 the proposed Fourteenth Amendment to the United States Constitution, which gave the vote to black men, caused controversy as women's suffrage campaigners such as Susan B. Anthony and Elizabeth Cady Stanton refused to endorse the amendment, as it did not give the vote to women. Others, such as Lucy Stone and Julia Ward Howe however argued that black men were enfranchised, women would achieve their goal. The conflict caused two organisations to emerge, the National Woman Suffrage Association, which campaigned for women's suffrage at a federal level as well as for married women to be given property rights, and the American Woman Suffrage Association, which aimed to secure women's suffrage through state legislation. In 1920 the Nineteenth Amendment to the United States Constitution gave women the right to vote.

Nordic countries gave women the right to vote in the early 20th Century – Finland (1906), Norway (1913), Denmark and Iceland (1915). With the end of the First World War many other countries followed-the Union of Soviet Socialist Republics and the Netherlands (1917), Austria, Czechoslovakia, Poland and Sweden (1918), Germany and Lunenburg (1919). Spain gave women the right to vote in 1931, France in 1944, Belgium, Italy, Romania and Yugoslavia in 1946. Switzerland gave women the right to vote in 1971, and Liechtenstein in 1984.

In Canada women's suffrage was achieved first on a provincial level in Alberta, Manitoba and Saskatchewan on 1916, with federal suffrage being granted in 1918. In Latin America some countries gave women the right to vote in the first half of the 20th Century – Ecuador (1929), Brazil (1932), El Salvador (1939), Dominican Republic (1942), Guatemala (1956) and Argentina (1946). In India, under colonial rule, universal suffrage was granted in 1935. Other Asian countries gave women the right to vote in mid of the Century – Japan (1945), China (1947) and Indonesia (1955). In Africa women generally got the right to vote along with men through universal suffrage – Liberia (1947), Uganda (1958) and Nigeria (1960). In many countries in the Middle East universal suffrage was acquired after the Second World War, although in others, such as Kuwait, suffrage is very limited. On 16 May 2005, the Parliament of Kuwait extended suffrage to women by a 35-23 vote, and women have been elected to Parliament.

5

Women Movements

The women's movement in India is a rich and vibrant movement which has taken different forms in different parts of the country. Urvashi Butalia contends that the absence of a single cohesive movement, rather than being a source of weakness, may be one of the strengths of the movement. Although scattered and fragmented, it is a strong and plural movement.

One of the most enduring cliches about India is that is a country of contradictions. Like all cliches, this one too has a grain of truth in it. At the heart of the contradiction stand Indian women: for it is true to say that they are among the most oppressed in the world, and it is equally true to say that they are among the most liberated, the most articulate and perhaps even the most free. Can these two realities be simultaneously true? During the 18 years that India had a woman as Prime Minister the country also saw increasing incidents of violence and discrimination against women.

This is no different from any other time: a casual visitor to any Indian city-for example Mumbai-will see hundreds of women, young and old, working in all kinds of professions: doctors, nurses, teachers, engineers, scientists... and yet newspapers in India are full of stories of violent incidents against women, of rape, sexual harassment, sometimes even murder. But to have a woman in the highest office of the State and to simultaneously have extreme violence against women are merely the two ends of the scale. As always, a more complex reality lies in between.

Fifty years ago when India became independent, it was widely acknowledged that the battle for freedom had been fought as much by women as by men. One of the methods M K Gandhi chose to undermine the authority of the British was for Indians to defy the law which made it illegal for them to make salt. At the time, salt-making was a monopoly and earned considerable revenues for the British. Gandhi began his campaign by going on a march-the salt march-through many villages, leading finally to the sea, where he and others broke the law by making salt. No woman had been included by Gandhi in his chosen number of marchers. But nationalist women protested, and they forced him to allow them to participate.

WOMEN'S MOVEMENT IN INDIA

During the last one decade, women's movement in India has faced sharper polarisation due to rise of cultural nationalism, that uses women to score points for identity politics, coupled with economic liberalisation that is wooing the elite women and breaking the backs of the working class women. In response to imposition of structural adjustment programme (SAP) and stabilization policies at the behest of International Monitory Institute, women's movements across the national boundaries have been debating various strategies and tactics of transforming the Neo-liberal Development Paradigm. World Social Forum and Regional Social Fora have provided democratic platforms for reflections on a just, sustainable & caring Global Economy.

These deliberations have convinced us that Another World is Possible and globalisation also bears the promise and possibilities of furthering women's rights and well-being. Gender sensitive strategic thinking can address practical and strategic gender needs of women. For example, more women in more areas of economic activities can be gainfully and justly employed. Information technology can enable women throughout the globe to share strategies and successes for stress-free and safe life. We should not forget that there is north in the South and there is south in the North. So we must strive for global solidarity and sisterhood of all women who are oppressed and exploited, degraded and dehumanised by the patriarchal class structure.

Feminists are playing a crucial role in motivating the nation-states and the global decision-making bodies to be pro-active in furthering women's entitlements in the households, economy and governance. Rapid pace of globalisation has brought massive uncertainties in women's lives. Multi-faced tragedies due to marketisation of poor economies and commercialisation of human relations, commodification of women's bodies especially in sexual trafficking, advertisements and beauty-contests promoted by the Trans-national corporations (TNCs) and Multi-national Corporations (MNCs), starvation deaths in the rural areas, havoc played by onslaught of new reproductive technologies (of both pro and anti-natalist varieties) violating dignity and bodily integrity of women, armed conflicts, increasing economic disparity, the feminisation of poverty, disasters in the name of mega development projects resulting into massive displacement of peoples, stressful life leading to increasing violence against women, the pandemic of HIV and AIDS, racist population control policies, persistent racism, casteism, sexism, chauvinism and extremism demand urgent attention in terms of the global effort to change macro-policies, programmes of the nation-state and actions at the local level by the government and non-government bodies.

WORSENING ECONOMIC CONDITION AND GROWING SECTARIAN VIOLENCE AGAINST WOMEN

Any fundamentalist propaganda that concerns itself with identity makes use of the gender question to impose rigid norms on women who are identified as repositories of culture and tradition. These norms manifest themselves in Son-preference and female infanticide (quotation from Hindu scriptures-"Be thy the mother of 100 sons". (Questions are asked to wife-" Did any heroes of *Ramayana* or *Mahabharata* have daughters? That shows daughters are inauspicious!"), Glorification of *sati* (widow-burning) — thousands of sati temples have flourished all over India and Global Association for Glorification of Sati has its head-quarter in Chicago (USA), Witch-hunting of widows as they are perceived to be inauspicious; dress code, general demeanour and the social construction of the ideal woman who submissively accepts the patriarchal norm imposed by fundamentalists agendas. In the last *Kumbh Mela* 60000 women devotees were deserted by their brothers, sons and relatives. Allahabad police tried its best to reach them to their respective families but the family members refused to have known them. Now, the government has made a special budgetary provision for abandoned widows at the pilgrimage centres and women in difficult circumstances.

Violence against women has escalated enormously, both in the private and public arena. Economic stress due to SAP (the mainstream economists call it 'economic reforms') manifests in the form of domestic and communal/caste violence).

Southern Women's Movements' Perspectives

NGOs wedded to safeguard the entitlements of women have been trying to convince the international financial, economic and commercial institutions, namely, World Bank, International Monitory Fund, World Trade Organisation and Organisation of Economic Cooperation and Development to withdraw existing conditionalities and rules of economic globalisation, and covertly and overtly, promoting the interests of patriarchal class system, all over the globe, defending the interests of TNCs and MNCs and imposing unrestrained commodification, thereby resulting into concentration and centralization of economic, financial and political power in the hands of the few. There is today a blurring division between the centre and the periphery as the economic and manufacturing situations are undergoing changes in our country. Globalisation has brought about structural changes that have been impacting gender. Apart from employment it affects sustainable development, leading to state withdrawing from commitments to social sector. This affects women adversely. The impact of WTO, taxation patterns and user fee concept are adversely affecting women. The Second National Commission of Labour is furthering the neo-liberal agenda so far as the working class is concerned, though it has separate chapters on women in the informal sector and child-labour.

SAROJINI NAIDU

The first to join was Sarojini Naidu, who went on to become the first woman President of the Indian National Congress in 1925. Her presence was a signal for hundreds of other women to join, and eventually the salt protest was made successful by the many women who not only made salt, but also sat openly in marketplaces selling, and indeed, buying it.

Sarojini Naidu's spirit lives on in thousands of Indian women today. Some years ago, Rojamma, a poor woman from the southern state of Andhra Pradesh, attended a literacy class. Here, she read a story which described a life very like her own. It talked about a poor woman, struggling to make ends meet, who was regularly beaten by her husband. Whatever he earned, he spent on liquor, and then, drunk and violent, he attacked her because she had no food to give him. Unable to stand the continuing violence, the woman went from house to house, to find every other woman who had the same story to tell. They got together, and decided they would pitch their attack where it hurt most: they would picket liquor shops and stop liquor being sold.

Their husbands then would have no liquor to drink, and the money they earned would be saved. Inspired by the story, Rojamma collected her friends together, and they began to picket liquor shops. The campaign spread like wildfire. In village after village, women got together, they talked, they went on strike, they beat up liquor shop owners, they refused to allow their husbands to squander money on liquor. And, they succeeded. The sale of liquor was banned in Andhra Pradesh, reluctantly, by the government for liquor brings in huge amounts of money. As a result, savings went up, violence levels dropped, and the lives of poor women began to improve.

The hundreds of thousands of Rojammas and Sarojini Naidus who are to be found all over India form part of one of the most dynamic and vibrant of political movements in India today, the women's movement. The trajectory of this movement is usually traced from the social reform movements of the 19th century when campaigns for the betterment of the conditions of women's lives were taken up, initially by men. By the end of the century women had begun to organise themselves and gradually they took up a number of causes such as education, the conditions of women's work and so on. It was in the early part of the 20th century that women's organisations were set up, and many of the women who were active in these later became involved in the freedom movement. Independence brought many promises and dreams for women in India-the dream of an egalitarian, just, democratic society in which both men and women would have a voice. The reality, when it began to sink in was, however, somewhat different. For all that had happened was that, despite some improvements in the status of women, patriarchy had simply taken on new and different forms.

UNFULFILLED PROMISES

By the 1960s it was clear that many of the promises of Independence were still unfulfilled. It was thus that the 1960s and 1970s saw a spate of movements in which women took part: campaigns against rising prices, movements for land rights, peasant movements. Women from different parts of the country came together to form groups both inside and outside political parties. Everywhere, in the different movements that were sweeping the country, women participated in large numbers. Everywhere, their participation resulted in transforming the movements from within.

Worried at this increase in political activity, Indira Gandhi's government declared a State of Emergency in 1975, putting a stop to all democratic political activity. Activists, both young and old, women and men, were forced to go underground or to stop all political work. It was only when the Emergency was lifted, some 18 months later, that overground political activity resumed. It was around this time that many of the contemporary women's groups began to get formed, with their members often being women with a history of involvement in other political movements.

One of the first issues to receive countrywide attention from women's groups was violence against women, specifically in the form of rape, and what came to be known in India as 'dowry deaths'-the killing of young married women for the 'dowry' or money/goods they brought with them at marriage. This was also the beginning of a process of learning for women: most protests were directed at the State. Because women were able to mobilise support, the State responded, seemingly positively, by changing the law on rape and dowry, making both more stringent. This seemed, at the time, like a great victory. It was only later that the knowledge began to sink in that mere changes in the law meant little, unless there was a will and a machinery to implement these. And that the root of the problem of discrimination against women lay not only in the law, or with the State, but was much more widespread.

In the early campaigns, groups learnt from day to day that targeting the State was not enough and that victims also needed support. So a further level of work was needed: awareness raising or conscientisation so that violence against women could be prevented, rather than only dealt with after it had happened. Legal aid and counselling centres were set up, and attempts were made to establish women's shelters. It was only when groups began to feel sucked into the overwhelming volume of the day-to-day work of such centres that they began to feel that it was not enough to do what they now saw as 'reformist' and 'non-campaign' work. Knowledge was recognised as an important need. India is such a vast country; what did activists in Karnataka, a state in southern India, know of what was going on in Garhwal in north India? And yet, everywhere you looked, there was women's activity, activity that could not necessarily be defined as 'feminist', but that was, nonetheless, geared towards improving the conditions of women's lives. In recent years, the euphoria of the 1970s and early 1980s, symbolised by street-level protests, campaigns in which groups mobilised at a national level, the sense of a commonality of experience cutting across class, caste, region and religion-all this seems to have gone, replaced by a more considered and complex response to issues. In many parts of India, women are no longer to be seen out on the streets protesting about this or that form of injustice. This apparent lack of a visible movement has led to the accusation that the women's movement is dead or dying. Other whipping sticks have been brought out: little has happened to improve women's lives, so how can the movement be called successful? Activists within the movement are urban, Western, and middle class, so the movement was considered an alien thing, a Western product. It has little to do with the lives of thousands of poor, rural, underprivileged women all over India. These allegations make the classic mistake: they judge a complex reality by that part of it that is most visible. Because urban, middle-class women are visible and articulate, therefore they must be the only participants in the women's movement.

BACKBONE

The reality is somewhat different. While the participation of urban, middle class women is undeniable, it is not they who make up the backbone of the movement, or of the many, different campaigns that are generally seen as comprising the movement. The anti-alcohol agitation in Andhra Pradesh, and similar campaigns in other parts of India were started and sustained by poor, low-caste, often working-class women. The movement to protect the environment was begun by poor women in a village called Reni in the northern hill regions of India, and only after that did it spread to other parts of the country. There are any number of such examples.

One of the biggest challenges women have had to face in recent years is the growing influence of the religious right in India. Right-wing groups have built much of their support on the involvement of women: offering to help them with domestic problems, enabling them to enter the public space in a limited way, and all the while ensuring that the overall ideology within which they operate remains firmly patriarchal. For activists too, this has posed major problems. It has forced them to confront the fact that they cannot assume a solidarity as women that cuts across class, religion, caste, ethnic difference. And yet, they must hold fast to such an assumption if they are to work with women: for how, as an activist, do you deal with a woman who takes part in a violent right wing demonstration one day, and comes to you for help as a victim of domestic violence the next?

Perhaps the most significant development for women in the last few decades has been the introduction of 33% reservation for women in local, village-level elections. In the early days, when this move was introduced, there was considerable scepticism. How will women cope? Are they equipped to be leaders? Will this mean any real change, or will it merely mean that the men will take a backseat and use the women as a front to implement what they want? While all these problems still remain, in a greater or lesser degree, what is also true is that more and more women have shown that once they have power, they are able to use it, to the benefit of society in general and women in particular. The women's movement in India today is a rich and vibrant movement, which has spread to various parts of the country. It is often said that there is no one single cohesive movement in the country, but a number of fragmented campaigns. Activists see this as one of the strengths of the movement which takes different forms in different parts. While the movement may be scattered all over India, they feel it is nonetheless a strong and plural force.

It is important to recognise that for a country of India's magnitude, change in male-female relations and the kinds of issues the women's movement is focusing on, will not come easy. For every step the movement takes forward, there will be a possible backlash, a possible regression. And it is this that makes for the contradictions, this that makes it possible for there to be women who can aspire to, and attain, the highest political office in the country, and for women to continue to have to confront patriarchy within the home, in the workplace, throughout their lives. As activists never tire of repeating: out of the deepest repression is born the greatest resistance.

INDIA'S COMMUNALIST VIOLENCE AGAINST WOMEN

In the colonial and post-colonial periods in India, both the state and the religious communities identified women as a site of concern. Yet at the close of the 20th century, the condition of women in India remains deplorable-a condition that should not be belittled on the ground that colonialism used it in order to discredit India's peoples and achievements.

Colonial Modernism and a New Patriarchy

The British colonial state, in order to justify and legitimize its rule and to dominate the colonized, always referred to the "backward" and "retrograde" social conditions of Indians, denigrating India's religions, customs, cultures, norms, values. One of its strongest claims was that women in India were extremely oppressed.

From the ban on sati to the age of consent controversy the state portrayed itself as the "protector" of women from obscurantist Indian males. A sati is a faithful/loyal/chaste wife. The ban on sati was a ban on the "self-immolation" of widows on the funeral pyres of their husbands. The ban came after protracted debates, with conservative Hindus asserting that the colonial state had no right to dictate law to them.

The next major disputes were over the remarriage of widows and the ban on polygamy. Remarriage was legislated, again in the teeth of stiff conservative masculine opposition. Polygamy illegalization had to await independence.

In the 1890s a three-way controversy arose over the age of marriage. Phulmoni, a young girl of 10, died as a result of sexual intercourse forced on her by her husband. For Hindu nationalist conservatives, the British were unable to understand the willing sacrifice of Hindu women. For some, the way out was simply to raise the age of consent to 12. For a few others, like Iswarchandra Vidyasagar, the point was to wait until a girl had matured physically and mentally for the childbearing function rather than mechanically setting an age.

There are two points to note. First, the oppression of women was very real, regardless of who was raking up the data in order to score brownie points. Second, there did exist a line, however thin, of men, and as the century progressed, of women, who were highlighting women's oppression rather than an issue between two groups of men in a struggle for power.

It is interesting to note that it was a Brahmin reformer, Pandit Iswar Chandra Vidyasagar, who stressed the liberal value of the rights of women as individuals. He pointed out that male control over women's sexuality was what kept women in their widow stage, while it was the British state which agreed to legislate only when provided with evidence that Hindu shastras, namely the Parashar Samhita, provided for widow remarriage.

Contrary to its assertions, the process of personal law codification by the British colonial state did not have "modernization" of India on the agenda. The British had conquered an extensive territory within which there lived different peoples with different laws and customs. In those areas where the politico-economic needs of the capitalist rulers and their colonialist state was paramount, there was no hesitation in the imposition of uniform laws entirely under their supervision.

But in other areas, eventually to be designated as "personal laws," notably for marriage, divorce, inheritance, adoption, rights of widows and guardianship, where contemporary English law talked about ecclesiastical laws (laws based on the scriptures), the British were willing to be flexible. In the formative period of colonialism the British were aware of the need for collaboration with the indigenous elites.

The flexibility was based on the aim of the colonial state to create a base for itself by pushing its homogenizing agenda, through negotiating with local elites. As a result, lawmaking in what came to be called "personal laws" was based neither on the principle of pluralism and respect for the customs of all the diverse groups nor on the principle of liberal individualism.

Beginning in 1772 the colonial state tried to codify the Hindu and Muslim laws separately to create monolithic and mutually opposed Hindu and Muslim communities. To explain these laws, to get at the proper interpretations, they called upon maulavis and Brahman pandits. This had two clear-cut consequences: 1) Despite all the condemnations of "barbaric" customs like sati, the state was willing to enact reforms in the sphere of personal laws only when there existed clear shastric or shariat-based (i.e. Hindu or Muslim) sanctions; 2) the rights of women were not paramount but expendable.

Thus the personal laws created by the British were themselves the result of an artificial homogeneity imposed by the state in its own interests, a homogeneity created often through negotiations with local religious and economic elites, who wielded power at the sanction of the colonial state.

In pre-British India, many Hindus and Muslims lived under laws based in local custom. So why was it necessary to retain a particular kind of Hindu or Islamic law only in one particular domain? Clearly, the state was providing support to Hindu upper caste, economically powerful, patriarchal elites. So the supposedly uniform Hindu or Muslim community, far from being the original social grouping, appears from the outset as the creation of the state. The creation of religious identities was pure politics. Muslims in colonial India lived under local laws/customs, and had different cultures. Muslims in the Punjab, the North West Frontier and the Central Provinces were governed by local customary laws.

Three groups had an interest in homogenizing all these forces-British imperialism; the ulama [Muslim religious authorities] and the conservative semi-feudal landlords; and also, the Westernizing liberal reformers. The conservatives wanted to establish their own control over the large-scale Muslim population. As for the Westernizers, the Government of India Act of 1935, followed by the elections of 1937, made it clear to them that if they wanted to win the Muslim seats, they had to make a stronger appeal to a much more homogeneous community. The two Acts which were passed in this period reflected the concerns of both groups. The Shariat Application Act of 1937 claimed that its stated purpose was to bring Muslims under the shariat instead of customary laws in order to recognize their property rights. In fact, women's right to property was supposedly the motivating factor for this law.

But an amendment by Muslim leader Muhammad Ali Jinnah kept the property of landed elements out of the purview of the act, under the pretext that it would lead to fragmentation of consolidated agrarian holdings. Moreover, individuals had the right to dispose of their wealth through wills. Thus an artificial community was homogenized while professing the protection of women's rights.

A similar situation came up in 1939. A majority of Indian Muslims were governed by the Hanafi School of Law in Sunni jurisprudence, a provision of which allowed Muslim women to come out of difficult marriages by converting to some other religion. The bill proposed in 1939, instead of making the terms of divorce easier, sought to debar Muslim women from the advantages they had earlier. In the name of protecting women, the act helped certain conservative elements to establish control over women's sexuality. So the laws that for the first time created the Muslim community also subordinated gender to community. Further, this process of creation of a common identity overlooked the space needed by the Shias, a minority within the Muslims of India. Only one school of Sunni jurisprudence was recognized.

Since the British had claimed that their rule would bring about the modernization of India, the majority of Indian responses also accepted this premise. But accepting the terrain of the British also meant accepting claims about religious authorities' "correct interpretations" of the scriptures, as the basis for law reform. Few deemed the need for reforms concerning women as a project needed for its own sake. Most reformers also accepted that community laws/shastric injunctions should be considered the basis for reforms. Even the best of reformers kept gender subordinated to community identity, with a clear prioritization of North Indian shastric traditions. Gender was thus a contested terrain between two sources of patriarchal interpretation and practice-colonial and indigenous.

COMPETING HINDU NATIONALISMS

There next developed a clear break between a "cultural nationalism," tinged with Hinduism, and a "militant Hindu chauvinism." The rise of this militant Hindu chauvinism in the early 20th century appears to have resulted from challenges to the upper caste and class power from peasants, from activists of the non-Brahmin movements, and others, especially the newly emerging non-Hindus. In the early twentieth century worries about a further decline of upper-caste hegemony were heightened by the prospect that untouchables might secede from the fold of Hindu community.

The struggle against this threat led to the creation of a reformed fundamentalism with a Hindu supremacist agenda. Tanika Sarkar has argued that this Hindu supremacist discourse also incorporated considerable manipulation of gender issues. In this discourse, upper caste Hindu women were seen simultaneously as the objects of Muslim lust, marginal figures within the community and, at the same time, mothers of the future leaders of the community who needed to learn the new politics. This new politics of community was based on the creation of an "other," which was usually the Muslim community. Two key figures in the development of this discourse were Dayanand Saraswati and V.D. Savarkar. Dayanand accepted the movement for social reform with the overt agenda of the liberal reformers regarding women. The reasons he gave, however, were exclusively about serving the interests of the community, in an ominously fascist way. For instance, he was in favor of widow remarriage because he wanted the optimum use of potential childbearing wombs.

For V.D. Savarkar creation of the Muslim "other" as opposed to the "self" of Indian (=Hindu) culture/civilization was a concrete political necessity. His major theoretical work is The Six Glorious Epochs of Indian History. Savarkar identified the Hindu community with the Indian nation. He replaces god with the nation as the crucial referent for moral decisions.

This is important because then the demands of the community/nation can be perceived as adequate justification for actions which, by traditional as well as by modern secular ethics, would be considered immoral. This is made explicit when Savarkar repeatedly criticizes Hindu heroes like Shivaji for humane Behaviour to Muslim women. (The incident of Shivaji capturing the daughter of the governor of Kalyan and sending her back with full honours was often celebrated by other communalists, particularly in Maharashtra, as a sign of Hindu tolerance in opposition to Muslim Behaviour to Hindu women.) Savarkar rejected the moderate form of Hindu communalism and advocated brutality toward Muslim women. The nation tracing its contours on the bodies of women: Women of the upper-class, upper-caste majority community were the custodians of the national honour-not honour for their own sakes, but for the male-defined community/nation. For the same reason, defiling the honour of the opposite community was best done through the women of the opposite community.

Savarkar's definition of a community was a purely political entity based on race and the joining of religious dogma, so as to mobilize the majority of Hindus while streamlining all differences, creating a monolithic entity.

Race theory was the normal basis of his creation of others, excepting Muslims: He lumped together all the Islamic peoples, to validate the construction of Muslims as the principal enemy to the Hindu nation. Savarkar's narrative consistently projected Muslim males as rapists who could be stopped only if Hindu men gave up their misplaced sense of chivalry and plunged into a "tit for tat" policy.

Since women were imagined as perennially threatened, a major step was taken when the Rashtra Sevika Samity (RSS) agreed to launch a separate women's wing. [RSS is a militant Hindu-communalist cadre group that forms a crucial component of the current governing party BJP-ed.] The RSS was founded in 1925 as a response to mass anti-colonial movements, as well as to the fear of united Hindu-Muslim action. Over the next two decades the RSS attempted to counter secular nationalism and never took part in any anti-British movement.

Gender fitted into this discourse in two ways:

(1) The revival of the narrative of continuous assault on Hindu womanhood;

(2) A distorted use of the census data and whipping up the fear that the Muslim population in India would overtake the "dying Hindus." This eugenic emphasis focused on the Hindu female body and its capability for bearing strong and heroic sons.

STATE AND COMMUNITY IN INDEPENDENT INDIA

The Indian constitution adopted in 1947 created a tension among the rights of:

(1) the abstractly equal individual, posited in articles 14 and 15;

(2) the historically/socially marginalized/deprived sections, so that substantive equality can be achieved (article 15, section 3, for example);

(3) the community (articles 25-30).

At the time of the adoption of the fundamental rights, Amrit Kaur, one of the members of the Constituent Assembly explained that the constitutional guarantee of freedom of religious practice might stand in the way of any progressive legislation in the future. In the communally charged atmosphere of the 1940s and early 1950s the constitution makers highlighted the need for national integration by proposing in the Directive Principles the eventual promulgation of a Uniform Civil Code (UCC). In the proposal for a UCC the concern for gender justice was submerged into a national integrationist perspective.

One secular act passed in this period was the Special Marriage Act of 1954, by which any two Indians could marry regardless of their religion. It is noteworthy that the first retrograde legislation also concerned this act. During the (1970s) emergency, Mrs. Indira Gandhi had an amendment to this act passed, whereby if two Hindus married they would continue to be governed by Hindu property laws instead of the Indian Succession Act of 1925.

When Hindu communalists claim that in the name of secularism the Indian state has always appeased Muslims, we should understand that the reality is different. The state has compromised with Muslim communalists in the same way it has compromised with Hindu communalists. Thus the bill which sought to bring about a uniform law for child adoption for all Indians was repeatedly, as shown by Kirti Singh, dropped because of resistance from so-called Muslim community heads. And this was done despite the support to this bill by many Muslim intellectuals, and despite the fact that this is not a law compelling anyone to do anything, but merely allowing people, if they so desire, to adopt children. Thanks to the resistance on this point, today one has to declare oneself as belonging under particular religions in order to adopt, as a couple, both CPI(M) members and atheists, discovered a few years back when they adopted a child.

Similarly the Shah Bano Case (1985) resulted in the Government of India succumbing to pressure from Muslim communalists and promulgating the Muslim Women (Protection in Divorce) Act. This law tried to take away from Muslim women the right to seek compensation under the secular and uniform Criminal Law. Out of a laudable desire to protect minorities from state action by majority communalism, scholars like Partha Chatterjee and Nivedita Menon have been arguing that empowering the state is the wrong way of protecting individual rights in civil society. According to them the abstract individual does not exist in civil society, but is embedded in the communities.

In the name of protecting the pluralism of civil society, this perspective grants a totalizing power to communities. Chatterjee assumes that the community has the right to regulate the life of individuals without any interference. Since the state is an outsider, the community is not obliged to explain why it is different.

Chatterjee's arguments, further carried forward in his 1998 essay "Communities in the East," end up glossing over the internal structure of the supposed communities in favor of a notion of moral bond and cultural authenticity. We see how in contemporary scholarship class and material critiques of capitalism have been increasingly replaced by a critique of colonial and post-colonial discourse. The politics of recognition has come to replace the struggle for emancipation.

Kumkum Sangari's response to this viewpoint is very important. For her there is no abstract disembodied patriarchy. Rather, there is a multiplicity of patriarchies located in a variety of institutions in the civil society, apart from the state.

Communalism Today

With the BJP in power, the RSS claim to represent the entire Hindu community and to equate them with the nation is getting substantial state support. Their strategies for whipping up support are diabolical. The BJP spokesperson K.R. Malkani has asserted that population growth in itself is not bad. (In Hitler's Germany, "Aryan women" were encouraged to have more children while even before the holocaust there were large scale sterilizations of Jewish women.) The old fantasy of getting Hindu women to bear many strong sons is being revived by the government, so that Hindu women should expect to become compulsory wombs, while Muslim women have to await their fate with trepidation. Malkani's thrust is not on reproductive rights or health. He is fed up with the frittering away of resources in futile population control projects.

Savarkar's call for "a tit for tat response" has been taken up even more enthusiastically. Having created with great care the image of the Muslim rapist, and having constantly called on Hindus to resist by counter-violence, the BJP and its allies in the Sangh fraternity implemented Savarkar's call in the Surat mass rape of the post-Babri Masjid period. Reports by women's and human rights' delegations made it clear that a rumor of Hindu women being insulted and molested by Muslims was spread and violence consciously organized.

This trend has been intensified since the BJP came to power, for instance, the rape of nuns in Jhabua, Madhya Pradesh. At that time, the general Secretary of the Viswa Hindu Parishad declared the incident as a patriotic Hindu reaction to Christian conspiracies concerning conversions. Home Minister L. K. Advani refused to condemn this statement in Parliament.

This politicizing of rape was reflected in the National Commission for Women (revamped by the BJP) document on

Rape: A Legal Study, which claims that women's condition had been consistently good in ancient India until the coming of the Muslims. The study asserts that women became insecure because of the Muslim invasions and that the protection they craved led to male domination.

Well before the BJP had come to power, Asha Sharma, an RSS activist, had attributed the occurrence of rapes to the fight for equal rights. The only way out of this is through a series of bans on freedom of expression and democratic rights of women. The rhetoric of freedom and modernity wears out here, showing what kind of women the Hindu right wants to construct. If women transgress the boundaries set out by the fascist ideology, they can expect violence.

Vijay Raje Scindia defended the burning of Roop Kanwar under the plea that voluntary sati was a traditional heritage. She even claimed it under the rhetoric of "freedom of choice." S. Mahajan, Minister in charge of Women and Children, declared in January 2000 that on 8th March, International Women's Day, she would institute sati awards for women who have combated great odds to win a goal in life.

CHOICES FOR THE WOMEN'S MOVEMENT

Combating the multiple patriarchies in Indian society calls for complex strategic thinking. In national women's conferences over the last two decades, communalism has never been off the agenda. A woman-centered strategy has been hard to develop, but certain directions are now clear. To say that a declaration of atheism is the precondition for united work is to ensure a ghettoized existence for the women's movement. Activists like Amrita Basu, Flavia Agnes, Fareeda Shaheed and Patricia Jeffrey have noted that despite their secular democratic strategy, feminists have failed to mobilize women the way Hindu communalists have done. They suggest that this is because the kind of identity which feminists project compel women to take a stand in defiance of their surroundings, while the communalists' discourse makes them feel empowered without having to take on the tremendous weight of the patriarchy.

It should be noted here that caste, a boundary marker distinct from communal identities, have also generated forms of gendered violence and its own regional politics which have done a disservice to women. This has been far less studied than communalism and this needs rectification.

It is also now clear that participation in concrete struggles within the artificially homogenized communities, like the attempt by Awaaz-e-Niswaan for dialogues within Islamic communities for greater rights for women is a step forward. Recently Sachetana, a feminist group, held a seminar where Sayeeda Hamid, a member of the National Commission for Women, explained that Muslim women organized in the Muslim Women's Forum had effectively argued on the basis of the Hadis (legal interpretation of the Koran) that Muslim Personal Law in India is flawed and unjust to women.

In Islamic law, a woman has the right to initiate divorce proceedings provided it is stated in the Nikahnama (marriage contract). Thus the Muslim Women's Forum is trying to pressure the Muslim Personal Law Board (one of those "community" head organizations, in fact created by law) to abolish the verbal talaq and to adopt a standardized Nikahnama drafted by the women, where women's right to divorce is recognized.

Feminists are also demanding compulsory marriage registration, irrespective of religious affiliation or lack thereof. This can be done by a provincial government no less than the central government. But none will do so. The leftist law minister of West Bengal told us in the Sachetana Seminar that compulsory registration was difficult due to "pressure from communities." The central government will not pass any such measure since in Hindu marriage registration is not needed. In fact Hindu marriages are often difficult to prove due to the absence of registration. There are a plethora of forms of Hindu marriage, yet courts recognize only the "saptapadi" form (which has a Vedic sanction). Thus in the absence of registration a Hindu woman, after believing herself married for a decade can find herself abandoned with no protection. Yet it is the so-called community heads who resist such reforms. Having said all this, there has been a redefinition of the feminist agenda. Many women were boldly calling themselves feminists in the 1970s and early 1980s. The preferred term today is women's rights activists. Yet the shift away from mass movements over prices, food supply, and the like has also meant that concerns of many worker and other low-income group women are not being taken up sufficiently. Just as there has been a deepening of the reformism of the left parties to the point where they are now more fervent champions of national capitalism than is the Indian big bourgeoisie itself, so there has been a retreat of the women's movement. This points to the need to organize coordinated movements,including local and national struggles that can unite women across communal divides.

CAMPAIGN FOR LEGAL REFORMS

While providing support to women facing problems concerning marriage, divorce, maintenance, alimony, property rights, custody of child/children and guardianship rights, the activists realised that the existing personal laws and most of the customary laws were discriminating against women. Hindu daughters were deprived of coparcenary rights in parental property as per the codes of *Mitakshara*. Christian women could not get divorce on the ground of husband's adultery; it had to be coupled with cruelty, bestiality and sodomy; while Christian husband can just declare his wife as an adulteress and divorce her. This antiquated law was enacted in the colonial period to serve the interests of the British bureaucrats who had their legally wedded wives in England and were cohabiting with the Indian (in their language 'native') women. Parsee daughters who married non-Parsee men lost their property rights and non-Parsee wives of Parsee husbands got only half the shares in husband's property as per the Parsee Personal Law. Shariat Law subjugated Muslim women by imposing *purdah*, allowing polygamy and unilateral divorce by men to his wife/wives and by depriving divorced Muslim women of maintenance rights.

Underlying philosophy of all these personal laws was that: women are not equal to men. They are governed by the patriarchal ideology. Irrespective of their religious backgrounds, these personal laws perpetuate patrilineage, patrilocality, double standard of sexual morality for men and women and perceive women as dependent on men. Individual women from different communities have challenged the constitutional validity of discriminatory aspects of the personal laws in the Supreme Court of India. Increasing number of educated workingwomen and housewives from all religious backgrounds have been approaching secular women's organisations. Main problems faced by them from their natal families have been forcible marriage, murderous attacks in cases of inter-caste, inter-class and inter-religious marriages, property disputes, incest and from their husbands and in-laws have been adultery, bigamy, polygamy, divorce, custody of child/children, property, incest etc. As the issue of personal laws is intertwined with the religious identities, the secular women's movement had to face tremendous hostility from the elite of the different communities, mass organisations, patriarchal secular lobby and the parliamentary parties cashing on block-votes.

Individual women (divorced, deserted, single and married under duress) are questioning discrimination in the customary laws. Tribal women in Maharashtra and Bihar have filed petitions demanding land rights in the Supreme Court of India. Several women's groups (*Saheli*, Delhi, *Vimochana*, Bangalore and Forum against Oppression of Women, Mumbai) and human rights lawyers team (The Lawyers Collective, Mumbai and Indian Social Institute, Delhi) have prepared drafts containing technical detail of gender just and secular family laws. In 1996, Ahmedabad Women's Action Group (AWAG) filed writ petition to declare Muslim Personal Law, which allows polygamy as void as offending Articles 14 and 15 of the Constitution. " The issue of women's rights and family law reform has been increasingly entangled within the polemics of identity politics and minority rights." Say a feminist lawyer, Ad, Flavia Agnes.

On April 23, 1985, the Supreme Court of India awarded lifelong maintenance to an old divorced Muslim woman, Shah Bano. The communal tone of the judgement – which, instead of highlighting the right to maintenance of a divorced woman, spoke of ' Muslim woman" and 'Muslim husband'-created unnecessary and harmful polarisation on religious grounds. Lawyers, women's groups, progressive and conservative people reacted sharply. Demonstrations, rallies, petitioning, signature campaigns, media war, public meeting, both for and against the Muslim Personal Law-all totally communalised the issue if gender justice (Vibhuti Patel, 1995). Human Rights Law Network, YUVA and College of Social Work, Mumbai have prepared domestic workers' bill to regularise terms and conditions concerning work condition and wages of the domestic workers who happen to be women from the depressed classes. Deepalaya, Justice and Peace Commission of St. Pius College has published a manual focusing on practical and operational aspects of legal battles, law and order machinery and community's initiatives such as people's courts, out of court settlement in presence of an impartial individual or a body.

WOMEN'S MOVEMENT AND POPULATION POLICY

When it comes to reproductive rights of women, most of the efforts of the women's groups in India have been directed against excesses committed in the name of family planning programmes.

Now, Indian Council of Medical Research, All India Institute of Medical Sciences and Institute of Research in Reproduction (IRR) has shown readiness to discuss scientific, medico-legal and operational dimensions of bio-medical researches conducted on human subjects. UNFPA and WHO have drawn guidelines about population policies that its focus shifts from targeting women for population control to women's reproductive rights. Ethical guidelines for bio-medical research are drawn. Still in the interior parts of India, poor women have been the main targets of the abusive sterilization operations and unsafe injectable and oral contraceptives.

Recent researches on adolescent girls and abortion have highlighted the problem of teenage pregnancies, trafficking of young girls for sex trades and complicity of the criminal justice system.

Campaign against sex determination resulted into central legislation banning amniocentesis, chrion-villai-biopsy and sex pre-selection techniques for femicide. But, much needs to be done to make the legislation effective in the real life. CEHAT and the Lawyers Collective have jointly supported a petition (Public interest Litigation in the Supreme Court of India) filed by Dr. Sabu George for effective implementation of the Act: In 1998, All India Democratic Women's Association challenged the use of the drug quinacrine as a method of female sterilization by filing a Public Interest Litigation case against Quinacrine. Women's groups are demanding that the population policy should focus on women's reproductive rights.

CAMPAIGN AGAINST PRE-BIRTH ELIMINATION OF GIRL CHILD

Prenatal Diagnostic Techniques (Regulation and Prevention of Misuse) Act was enacted in 1994 by the Centre followed by similar Acts by several state governments and union territories of India during 1988 (after Maharahstra legislation to regulate prenatal sex determination tests), as a result of pressure created by Forum Against Sex-determination and Sex-preselection. But there was a gross violation of this central legislation.

In response to the public interest petition filed by Dr. Sabu George, Centre for Inquiry into Health and Allied Themes Mumbai) and MASUM fought on their behalf by the Lawyers Collective (Delhi); the Supreme Court of India gave a directive on 4-5-2001 to all state governments to make an effective and prompt implementation of the Pre-natal Diagnostics Techniques (Regulation and Prevention of Misuse) Act (enacted in 1994 and brought into operation from 1-1-1996). Now, it stands renamed as " The Pre-conception and Pre-natal Diagnostic Techniques (Prohibition of Sex Selection) Act".

Recently enacted Prenatal Daignostic Techniques (Prohibition of Sex Selection) Act, 2003 tightens the screws on sex selection at pre-conception stage and puts in place a string of checks and balance to ensure that the act is effective. The Pre-natal Diagnostics Techniques (Regulation and Prevention of Misuse) Amendment Act, 2002 received the assent of the President of India on 17-1-2003.

The Act provides "for the prohibition of sex selection, before or after conception, and for regulation of pre-natal diagnostic techniques for the purposes of detecting genetic abnormalities or metabolic disorders or sex-linked disorders and for the prevention of their misuse for sex determination leading to female foeticide and for matters connected therewith or incidental thereto".

Under the Act, the person who seeks help for sex selection can face, at first conviction, imprisonment for a 3-year period and be required to pay a fine of Rs. 50000. The state Medical Council can suspend the registration of the doctor involved in such malpractice and, at the stage of conviction, can remove his/her name from the register of the council.

The Pre-Natal Diagnostic Techniques (Regulation and Prevention of Misuse) Amendment Rules, 2003 have activated the implementation machinery to curb nefarious practices contributing for MISSING GIRLS. According to the rules this all bodies under PNDT Act namely Genetic Counselling Centre, Genetic Laboratories or Genetic Clinic cannot function unless registered. The Bombay Municipal Corporation has initiated a drive against the unauthorised determination of gender of the foetus as per the directive of the Ministry of Law and Justice. All sonography centres are required to register themselves with the appropriate authority-the medical officer of the particular ward. The registration certificate and the message that under no circumstances, sex of foetus will be disclosed, are mandatory to be displayed.

The shortcomings of the PNDT Act (2003) lie in criteria set for establishing a genetic counselling centre, genetic laboratory and genetic clinic/ultrasound clinic/imaging centre and person qualified to perform the tests.

- The terms genetic clinic/ultrasound clinic/imaging centre can't be used interchangeably. But the Act does.
- Moreover, The amended Act should have categorically defined persons, laboratories, hospitals, institutions involved in pre-conception sex-selective techniques such as artificial reproductive techniques and pre-implantation genetic diagnosis.
- Who is a qualified medical geneticist? As per the Act, " a person who possesses a degree or diploma or certificate in medical genetics in the field of PNDT or has minimum 2 years experience after obtaining any medical qualification under the MCI Act 1956 or a P.G. in biological sciences". Many medical experts feel that a degree or diploma or 2 years experience in medical genetics can't be made synonymous.
- As per the Act, an ultrasound machine falls under the requirement of genetic clinic, while it is widely used also by the hospitals and nursing homes not conducting Pre-implantation Genetic Diagnosis (PGD) and PNDT.

Ban on the Advertisements of SD & SP Techniques. Another important initiative that has been taken is against any institution or agency whose advertisement or displayed promotional poster or television serial is suggestive of any inviting gestures involving/supporting sex determination.

MASUM, Pune made a complain to the Maharashtra State Women's Commission against Balaji Telefilms because its top rated television serial's episode telecast during February 2002 showed a young couple checking the sex of their unborn baby. The Commission approached Bombay Municipal Corporation (BMC) and a First Investigation Report (FIR) was lodged at the police station. After an uproar created by the Commission, the Balaji tele-film came forward to salvage the damage by preparing an ad based on the Commission's script that conveyed that sex determination tests for selective abortion of female foetus is a criminal offence. Now there is another battle brewing. The women's groups insist that the ad should be telecast for 3 months before each episode, while the Balaji Tele-films found it too much.

We need to counter those who believe that it is better to kill a female foetus than to give birth to an unwanted female child. Their logic eliminates the victim of male chauvinism, does not empower her.

The techno-docs don't challenge anti-women practices such as dowry, instead display an advertisement, "Better Rs.5000 now than Rs.5 lakhs later" i.e. Better spend Rs.5ooo for female foeticide than Rs. 5 lakhs as dowry for a grown up daughter. By this logic, it is better to kill poor people or third world masses rather than let them suffer in poverty and deprivation. This logic also presumes that social evils like dowry are God-given and that we cannot do anything about them. Hence victimise the victim. Investing in daughter's education, health and dignified life to make her self dependent are far more humane and realistic ways than brutalising pregnant mother and her would be daughter. Recently series of incidents in which educated women have got their grooms arrested at the time of wedding ceremony for demand and harassment for dowry, is a very encouraging step in the direction of empowerment of girls. Massive and supportive media publicity has empowered young women from different parts of the country to cancel marriages involving dowry harassment. They have provided new role models.

Hence, our slogans are:

"Eliminate Inequality, not Women", "Destroy Dowry, not Daughters",

Say "No" to Sex-determination, Say "Yes" to Empowerment of Women,

Say "No" to Sex Discrimination, Say "Yes" to Gender Justice.

Philosophical and medical details of NRT need public debate without iron wall of secrecy, in all Indian languages as NRT is penetrating even in those areas where you don't get even safe drinking water or food. Technologies for population control are primarily concerned about efficiency of techniques to avert births rather than safety of women. Women have to put up with the side effects of NRTs. New reproductive technologies are provider/doctor controlled, not women controlled. Hence the women's groups repeatedly state that NRTs have inherently anti women bias. In the petition filed by CEHAT-MASUM in the Supreme Court of India and supported by the women's rights groups, Dr. Sabu George, the petitioner's demand of expansion of the scope of the Pre Natal Diagnostic Techniques Act to include sex pre-selection techniques and effective implementation of the PNDT ACT has not only been accepted but also rules have been formulated for its implementation. The state governments are also organising state level seminars for doctors from the government and private sectors to focus on raising awareness to the fact of sex selective foeticide as a discriminatory practice. They are also trying to deal with the issue from the point of view of responsibility of science towards gender justice, medical ethics and human rights. Recent publication of CEHAT "Sex Selection-Issues and Concerns" selected important writings of spokespersons, which have examined the problem of "missing girls" from these angles.

There is a need to clarify the gender-just position from the anti-abortionist position. "Women should have a right to their bodies and unconditional access to abortion is not in conflict with the claim that sex selection and sex selective abortions are unethical. It is not the abortion which makes the act unethical, but the idea of sex selection."

We have a great task in front of us i.e. to change the mindset of doctors and clients, to create a socio-cultural milieu that is conducive for girl child's survival and monitor the activities of commercial minded techno-docs thriving on sexist prejudices. Then only we will be able to halt the process of declining sex ratio resulting into the phenomenon of missing girls. To stop a gender imbalanced society we will have to convince doctors and clients, state and civil society that "Daughters are not for slaughter".

CAMPAIGN AGAINST SEXPLOITATION

Women's rights organisations in Kerala and Goa have consistently opposed tourism driven sexploitation of children and young women. Global tourism industry has given rise to mushrooming of bars and nightclubs through out Asia.

Prostitution

Series of raids by the Bombay police in the red light areas " generated public opinion that strongly called for joint cooperation of the Government and non-government agencies in the matter of rehabilitation." Several women's rights groups and health groups are working in collaboration with refuge homes for rehabilitation of the ex-prostitutes in a humane manner.

Child Sexual Abuse

Women's groups have taken up the cases of child sexual abuse within childcare institutions. In response to sexual assault of a deaf-mute juvenile in the observation home, Forum Against Child Sexual Exploitation (FACSI) came into existence. Juvenile Welfare Board situated in the premises of the observation home took 10 days to respond to the event and that too after massive pressure exerted by FACSE which conduced thorough inquiry and submitted its report to the National Commission of Women.

In its recommendations it demanded formulations of code of conduct for the child care institutions. Transparency in its functioning, regular inspection, social audit by the citizens groups were some of the crucial measures for checking and controlling abuse. In case of child sexual abuse, FACSAE suggested that the institution must launch a public inquiry or constitute a truth and reconciliation commission.

WOMEN'S MOVEMENT AND THE DEVELOPMENT AGENDA

During 1970s and 1980s, the women's movement highlighted marginalisation of women from the economy. The efforts of women activists were directed in agitation and propaganda for women's rights, street fighting against escalating violence against assertive women and team building to counter sexual harassment at work place.

In the 1990, the women's movement is demanding its legitimate place within the mainstream with its own agenda of empowerment of women with partnership with men (Martha Nussbaum and Jonathan Glover, 1995). It has been able to identify its allies in all sections of society. Its horizontal and vertical networking has created congenial atmosphere to execute development agenda with the help of effective use of information technology, communication channels, modern managerial practiccs and efficient law and order machinery.

The most difficult areas have been providing educational opportunities for the poverty groups, low-cost housing, environmental and occupational safety and human rights concerns.

Development thinkers and workers need safety nets to operate without pressure from the local bullies and vested interests. Bullies of each and every communities are increasingly taking advantage of development workers/teachers/ academicians because they are non-hierarchical in their functioning and also because they are not commercial minded in their day-to-day affairs. When individual women activists sense threat/pressure in advance, they do change their accommodation and jobs.

This is another form of sati. The state, political parties and beneficiaries of women's groups too have duty to ensure democratic and multicultural atmosphere within which the women activists can take judicious and gender-just decisions about allocation of developmental resources and development funding for construction of schools, community centres, sports-clubs, libraries and reading rooms, low cost hospitals and low cost housing for the poverty groups leading settled life.

Women's Movement and Peace Initiatives

The most important contribution of the women's movement has been its commitment for peace-initiatives in the disturbed areas torn by communal conflicts, ethnic tensions and mob violence. Its work in the refugee camps has been acknowledged by the state. Media publicity on this issue is extremely important so that such work can be replicated in the places where such groups don't exist. Indian women's movement has played a crucial role in the global peace initiative (Women for Peace, 1994). Women's groups were at the forefront in terms of offering support to the survivors of communal carnage in Gujarat in 2002. Women's Movement in INDIA and Decision Makers in the Educational Institutions.

To incorporate a gender perspective in the academic curricula, our decision-makers will have to be prepared for numerous reforms in the existing syllabi and teaching methods. Conceptual issues regarding gender perspective will have to be integrated in all subjects within humanities, social sciences, technical training institutes, Academies on essential services such as railways, road transport, police, military and paramilitary forces, health-care, school of architects, engineering and science colleges so that we can get gender-aware human resource for area development, town planning, travel and tourism, public health projects, industrial growth and disaster management.

Fine arts faculties, communication schools, sports department, music colleges and libraries should integrate relevant research findings generated by the women's movement in their course content. The most difficult task in this direction is-identification of motivated teachers who are ready to evolve course-content on women, which can be integrated in the mainstream discipline.

This exercise will have to be supplemented with textbook writing, translations and funding. Vice-chancellors of our universities need to be convinced about foundation course on women and Development.

Educated women (with specialization to deal with technical aspects) of the women's movement can be invited as resource persons to provide inputs in curriculum development. Sexual harassment of women employees, contract labour, Ph.D. students, women field workers and women teachers should be handled with utmost sensitivity, by the heads of the institutions and academic council. Witch-hunting of women academicians fighting for women's rights must stop.

THE UNIVERSAL MISSION OF WOMAN

Woman's essential mission in the world is to be for mankind a living example of the spirit of total dedication to God. To love God with her whole heart, her whole mind, her whole strength, and to radiate that love to the world--this is the universal task of woman. It is true that every human being is made for the love of God and is meant to be totally consecrated to His praise. In what sense, then, can we say that it is the particular mission of woman to be both an example and guide of man along the way of dedication?

There are two poles, two principles in human nature. Father Gerald Vann, O. P., in his recent book, "The Heart of Man," distinguishes these two basic tendencies as "man the maker" and "man the lover." Both principles are present to some extent in every human being, but man the maker is realized most perfectly in man; man the lover in woman. It is the maker who asserts, who imposes his idea and his will on the surroundings. The race takes its forward motion along the way of organization and invention from him. It is man the lover who gives, who yields his own will and gladly surrenders not only his will but his very self to the beloved.

Mankind has always recognized that love plays a far greater role in woman's life than in man's. Every woman when she looks into her own heart finds there the deep desire to surrender herself completely in love. Woman is by nature total in her giving; love absorbs her whole being. Byron was expressing the common experience of mankind when he wrote:

"Man's love is of man's life a thing apart

'Tis Woman's whole existence."

In relation to God, we must all fulfill the role of the lover, awaiting the divine initiative, surrendering completely to the divine will. As C. S. Lewis writes so beautifully, "Our role must be always that of patient to agent, female to male, mirror to light, echo to voice. Our highest activity must be response, not initiative. To experience the love of God in a true and not an illusory form is therefore to experience it as our surrender to His demand, our conformity to His desire." Christian tradition has often expressed man's relation to God in the beautiful phrase: the soul is the bride of Christ. But woman's nature has the greater innate affinity for the bridal role, for the act of loving surrender. That is why woman has been throughout Christian history a symbol and example of the spirit of complete consecration to God. Woman's natural capacity for wholehearted giving of herself in love is the basis for her glorious supernatural vocation. It is her function to help to lead mankind to God by becoming herself a radiant example of total dedication to His will.

The lover's surrender opens the way for the action of God's grace in the world. "The world can be moved by the strength of man, but it can be blessed in the real sense of the word only in the sign of woman," writes Gertrude von Le Fort. It is first of all to Our Lady that these words apply. In her, the universal mission of woman, the lover, was fulfilled most completely. Her "fiat" is the perfect expression of the creature's wholesouled surrender to the creator, and through her surrender the fullness of blessing entered into the world. These words may be applied, too, to the universal task of womankind, for it is the function of every woman to re-echo the "fiat" of Mary and thus to become a source of blessing to humanity.

Woman as Mother of Mankind

Woman helps to lead society Godward by her direct service of mankind as well as by her example. Total dedication to God implies wholehearted service of man. A loving care for one's neighbor is but the necessary practical expression of a genuine love of God. In woman, the care for one's neighbor has the character of maternal love, with its warm personal devotion and generous sacrifice of self. Spiritually as well as physically, woman is the mother of mankind, the fountain and nurturer of life.

Through her relation to "man the maker" woman exercises a strong spiritual influence on the whole of a culture. Man leaves the imprint of his personality in the creations of his mind--works of science and art, monumental buildings and commercial empires. But woman's masterpiece is life itself. She is not interested in abstract or technical achievements but in persons, and in bringing persons to God. She stays in the background, the great inspirer, whose warm sympathy and encouragement spur man on.

Intuitively she perceives what is best and noblest in his proposals and helps to develop it. With her deep awareness of the sacramentality of life, she helps man to see matter as the image of spirit, inspiring him with her vision of the divine poetry of creation and the symbolism of human action.

In the life of every great man one finds this vital influence of a noble woman-Monica and Augustine, Paula and Jerome, Scholastica and Benedict, Clare and Francis, Blanche of Castile and King Louis, Clothilde and Clovis, Beatrice and Dante. Woman's influence is subtle and hard to define but nonetheless real. When she no longer fulfills her role as spiritual mother, culture becomes gross, materialistic, brutal, and loses grace and beauty.

The Three Spheres of Woman's Dedication

Woman must needs fulfil her universal mission of dedication to God and loving service of mankind in some concrete set of circumstances. There are three spheres in which she can carry out her primary task: religious life, marriage, and single life in the world. In the designs of God's

Providence, some women in every generation, the "first fruits," are meant to consecrate themselves to God in religion; most women are called to dedicate themselves to Him in marriage; and very few are intended for the life of the unmarried woman in the world. But whether she becomes a nun, a mother of a family, or a single woman in the world, her essential function remains the same: to be a living example of the spirit of surrender and love, the spiritual mother of mankind.

The virgin consecrated to God by her vow of chastity has always been regarded with highest honour in Christian civilization. Consecrated virginity diffuses a fragrant atmosphere of purity and spiritual integrity throughout society, which contributes to preserve the sanctity of marriage and the dignity of womanhood. The greater the respect and esteem shown to virginity in a society, the higher the position of all women will be. It is significant that the Protestant revolt which has had so many unfortunate consequences for the position of woman began with Luther's attacks on virginity and his liquidation of convents and monasteries.

The topic of woman's contribution to society through the religious life, however, demands a separate article for adequate treatment. The present discussion will be confined to the role of woman in marriage and in the single life in the world.

Woman in Marriage

Woman's nature is admirably adapted to her functions as wife and mother. The responsibilities of the family develop her powers and mature her spiritually, mentally and physically.

Spiritually, a woman becomes mature through surrender, through finding the particular role in which she can accomplish her total dedication to God. The young woman who has found her vocation in life in marriage and is wholly given to her task of bringing her family to God is a mature person whatever her age. She will have that air of serenity and peace which are the sign of the basic fulfilment of her being.

The woman who has never surrendered wholeheartedly to any purpose outside herself remains immature all her life, like a bud which never unfolds itself. In marriage, woman can develop a spirit of selflessness which makes her dedication deeper and richer with the years. Her service to her family both expresses her love of God and increases her power of loving. The woman who has no outlet for her love, no one for whom she can spend herself, is apt to become hard, bitter, selfish, because she has no one but herself to consider. The woman who is constantly concerned with the needs of her family can unfold the qualities of love, tenderness, and unselfish devotion which make her truly great and truly happy.

Mentally, a woman's mind matures under the stimulus of the varied practical activities she performs for those she loves. In the concrete, living experience of the family, she can develop sound judgment and a keen insight into human nature. Lombroso's observation can readily be verified. "The mother of a large family who has had no time to study, having been occupied with her children and her household, has more life, more breadth of ideas, than the old maid of the same age who has done nothing else than to potter about at universities and libraries." The responsibilities of her family life exercise all woman's mental powers. Her intuition and powers of observation are called into play constantly to discover the unexpressed desires of her family, particularly the needs of the helpless child. She has need of her intuition, too, as well as her tact, to help her solve the hundred problems of human relations and practical affairs that arise in the course of her day. Providing for the family helps to develop woman's natural ingenuity and inventiveness.

It is to the ingenuity of women intent on meeting the needs of their families that we owe the discovery of many of the most important arts: horticulture, for example; the creative arts of weaving, pottery, basketry; the domestic arts of food preparation and preservation; the uses of medicinal herbs in healing.

Physically, too, marriage and child bearing represent a development and completion for the normal woman, giving her new beauty and vitality. The mother of a large family experiences a physical fulfilment with the birth of each child which gives her fresh vigour and health.

Dr. Alexis Carrell observes that women attain their full development as a rule only after the birth of several children. He writes in "Man The Unknown": "Women who have no children are not so well balanced and become more nervous than the others. The importance to woman of the generative function has not been sufficiently recognized. Such function is indispensable to her optimum development. It is therefore absurd to turn women against maternity.

The Gigantic Task

In a well balanced society, where the family performs all its proper functions, the home is a society in microcosm, presenting all the problems of human relations, all the variety of human activities. The home is at once an economic and industrial centre, preparing goods for family use; a school in which the young are introduced to the universe; a sanctuary for rest and relaxation; a temple dedicated to the praise of God. It is woman's function to organize and direct this complex undertaking, a role which demands intelligence talents and spiritual qualities of a high order. Chesterton describes the vastness of woman's task in the family in the following passage from "What's Wrong With the World":

"To be Queen Elizabeth within a definite area, deciding sales, banquets, labours, and holidays; to be Whiteley within a certain area, providing toys, boots, sheets, cakes and books; to be Aristotle within a certain area, teaching morals, manners, theology and hygiene: I can understand how this might exhaust the mind, but I cannot imagine how it could narrow it. How can it be a large career to tell other people's children about the Rule of Three and a small career to tell one's own children about the universe? How can it be broad to be the same thing to everyone, and narrow to be everything to someone? No; a woman's function is laborious but because it is gigantic, not because it is minute."

One of the greatest of woman's responsibilities is her task as educator, transmitting the fundamental heritage of civilization, the traditions of culture and religion, to the new generation. The child receives his first introduction to civilization from his mother. The first formation of his mind and character belong almost entirely to her. She gives the child his first concepts of reality, his basic acquaintance with his mother tongue.

The child's ideas of God, of right and wrong, of repentance for faults, his first meeting with God in prayer--all come through the mother's teaching. She socializes the young human being, training him to honesty, courage, generosity, developing self-control, responsibility, and all those other virtues without which society cannot exist. She molds the men and women of the future. No other influence is as strong as the mother's in forming and preparing human beings for life.

Woman not only transmits the foundation of culture to the child; she is the great keeper of tradition in society, the custodian of manners and morals, conserving the gracious customs and fundamental standards of the race. She inspires and enforces the code of social Behaviour as, for example, the great chatelaines of the middle ages upheld the noble code of chivalry, and the hostesses of the seventeenth century salons cultivated the refinement of taste and manner. She keeps alive those religious customs and traditions in the home and community which link the daily life of man to God by so many intimate bonds. She is the guardian of the moral standard, especially in all that concerns the family. In this respect, as in so many others, the modern woman has abrogated her traditional role with tragic consequences for society.

It is impossible to exaggerate the importance for society of woman's achievement in the family. The family is the foundation of all the larger social structures, the basic cell on which all other agencies depend for the very existence and first formation of their members. A nation can flourish only to the extent that it is composed of healthy, flourishing families. But the family can endure only if the woman spends herself wholeheartedly to create a real home. If the woman looks down upon her function and neglects her task in the family, nothing can take her place; the family will disintegrate and with it the whole society. This should be abundantly clear to us when we see how powerless the most elaborate schools and the most advanced methods of social work are in the face of the rising tide of juvenile delinquents from neglected and broken homes.

It is superficial to think as women that we must be in the forefront of public affairs, politics, or business to influence the course of the world. "Not in the branches of a tree but in its roots do force and power reside," writes Gertrude von Le Fort. Woman is at the very roots of social life. If she keeps the sources of life pure and healthy, the entire social order will be renewed and reinvigorated by her effort.

Woman in Single Life

The other sphere through which woman can carry out her mission is the state of single life in the world. In normal times, only a few women are called to this vocation. But in our time, due to the war and to other abnormal social conditions, many women will remain unmarried. We should realize that this circumstance falls within God's Providence, and that He has destined the single woman to fulfil an important role in the modern world. The task of the unmarried woman is, by her whole hearted surrender to God, to make virginity spiritually fruitful in the world. In embracing virginity, she should radiate purity and nobility of soul. Her very existence, like that of the virgin consecrated in religion, should be a strong positive influence upholding the dignity of womanhood and the sanctity of marriage.

By developing her capacity for spiritual motherhood, she should become a source of strength and comfort and inspiration to mankind. Never has the world been so full of misery, so desperately in need of the healing influence of woman's love. The mission of the unmarried woman in this time is to give the full riches of her maternal love and devotion to alleviate the sufferings and renew the hope of mankind. In order to accomplish her vocation, the single woman must find an appropriate sphere in which she can carry out her dedication to God through loving service of human beings. She must strike out on new paths, searching for types of work in which she can use her womanly talents and develop her woman's nature. In the education and formation of the young; in agriculture, tending growing plants and animals; in the care of the sick, the weak, the poor, the helpless, woman finds fields of activity appropriate to her capacities as nurturer of life.

Unfortunately, work as it is carried on in these fields today often affords small opportunity for the use of woman's characteristic talents. In medicine, in education, in social work, we suffer from depersonalization, from too much large scale organization and mechanical routine, from too much concern with the physical aspects of the process. We need women to pioneer in these fields again, bringing with them their gift for warmly personal service and creating truly womanly occupations. We need women who will help to restore the emphasis on the spiritual, and who will make the work of healing, of teaching, of relieving the distressed a full expression of living charity between human persons.

How did We Lose the Concept of True Womanhood?

As we look over the modern world we may be tempted to echo King Solomon's cry: Who shall find a valiant woman? On every hand we see modern women turning away from this type of the greathearted woman. How does it happen that we have lost the concept of the woman of love and sacrifice and have accepted the ideal of the professional woman in its place?

Three major factors have contributed to the destruction of the womanly ideal: the Reformation, and the consequent secularization of western culture; the Industrial Revolution; the Feminist Movement. The Reformation was an ultra-masculine movement with small regard for woman's qualities and woman's functions. As society lost its Catholic sense, it lost also the concept of total dedication, the understanding of the sacramentality of life, the regard for the sanctity of marriage--all principles intimately connected with woman's mission and dignity. At the same time, "the masculine desire to dominate the woman found expression in the law." Public opinion looked down upon woman's sphere. "Kirche, kuche, and kinderstube" ("Church, kitchen, and nursery") were linked together and treated with scant respect as fit only for women.

Along with the intellectual devaluation of woman's activities came the profound economic and social changes created by the Industrial Revolution. Seventy-five years ago the woman in the home was still the centre of a variety of economic enterprises of unquestioned value and importance. But one by one almost all the activities through which a woman served her family, developed herself, and earned the esteem of society, have been lifted out of her hands and transferred to the factory. The sphere in which most women had found their means of dedication was severely curtailed. At the same time, economic necessity forced many women into the labour market to help support their families and thus led them further away from a womanly pattern.

The third influence which has contributed to the loss of a true concept of woman's function is the feminist fallacy. Feminism was born of woman's natural reaction against the depressed condition in which she found herself in a secularized, masculine, industrial culture. The feminists vociferously demanded equality, but unfortunately they conceived equality on a masculine pattern. Their whole struggle for woman's rights has simply helped to destroy the difference between the sexes and has worked to make the woman a slavish imitation of the man. Feminism is an abject surrender to the masculine ideal as the only ideal. The feminist has completely lost faith in herself as a woman. Her effort to prove herself "just as good as a man" betrays her insecurity and is a tacit admission of inferiority. Woman's struggle for freedom has led her deeper and deeper into a morass of conditions which frustrate her nature and her mission. Chesterton's bon mot is more than a witty pun: "Twenty million women rose to their feet with the cry: 'We will not be dictated to' and proceeded to become stenographers." It is a summary of woman's situation in the modern world. Women rebelled against the confinement of the home; they find themselves now confined to the mechanical routine of the typewriter and the assembly line, rendered all the more monotonous for a woman because of its exceedingly impersonal character. Woman is made for marriage and motherhood; the modern woman in the name of freedom urges easy divorce and artificial sterility. Woman is well adapted to the universal activity of the home; her demand for freedom leads her to a narrowly specialized education and still more narrowly specialized career. Woman is made for love, for the giving of herself in personal, devoted service. In the modern world she has found her way to a position of lonely and selfish independence.

Towards a Solution

The problem of woman's role is fundamental and no simple, facile solution will meet it. It is not surprising that a society which has lost its sense for divine things and for man's own nature should have lost also the true concept of woman. The unnatural position of woman in our society is but one aspect of the disintegration of modern culture. Nothing short of an intensive and all-embracing renewal of the modern world in the Christian spirit will restore woman to her proper functions. What can we do as women to restore a true concept of womanhood?

(1) *Know Thyself*: As women, our first task is to regain our self-respect in the light of a clear concept of our nature and our role. We must grasp the full splendor of the divine idea of woman as it is revealed to us in the sacred writings, climaxing in the figure of Our Lady. If we have the courage to be ourselves and to follow our spiritual mission, then the world will once again recognize and reverence the immeasurable dignity of womanhood.

(2) *Restore the Christian Family*: We must strive in all ways to restore the family to its rightful dignity and full vigour as the basic cell of the social organism. The

family must regain the entire range of its functions, the full scope of its gigantic task--religious, educational, cultural, economic. As women it is our particular responsibility to develop a new pattern of integral Christian life in the family, in which common prayer, work, study and recreation will build the bonds of unity and draw the family heavenwards.

(3) *Create Womanly Work*: If woman is to give the full benefit of her special qualities to society, it is of the utmost importance that we create, especially for the unmarried woman, many types of womanly work. We need pioneers of vision and imagination to take the lead in developing occupations which give woman the opportunity to mature and use her distinctive gifts. We must be alert to discover appropriate spheres of activity in which woman may realize her dedication to God in loving service of humankind.

(4) *Become Radiant Examples of the Spirit of Total Dedication*: Most important of all we must fulfil our primary mission to radiate the spirit of dedication in the world. Never has there been a period in the history of the race when the need for woman's spiritual mission was so great. At the root of all the disorders of our sad, sick world lies man's attempt to assert his independence of God. To bring tranquillity and joy into the chaos of modern society, the first necessity is a profound renewal of spirit, a wholehearted surrender of man to God, a humble and joyful acknowledgment of our complete dependence on Him. To light the way to this surrender is the spiritual mission of the women of the twentieth century, the task of woman in the modern world.

WOMAN'S FUTURE POSITION IN THE WORLD

To be strictly logical one should not treat of woman apart from the rest of the human race, for this is in a manner to admit that women are a distinct class, not affected by conditions, environment, etc., as men are. But we find a "woman question" actually existing. A great deal of discussion has been going on as to what is proper for woman, what her real nature is, and how many of the duties and privileges of man she should be admitted to. Women do not occupy the same position, socially, politically, economically, or intellectually that men do, and her powers are not equal to her brother's. She is daily reproached for trying to be other than she is, and reminded that her very nature forbids her presuming to climb out of the subserviency and inferiority which are now undeniably her portion. Thus a "woman question" is forced upon us whether we will or not. It is to discover, if possible, whether she may ever become equal to and like man without perverting her inherent nature, that this inquiry is made.

It is impossible to ascertain whether there ever was a time when woman stood an equally strong intellectual and physical being, on an equal footing with man, or not. If it ever existed, its memory is now very hazy. Yet there are writers who refer to it as a fact. August Bébel, in "Woman: Past, Present, and Future," refers to it thus: "We have no grounds for assuming that in this primitive state men were physically or mentally superior to women.... Certain savage tribes were governed by women instead of men owing to the superior strength of the former.... Primeval woman, although the equal of man in bodily and mental power, nevertheless became his inferior when periods of pregnancy, birth, and lactation forced her to look to him for assistance, support, and protection."

And in a more mystical sense Olive Schreiner refers to the time: "And he answered: 'Listen and I will tell you. Ages and ages long she has lain here, and the wind has blown over her. The oldest, oldest man living has never seen her move; the oldest book records that she lay here then as she lays here now. But listen! Older than the oldest book, older than the oldest recorded memory of man, on the rocks of language, on the hard baked clay of ancient custom, are found the marks of her footsteps. Side by side with him who stands beside her, you may trace them, and you may know that she who now lies here once wandered free over the rocks with him.'"

Matilda Joslyn Gage, in her "Woman, Church, and State," lays great emphasis upon the days of matriarchy, when women, as mothers of the race, ruled the people. But we have no evidence that any such period ever existed. Letourneau shows that cases have been where inheritances descended and relationships were determined through the women of the tribe.

Accompanying this usage, a certain importance adhered to the mothers of the tribe. It is true, women attained powerful and prominent positions in the old civilizations that have come and gone. The mythical lost Atlantis was peopled with great women of divine aspect. There were queens in the days of Solomon; and the Helens, Cleopatras, and Hypatias of history dot the dark pages with glints of a glory to come. A matriarchy never existed; cases of matriarchy have been known. Woman never stood beside man his equal in all things; women have ruled in isolated instances.

Be that as it may, woman's subordination came to be complete. She was first knocked down, dragged away senseless, and made a slave. She was bought and sold, or traded; she became a thing, a piece of property, a bond slave. Her degraded position among men became a custom, then an institution, then a tradition. There were centuries of "dark ages for her, into whose gloom no ray of light ever pierced, and from whose depths little has come down to us to tell the sombre story."

Slowly, very slowly man developed in intellect and acquired a rude knowledge of art. The woman in his tents could not remain very far behind him, and in time arose to some degree of companionship. That he treated her with a little kindness, and even appealed to her in times of weariness or perplexity for sympathy or counsel, was due, not to his traditions and creeds conceived in another grade of civilization, but to changed conditions and his own developed nature. There might even have arisen a "woman's rights question" in those old Mosaic days, had not the priests, who feared any loosening of their control over the people, issued a "Thus saith the Lord," and so riveted her chains for another three thousand years. "Thy desire shall be unto thy husband, and he shall rule over thee," settled the problem for the time.

"Economic dependence is the basis of all slavery," Bébel says; and he is right. All forms of slavery had their inception in some kind of economic dependence, but the slavery often exists long after the dependent condition has passed away. A thing, once established, once made an institution, is very apt to outlast the economic phase which determined its existence, and become a very troublesome matter. Institutions are crystallized ideas; they stand still: people grow--grow beyond and outside of them. Yet there they remain, unwieldy, mischief-breeding; to get rid of them at all is to tear them out by the roots at great cost of life and suffering. The bonds made ages ago, by economic conditions prevailing at the time, have become sacred; they bear another strength than that which they possessed when first formed. Though no longer with any economical basis for existing, they are even more effective in power than when first established.

Individually men are not to blame for the inferior position of women. They accepted a condition, a chain of customs, as they found them. Though long past the time when constant danger from without rendered it necessary that his whole family give him implicit obedience, the habit of expecting filial deference is fixed. Though the days of absolute property in wives have gone by, the sense of proprietorship in and responsibility for wives still prevails. That sentiment which played upon the superstitious fears of woman, setting a sort of mental watchdog to guard the master's property in his absence as well as when present, still exists in a modified form in the demand for perfect chastity in woman not expected man. The old feeling of ownership, which led men to seclude their women, has softened into that modern sentiment which would keep women guarded from the public gaze in every respect. The stern commands of old are toned down into "what is expected of womanly women," but that expectation is as binding as any chain or title deed to person could be.

Thus, through ages of subserviency, of which there were many grades, women have come to be what they are: emotional, since any prominent display of other faculties has been unnecessary in that "sphere to which it has pleased God to call her;" deceitful, since deceit has been her only weapon; illogical, since the encouragement of her reasoning powers would have often placed her in direct opposition to her master; vain, since her personal charms were long the only qualities for which she was considered; weak-minded, since strong brains were not desirable in that function to which man wished to limit her. So from long persisting conditions woman has come to be the creature she is.

But the change in woman's position and in the manner in which woman is considered during the last fifty years has been a remarkable one. We scarcely realize its greatness until we begin to compare the prominent women of today with women of the last century. It is perhaps correct to say that Mary Wollstonecraft began the modern woman's-rights movement. Her work, "The Rights of Women," written toward the close of the last century, is read more widely now than at the time of publication. It was many years before an organized effort was made to secure political equality for women. The movement, which has lasted through the lifetime of some of America's noblest women, though a little too narrow for modern sociological students, has been a great element in the remarkable change. Unconsciously it has builded better than it knew, and helped to widen the field and elevate the aspirations of women far more than the originators ever intended.

The introduction of machinery has been the most potent factor in the transition. When the work of the world was done in the home, when the spinning-wheel, the loom, the soap vat, the "pig-killing," the bake oven, and the slender needle were institutions in every household, naturally "woman's place" was at home. But spinning-wheel and loom turned into great cotton and woollen mills; the pork-barrel became the vast packing-houses of our large cities; the needle was reserved for mending, and great clothing establishments took its place; the old lye barrel gave way to immense soap factories; and family ovens were relegated to the past, for the bakeries that now supply the staff of life.

It was no longer profitable to make these things in the seclusion of the home; and women followed the machines and went in great crowds to the factories. The demand for women's work came at a time when a new restlessness was pervading the inner sanctum of the home. Secluded and protected, kindly treated though they might happen to be, women began to feel that they were not living full, true lives. They felt that all their faculties were not being developed, that all their powers for giving and receiving happiness were not being called out. Though the duties of motherhood might for the time being occupy all their time and energies, it was also true that not all women were mothers of children, nor were the mothers always mothers of young children. A woman's life stretches over many periods, as does man's. In a lifetime she is capable of being much more than a mother, as man is expected to be much more than a father.

The restlessness was natural. Women came out into the world and became acquainted with each other and with their working brothers; they took a broader view of life; and something of that feeling of fraternity to which men had attained in their clubs, lodges, and unions, began to take lodgment in their breasts. For the "old" woman had no conception of the brotherhood of the human race. She loved her own passionately, and she loved her immediate friends; she loved her church and believed in a vague way that she "loved all men," as a good Christian should. But of the real solidarity of the human race, of the truth that "an injury to one is the concern of all," she had no conception. The "new woman" has a very fair realizing sense of this great social truth today. And therefore, though she may be more of a slave in the factory than she was in the narrow confines of home, she has come up higher. She has reached greater opportunities for full, well-developed existence; and though she makes some mistakes, she is far advanced in her evolutionary progress.

But as yet she is no happier, and men are not pleased. They think she has taken their places in the workshop, in the office, and at the business desk; they fear to lose the sweet, clinging, fragile, wheedling little creature they imagine they love; and they have not reached a conception of what the free, self-poised, capable, womanly woman of the future will be. They are not very well satisfied with the crude sample of the "new woman;" and they are in a manner drawing away from her in the consciousness of a lofty superiority which never needs a transitional stage.

Women themselves are not happy, because they are not yet accustomed to the new order--an order that is as yet chaotic and undefined. Just out from the unwholesome hothouse air of their old seclusion, the atmosphere of comparative freedom and independence strikes too harshly upon them, and they shiver. They cannot go back, and they cannot yet breathe easily. They can do wonders in adaptation, but they cannot find their equilibrium in half a generation of partial freedom. The adjusting process hurts; it always does. What is it that woman wants? What is it she hopes to attain? What is it she lacks that men are not willing to give? It is no wonderful thing; nothing preposterous or presumptuous. She simply wants to be a human being, not a slave, not a toy, not a queen. She wants the equal personal liberty that every man demands in order to become a fully developed, well-balanced, happy, and useful being. Only this and nothing more.

With this emancipation--this "liberty to do whatsoever one wills so long as one [does not infringe] on the equal right of others to do as they will"--she needs not even the chivalry of old. Kindness, sympathy, love from equals she needs in common with man. She needs not that spirit of worship which some men who think they are "advanced" seem willing to pour out upon her; she needs not that undue devotion on account of her motherhood which many good people believe is right and just; she needs not that right which Robert Ingersoll declared she must possess when he said: "Women should have all the rights that men possess and one more--the right to be protected." The right to be a human being includes that right when necessary. If every individual in the world possesses an equal right to life, liberty, and the pursuit of happiness, the right of opportunity at nature's table, the right to develop to the highest she is capable of becoming, the rights of motherhood and womanhood are conceded. No better protection is needed than that which any enlightened human being will naturally give to another if circumstances make it imperative. A free woman will not choose to be "protected" in the old sense. Protection has ever been an implication of weakness and a willingness to occupy a subordinate position. Nations which call upon other nations for protection must needs give up for that protection some portion of their independence; and industries that can flourish only under "protection" create slaves in their turn.

A great fear seems to exist that if women were perfectly free to become whatever they see fit many dire calamities would happen. Woman would become "mannish;" she would lose her delicate sense of morality; and she might slight that one great duty to which she has been almost wholly consigned for so many ages. But why do we hesitate to trust woman free, when she has fulfilled so many precious trusts in bondage? I have no fear that motherhood and love is a great part of the sweetness of life, and free women are not likely to yield up any part of their happiness. This one great fear seems to lie at the bottom of every objection to the full freedom and equality of woman--the fear that she will refuse to do her duty by the human race. It is the last prejudice, the last of the old traditions, that man is willing to let go. He will go so far as to admit the right of suffrage, to accept equal property rights, to grant equal opportunities in all the fields of human activity, but he cannot rid himself of that sacred old tenet: that a woman cannot be a good wife and mother if she have any other interest in life besides her home and children. Even very radical thinkers still at times declare that "woman's crowning glory is motherhood;" and only insist on equal opportunities and unequal consideration that she may be more fully and perfectly the mother. I am aware that I am proving myself a startling heretic to generally accepted ideas, but I most emphatically dissent.

I am aware that throughout the realm of nature the one blind impulse of every living thing is to reproduce itself. Everything else seems to be sacrificed to this one object. In the lowest living organisms individual identity is completely lost in the separation which creates two where one existed before. A little higher up in the scale extinction follows reproduction; and for many degrees in the ascending gamut the sole purpose of existence seems to be simply reproduction. But as the higher forms of life evolve, in both the animal and the vegetable kingdoms, more and more of life is utilized in other ways. Trees live to give shelter and shade, and they minister to our sense of beauty through many years; the higher animals have many uses, and many years of animal enjoyment, aside from the function of reproduction.

In the lower grades of human life the power of reproduction seems the most important part of existence. But as the race advances, develops, acquires knowledge, the existence of its members becomes rich and full with the wealth of life itself. The individual becomes an emphasized, distinct identity. It is something to the world that a bright, sound individual lives, acts, and thinks, even though it is never reproduced. The male portion of the race already feel as though fatherhood were a mere incident in their lives, and would be insulted were you to intimate that fatherhood should be the crowning glory of their lives. They know that they possess powers and capabilities that the world needs and appreciates, and that fatherhood, blessed though it be, is not the fullest and best manifestation of their existence. The idea is in every way as applicable to woman as to man. Why should all the faculties and energies of woman be turned to the fulfilment of this one function of her being?

It is flattering to man to think that it takes all of a woman's whole life to carry out her duty to him and his children. But if he only knew it, the entire devotion of her powers to this one purpose is the poorest preparation for wifehood and motherhood that can be made. Even the man himself feels a sort of undefined contempt for the woman who is nothing but wife and mother. A woman becomes morbid who simply retires within herself to brood over her fitness or unfitness for her "crowning glory." It is distorting, dwarfish, narrowing. Her child is unfavorably affected by this intensity of thought centred upon its embryonic existence. It is like that unwholesome "self-analysis" which has ever made up so great a part of the old religious creeds, and which still crops up in modified forms in the "new philosophies."

Let the woman live for herself, not for unborn children. Let her fill her life to the brim with happiness, knowledge, mental and physical activity; let lofty emotions and vigorous thoughts fill her being; let her whole existence expand to its fullest extent; let her forget her motherhood; she will be the better mother for first being a perfect woman. And to be this she must first be free. It will not do to ask what she will do with her freedom, to criticise, to judge; one must only wait. "The cure for the evils of liberty is more liberty."

Do not fear for the result. The trend of human evolution is upward and onward. The plant allowed to grow freely, in the sunlight, with warm rich soil and pure fresh air, will develop to its very highest possibilities. Cramp it, interfere with it, abstract either light or warmth, and it becomes a stunted, pale, sickly growth. Looking upon it, no one could tell what it might have become under proper conditions.

Do not fear that woman thus freed would become a poor mimicry of a poor sample of a man. To become "mannish" is in the eyes of conventional society worse than to commit a crime. But what do we mean by this term? If it is anything reprehensible, believe me, it is as bad in man as in woman. Does it apply to the manners, morals, or the intellect? It is very vague at best. For those qualities which we call "good" are as beautiful in man as in woman. We love bravery, self-poise, strength, honour, truthfulness in one as well as in the other. We love gentleness, kindness, sympathy, tact in both sexes. We see today timid men and brave women; weak-minded men and strong-minded women; deceitful men and truthful women; vain men and self-forgetful women. Under equal and similar conditions the virtues and vices would be diffused much more equally. For I hold another heresy: that there is no sex in intellect, sentiment, or morals. The same environment, the same treatment, the same teachings would result in a similarity of characteristics. There will never cease to be variety, but we should not find a greater tendency toward any particular group of faculties in one sex over the other.

True, some scientific scholars declare that it is a physical impossibility for woman under any condition to become man's equal in physical and mental strength, or to become free from her emotional disturbances and sensitiveness of nerves. The shape, size, and quality of the brain, they say, preclude this; her peculiar functions, the time and energy necessary to the bearing of children and the nourishing of them, prevent a change from her present nature. Nevertheless this is not a demonstrated truth; no one knows by actual experiment whether it is true or not. The fact that all human creatures are the subject of environment and of hereditary conditions signifies that woman is no exception. There is every reason to suppose that under like conditions with men, women would develop in a manner as men do. Woman's peculiar functions should not create the sharp distinctions now seen. Weakness, dependence, emotionalism, vanity, deceitfulness have been cultivated in woman; these traits have been considered her greatest attractions; tradition, custom, public opinion have fixed them upon her, and it will take long to eliminate them.

There is no reason why woman should devote more of her time and energies to motherhood than man does to fatherhood. Work, activity, interest in other things, both while carrying and nourishing children, are better than idleness. No special training, no particular occupation or exercise of one's faculties, or the cessation of activities, are necessary as a preparation for motherhood. The life which makes a woman all she is capable of being as a human being is the only one essential to the rearing of good children. So little is required of a mother that need interfere with ordinary duties and occupations, that it is difficult to see how motherhood should have, in itself, such a wonderful differentiating effect.

Woman has been considered too much as woman, and not enough as a human being. The constant reference to her sex has been neither ennobling, complimentary, nor agreeable. Either as slave, toy, pet, or queen, this ceaseless thinking of her sex instead of herself has been degrading. To finally arrive at her best she simply needs consideration as a fellow member of society.

Do not fear liberty. Just now the results of the beginnings of freedom do not seem very satisfactory. Woman seems to be an intruder; she cannot overcome at once the prejudices that had their inception in the time of her complete economic dependence. She herself is dissatisfied. She is not as lovable perhaps. She has lost some of the charm of clinging womanhood which at best man only heeded in his leisure moments, and has not yet gained the poise and individuality that will draw him to her as a companion. She is dissatisfied with the old gallantry, and has not yet attained the spontaneous recognition and respectful love she longs for. But this will come. There will be a time when men and women, equal human beings, clasping hands and looking each other in the eyes on a level--not leaning on each other, but upright--will feel a true fellowship; and mutual admiration and respect will exist between them. Then will love be sweeter, purer, more beautiful than the world has ever known.

6

Initiatives for Women Development and Empowerment

DEVELOPMENT THROUGH ENTERPRISE

One of the important factors in the development programmes and plans of developing countries is the growth and expansion of public enterprises and the public sector. Initially, public enterprises operated principally in the infrastructure and the public utilities, but their range of activity has now considerably expanded. Being part of the broader stream of the public sector in developing countries, public enterprises are important instruments of national and collective self-reliance and are oriented towards increasing the countries autonomy in using and developing their natural and human resources in order to increase the well-being of the population as a whole.

One of the responsibilities of public enterprises is the promotion of the integration of women ınto the developmental process and of a conscious policy directed towards the advancement of women. The responsibilities of public enterprises in this regard, however, differ in accordance with their scope and nature, their mandate and function, their scope and coverage of national planning and the legislative framework. But, by and large, they cover a wide range of commercial and; or non-commercial functions of great importance in everyday life.

Practical experience in the operation of public interprises in developing countries has shown that they generate progressive social change in these countries, including positive moves towards involving women in the main streams of development. However, the public sector in general and the public enterprises in particular are still not strong enough to constitute a major or even a very important factor in involving women in the transformation of their socio-economic position and are thus not making a sufficient response to this complex task.

Within the framework of the national development programmes, the public enterprise in general, and each specific enterprise in particular should be provided with guidelines indicating the special steps expected from the enterprise for the promotion of the role of women in developing countries, which might include the following:

— More emphasis on clarity of aims and objectives, a regular review of the current status of women, including job profiles for the improvement of the position of women in training programmes, social welfare measures relating to child bearing and child rearing, provision of creches and the allocation of specific responsibilities to appropriate national institutions;

— preparation of concrete action plans which should include both short-term and long-term strategies in the area of manpower planning, recruitment systems promotional opportunities, incentives, training and women's representation at the management level. These strategies should also envisage a regular procedure and criteria for the evaluation of the performance of public enterprises in terms of the fulfilment of economic and social objectives;

— identification of areas of activity in which women are currently not represented but can be recruited. The human resources development plans should include a specific component on the employment of women;

— efforts should be made to involve more women in on going training courses, particularly management training, as well as to develop the curricula of these courses with an emphasis on the role and responsibilities of public enterprises in the advancement of women;

— in view of the need to involve more women at higher levels of management, special training programmes for the induction of women at these levels of enterprise management could be stimulated and developed as a short-term measure;

— Fuller involvement of women workers and men workers alike in decision-making processes as well as in forms of management at all levels of enterprise organisation, which is seen as an essential means of their advancement, parallel with the improvement of public enterprises' management patterns and efficiency;

— public enterprises should exploit their opportunities of generating employment in down-stream activities with which they are related. This is of particular significance in the case of sub-contracting to public sector ancillaries. Some cases of sub-contracting to women's cooperatives and to regional development corporations which stimulate small business could also promote both employment and entrepreneurship among women. However steps must be taken to ensure that such practices are not deterimental to the position of women or to the overall regional development;

— an agreed system of performance evaluation arising from the predetermined corporate plans should identify the evaluation criteria for each social objective including the objective of advancing the status of women. Whenever possible, an attempt should be made to quantify the criteria;

— the existing or/and newly created mechanisms at the national level responsible for scrutinising the policies and practice of public enterprises and evaluating their operations and contributions towards the socio-economic objectives of development could advise governments on the formulation of policies through which public enterprises could act as model employers and real promoters of the status of women, and could also undertake regular evaluation and monitoring of these efforts of public enterprises.

In view of the need to implement the socio-economic objectives of development and the advancement of women, due consideration should be given to the role of private enterprises. Governments should seek appropriate ways and means to ensure that public and private enterprises share the responsibilities for the improvement of the status of women. Some suggestions in this connections might be, for example:

- — private enterprises are established in developing countries under various systems of public licensing which include certain provisions for the enforcement of laws and these could be used for regulating the working conditions of women;
- — similarly, credit/banking agencies which give loans to private enterprises for equity and working capital could give specific incentives for the promotion of the advancement of women;
- — it may expected that the linkages between the public and private enterprises could promote the realisation of some of these ideas.

POLITICAL PARTICIPATION AND THE ROLE OF WOMEN IN DECISION MAKING

The political status of women in developing countries and the levels and quality of their political participation, are far from adequate, considering their share in the population structure, their part in social and economic reproduction, as well as their actual and potential role in the national development process. The unfavourable economic and social position of women in developing countries is directly reflected in the level of their participation in decision-making process at all levels. In many developing countries a large portion of the women actively participated in the national liberation movements and in the creation of national political structures. However, they were often under-represented in the decision-making processes, in public and political life. Studies on women's participation have revealed that they are more active at the informal levels, which are closer to their problems than in formal political activity. This passivity of women in formal political activity is both a symptom and a cause of some major developmental problems.

The political participation of women has always been indicative of their position in general. Today, there are only very few developing countries where national law excludes women from formal political processes. However data on a global basis indicate an enormous disparity between women's formal political equality and their actual participation in decision-making processes.

Having understood this problem and recognised it as an important barrier to social and economic progress and development changes, most developing countries have been adopting and trying to implement policies and measures which would mitigate and remove it. Many of these efforts and measures have been promoted through the implementation of UN instruments, such as the Convention on Equal Political Rights of Women, the Convention on the Elimination of All Forms of Discrimination Against Women, etc.

There has been general recognition among those in authority in developing countries of the great importance of women's participation in the efforts towards social and human welfare. A general summary of the findings of numerous studies in this field shows that the number of women who actively realise their role in development and their rights in developing countries is continuously increasing, as is the importance of their participation in representative and legislative for at the national, regional and particularly at the local level. Women are especially active and are gaining increasing representation in local self-government bodies. The number of women in executive orans, in the judiciary, and in particular among high officials and in the political structures and public services is small and inadequate, but nevertheless growing. Their representation in the upper management echelons in the economic, scientific, cultural and social fields is unsatisfactory, but it cannot be said that the situation is not improving. In some regions political education and economic emancipation of women, as well as the creation of better family and household conditions have led to increased participation of women in political parties, trade unions, various movements, etc.

The need for effective and extensive popular participation, promotion of grass-root organisations and institutional mechanisms to facilitate such participation has already been recognised. There will have to be a commitment from governments to provide opportunities for greater participation of women in political and other fields of life and to eliminate all forms of discrimination. Examples of decentralised planning and decision-making, such as community development programmes, may be seen as positive moves towards the realisation of such commitments.

In many developing countries genuine forms of popular participation have been established and are operating successfully, workers participation in management, industrial democracy, co-determination, self-management, etc. Most of these relate to the sphere of the economy, the public sector and public enterprises, but are often accompanied by various forms of citizens involvement in running the community's affairs at the local and regional levels. Workers and citizens involvement in the conduct of economic and community affairs also includes forms of direct sharing in the management of public and social services, cooperative, consumers associations, etc. All these forms, which have given women art opportunity to enlarge the scope of their participation in public and political life, have had a significant impact on the overall activisation of women in society in the mainstream of development processes. Such forms and experiences of workers, citizens and generally popular participation involving women equally, generate development and contribute to the realisation of human rights. This is being recognised by many international and UN fora and documents and should be fully considered by the development countries in applying strategies for the advancement of women.

Taking into account the overall context—constrained national economies, inequalities in societies and the high barriers to greater participation of women in political life—an organisational base is crucial for the promotion of a more dynamic role for women in the process of development. However, a supportive infrastructure (government, the academic system, education the media, etc.), is often also important.

Non-governmental organisations— ranging from international to national and grass-root level organisations—have a long history of fighting for political rights for women, campaigning for changes in laws and national policies and participating in democratic and civil rights movements peace movements and ecological movements. The UN Decade for Women witnessed a reactivisation of women's organisations and the emergence of new women's groups with an increasing emphasis on collective action for articulating women's concerns and increasing women's visibility to development planners and decision makers. There is a decisive shift now from social welfare work to involvement in income-generating projects, consumer rights and workers' right issues. The Decade also saw the emergence of radical action groups protesting against sex violence against women and curbs on women's liberties and rights. Self-help action groups have also emerged at the grass-root level to articulate women's employment needs and increase their access to credit, developmental inputs and services.

The importance of the role of non-governmental organisations lies particularly in their function as mobilising mechanisms and organising agencies of working women, protecting their interests, particularly in the informal sectors and providing necessary support services. Further they act as mediators between government and the people and between coordinating agencies for the provision developmental inputs and services, as well as pressure groups and catalysts for the development of cadres and local leadership potential and organisational skills.

ORGANISED ACTION FOR BETTERMENT

The need for collective organisations of workers to safeguard their interests is acknowledged. However, in surplus labour economies and in economies in which women are largely employed in the informal sectors, it has proved extremely difficult to set up such organisations. In the organised sector, even where women are members of the trade unions they do not exercise authority within them because of their low position in the occupational hierarchy and they are by and large excluded from collective negotiation with employers. Female membership in trade unions is low, since there are no pressure on unions alter their priorities. In some countries, trade unions have created women's wings to specifically articulate the need of women workers. There are also examples of separate women's trade unions, workers organisations, particularly of women workers in the informal sectors of the economy who remain outside the purview of small producers is a must, but supportive structures are equally essential for survival of such organisations. There is a school of thought which maintains that separate women's organisations only divide the workers' movements. And in some cases such organisations neither succeeded in involving more women in public and political life nor did they gain social support. Nevertheless, separate women's organisation, particularly organisations of the most disadvantaged groups of women workers, may play an effective role in protecting women's rights and thus contribute to the advancement of the status of women, also through joint trade union organisations.

DEVELOPMENT OF RURAL WOMEN

In rural areas women are most hardpressed by the burden of different types of work. They are always in a more disadvantageous position as compared to urban women, what to speak of men. More so, are the conditions of rural women of hilly regions. They toil throughout the day collecting fuel wood and drinking water from distant places, doing various household works and in addition they also work in agricultural fields, look after domestic animals and their own children.

To improve any society, development of both male and female should be on equal footing. Stress should be given more on the female child to compensate the already advantageous position of a male child. Government has made policies from time to time to give free primary education to rural children. A girl child is usually deprived of these privileges. To strengthen the already existing general education, instituted by the government of the development and upliftment of the lots of rural technological education should be introduced.

Both formal and informal education can be gainfully utilised to enlighten the rural women though mobile library, large scale mass media application and distant education. Open universities can play an important role in this regard. Local level education may be imparted to the target people through non-governmental organisations (NGOs) like Village Cooperation, Mahila Mandals and village societies and governmental organisations (GOs) like Primary and Secondary schools, Panchayats, Balwaris and Anganbaris.

Education will render knowledge of sanitation, hygiene cleanliness and thereby improve the scientific temperament of a child. By natural instance a girl child is more attached to her surroundings and would help improve it—if she is substantially educated. As a mother, she can help in educating her own children and as a teacher she can improve the lot of many more.

Nearly 80% of the population of India reside in rural areas. Literacy rate in rural areas is very low as compared to urban areas (29.65% vs. 54.6% according to 1981 census). Rate of female literacy in rural areas is still lower. These women are most hardpressed by the burden of various types of manual work.

Worse is the condition of those residing in hill areas. They toil throughout the day collecting fuel wood, and drinking water from distant places, doing household chores like cooking, washing, house-cleaning, dehusking and grinding food grains and in addition they also work in agricultural fields, look after domestic animals and of course their own children. In the Himalayan region, because of undulated land surface, all these works turn out to be more strenuous and drudging.

Women's Participation in Education

To improve any society, development of both male and female individuals should be on equal footing. Swami Vivekananada had said decades back that, "As a bird cannot fly on one wing, no society can make progress unless its women too join men in all activities". Stress on the education of the female child should be more but the scenario is just the reverse. It is the male child who is more privileged and gets a better chance in every aspect.

Effects of Educational Policies on Rural Women

The Policy makers of our country have emphasised long back that there should he an intensified effort in Human Resource Development, with education playing its multifaceted role. Government has made provision for free primary education to rural children.

But a girl child is usually deprived of these privileges. She is the one who is wanted back at home to do the household chores or to look after the younger brothers and sisters when the mother is away at work or she herself is engaged elsewhere to earn for the family.

Rural Areas and the Rural Women

Educational institutions of the type imparting general education and rural technology to rural folk in a three tier system, i.e., Children—Middle aged—and Old age people will be very useful. The Department of Education started National Literacy Mission programme to improve the educational status of rural women.

The main objective of this mission is aimed at provision of functional literacy to 50 million adults in 15-35 age group by 1995. The focus of the mission is on rural areas with a special concern for women and persons belonging to scheduled castes/ scheduled tribes (Singh and Bose 1991). Apart from programmes run by Government agencies a large number of voluntary agencies will be identified which will help in Adult education and continuing education programmes, organising training programmes for the instructors and supervisors, preparing and publishing, learning materials and audio and video materials for educating these people.

Formal and Informal Education

It has been observed that rural women in general are more receptive to progressive ideas and they want to learn more so that their economic condition is improved. Given a chance, they will make full utilisation of these schemes.

Mobile library is good help in imparting general education; mobile schools in vans, sent to remote areas can also render education to rural women and children. Distant education through media and other measures too, should be adopted. There is necessity of more Open Universities; may be one in each state to cater the needs of these people. Already many Universities are being involved in a big way through the Mass Programme for literacy. However, these programmes should be based on the needs and interest of women learners from rural areas. Any developmental activity, be it general education or technical education, must ensure adequate participation and representation of women.

Organisational Efforts

Through agencies like Village Cooperatives, Mahila Mandal and Village Societies, women in rural areas can be trained in various activities. Usually, the trend is to select mainly menfolk for training in fields of agriculture, animal husbandry, fishiculture, poultry, sericulture, apiary and others. Of the rural women, 54% are engaged in marginal occupation like collection of fish, firewood, cowdung etc. through which they supplement the family income.

Along with men, if women are also trained in various educational, technical and professional fields, they would be able to better their economic conditions. Moreover success of Balwaris and health programmes in some parts of the country, mainly carried out by trained women, has brought to light the fact, that there is unassumed potential in women that can be tapped and used for rural development (Dwivedi 1991).

Scientific Outlook through Education

Education will render the knowledge of sanitation, hygiene and cleanliness and thereby improve the scientific temperament of those who are educated. By natural instinct, a girl child is more attached to her surroundings and would help to improve it—if she is educated properly.

Protection of our environment and protection of our forests against indiscriminate felling are two important aspects where education and training rendered to rural women will prove beneficial. She can play a significant role in conserving the eco-system and preventing further deterioration of our environment. As a loving child, she can influence her parents to plant a few more trees in the surrounding; she can stop her brother from destroying these trees; and as a wife, she can exert tremendous influence on her husband not to cut down trees of the forest. If she is aware of the harms caused by deforestation, she can offer to use alternate resources for cooking rather than cutting down a tree.

Usually a man does not have so much attachment to the trees and plants as women have. Neither do they think of the long-term effects as women do and hence, at the time of need, they will not hesitate to cut down a tree. Woman, by nature is a binding force and has a broader vision of realising the consequences of such arbitrary felling of trees. They would rather take the pains to go and collect dead wood and dry leaves to use these as fuel than cut down a tree in a haste.

It was a group of village women, who in the face of armed opposition, prevented a logging company from cutting down a forest by simply remaining hugged to the trees. This movement—known as Chipko Andolan still continues in many villages in northern hilly areas of Uttar Pradesh. These women could realise that with the dwindling of forests, they must travel increasingly further to gather firewood and also they understood the relationship between deforestation, soil erosion and drying up of water resources.

Problems Specific to the Hill Regions

Why the emphasis is on the Himalayan region? The hilly tracts of the mighty Himalayas have problems of their own. The agricultural fields are on the slopes of the hills. To reduce flow of water and check erosion, what is practised here is called "Terrace Cultivation." About 50% or more work of the agricultural fields are done by rural women and hence, they must have the knowledge of soil erosion, how it can be checked, what are the consequences if it remains unchecked and how "Terrace Cultivation" helps checking soil erosion. Deforestation is already creating havoc coupled with 'Jhoom' cultivation. There has been unprecedented increase in 'Shifting' or 'Jhoom' cultivation, particularly in the North-Eastern States in the Himalayan belt. In addition, mining and quarrying on the hill slopes has led to destruction of natural vegetation and unbalancing the fragile eco-system.

This in turn will destabilise the complete Himalayan range which is protecting the Indian subcontinent against the vagaries of extreme weather conditions prevailing in the northern regions. Besides, it will also lead to loss of many valuable genetic resources. All these can be checked with the help of proper education and adopting appropriate technologies for the rural women to combat with these situations.

EMPOWERMENT OF WOMEN AND DEVELOPMENT OF CHILDREN

Women and children, who represent more than two third (67.7 per cent) of the country's total population, constitute the most important target groups in the context of the present day developmental planning. Therefore, their concerns are placed on the priority list of the country's developmental agenda.

Needless to say, they have the strength and support of the Constitution.

Empowerment of Women

Women, as a separate target group, account for 407.8 million (including girl children) as per the 1991 census and constitute 48.1 per cent of the country's total population. Depending upon the developmental needs of the individual age groups, the entire female population has been categorised into five distinct sub-groups, viz. i) girl children in the age-group 0-14 years, who account for 153.85 million (37.8%) and deserve special attention because of the gender bias and discrimination they suffer from at such a tender age; ii) adolescent girls in the age group 15-18 years, who account for 38.70 million (9.5%) and are very sensitive from the view point of planning because of the preparatory stage for their future productive and reproductive roles in the family and society; iii) women in the reproductive age group of 15-44 years, numbering 183.67 million (45.1%) who need special care and attention because of their reproductive needs; iv) women in the economically active age group of 15-59 years, who account for 226.04 million (55.5%) and have different demands like those of education/training, employment, income generation and participation in the developmental process, decision making etc.; and v) the elderly women in the age group 60+, numbering 27.17 million (6.7%) who have limited needs mainly relating to health, emotional and financial support.

The principles of gender equality and equity and protection of women's rights have been the prime concerns in Indian thinking right from the days of Independence. Accordingly, the country's concern in safeguarding the rights and privileges of women found its best expression in the Constitution of India. While Article 14 confers equal rights and opportunities on men and women in the political, economic and social spheres, Article 15 prohibits discrimination against any citizen on the grounds of sex, religion, race, caste etc.; and Article 15(3) empowers the State to make affirmative discrimination in favour of women.

Similarly, Article 16 provides for equality of opportunities in the matter of public appointments for all citizens. Yet, another Article 39 mentions that the State shall direct its policy towards providing to men and women equally the right to means of livelihood and equal pay for equal work. Article 42 directs the State to make provisions for ensuring just and humane conditions of work and maternity relief. Article 51 (A) (e) imposes a fundamental duty on every citizen to renounce the practices derogatory to the dignity of women. To make this de-jure equality into a de-facto one, special legislations have been enacted from time to time in support of women.

In the earlier phase of developmental planning, the concept of women's development was mainly 'welfare' oriented. During the Sixties, women's education received priority along with the measures to improve maternal and child health and nutrition services.

During the Seventies, there was a definite shift in the approach from 'welfare' to development' which started recognising women as participants of development. The Eighties adopted a multi-disciplinary approach with a special thrust on the three core sectors of health, education and employment. Accordingly, priority was given to implementation of programmes for women under different sectors of agriculture and its allied activities of dairying, poultry, small animal husbandry, handlooms, handicrafts, small scale industries etc.

Recognising the role and contribution of women in development, the early Nineties made a beginning in concentrating on training-cum-employment cum-income generation programmes for women with the ultimate objective of making them economically independent and self-reliant.

The Strategy for the Ninth Plan

'Empowerment of Women' being one of the nine primary objectives of the Ninth Plan, every effort will be made to create an enabling environment where women can freely exercise their rights both within and outside home, as equal partners along with men. This will be realized through early finalisation and adoption of the 'National Policy for Empowerment of Women' which laid down definite goals, targets and policy prescriptions along with a well defined Gender Development Index to monitor the impact of its implementation in raising the status of women from time to time.

NATIONAL POLICY FOR THE EMPOWERMENT OF WOMEN

The principle of gender equality is enshrined in the Indian Constitution in its Preamble, Fundamental Rights, Fundamental Duties and Directive Principles. The Constitution not only grants equality to women, but also empowers the State to adopt measures of positive discrimination in favour of women. Within the framework of a democratic polity, our laws, development policies, Plans and programmes have aimed at women's advancement in different spheres. From the Fifth Five Year Plan (1974-78) onwards has been a marked shift in the approach to women's issues from welfare to development. In recent years, the empowerment of women has been recognized as the central issue in determining the status of women. The National Commission for Women was set up by an Act of Parliament in 1990 to safeguard the rights and legal entitlements of women. The 73th and 74th Amendments (1993) to the Constitution of India have provided for reservation of seats in the local bodies of Panchayats and Municipalities for women, laying a strong foundation for their participation in decision making at the local levels.

India has also ratified various international conventions and human rights instruments committing to secure equal rights of women. Key among them is the ratification of the Convention on Elimination of All Forms of Discrimination Against Women (CEDAW) in 1993.

The Mexico Plan of Action (1975), the Nairobi Forward Looking Strategies (1985), the Beijing Declaration as well as the Platform for Action (1995) and the Outcome Document adopted by the UNGA Session on Gender Equality and Development & Peace for the 21st century, titled "Further actions and initiatives to implement the Beijing Declaration and the Platform for Action" have been unreservedly endorsed by India for appropriate follow up. The Policy also takes note of the commitments of the Ninth Five Year Plan and the other Sectoral Policies relating to empowerment of Women.

The women's movement and a wide-spread network of non-Government Organisations which have strong grass-roots presence and deep insight into women's concerns have contributed in inspiring initiatives for the empowerment of women. However, there still exists a wide gap between the goals enunciated in the Constitution, legislation, policies, plans, programmes, and related mechanisms on the one hand and the situational reality of the status of women in India, on the other. This has been analyzed extensively in the Report of the Committee on the Status of Women in India, "Towards Equality", 1974 and highlighted in the National Perspective Plan for Women, 1988-2000, the Shramshakti Report, 1988 and the Platform for Action, Five Years After-An assessment"

Gender disparity manifests itself in various forms, the most obvious being the trend of continuously declining female ratio in the population in the last few decades. Social stereotyping and violence at the domestic and societal levels are some of the other manifestations. Discrimination against girl children, adolescent girls and women persists in parts of the country. The underlying causes of gender inequality are related to social and economic structure, which is based on informal and formal norms, and practices.

Consequently, the access of women particularly those belonging to weaker sections including Scheduled Castes/ Scheduled Tribes/Other backward Classes and minorities, majority of whom are in the rural areas and in the informal, unorganized sector – to education, health and productive resources, among others, is inadequate. Therefore, they remain largely marginalized, poor and socially excluded.

Goal and Objectives

The goal of this Policy is to bring about the advancement, development and empowerment of women. The Policy will be widely disseminated so as to encourage active participation of all stakeholders for achieving its goals. Specifically, the objectives of this Policy include

(i) Creating an environment through positive economic and social policies for full development of women to enable them to realize their full potential

(ii) The *de-jure* and *de-facto* enjoyment of all human rights and fundamental freedom by women on equal basis with men in all spheres – political, economic, social, cultural and civil

(iii) Equal access to participation and decision making of women in social, political and economic life of the nation

(iv) Equal access to women to health care, quality education at all levels, career and vocational guidance, employment, equal remuneration, occupational health and safety, social security and public office etc.

(v) Strengthening legal systems aimed at elimination of all forms of discrimination against women

(vi) Changing societal attitudes and community practices by active participation and involvement of both men and women.

(vii) Mainstreaming a gender perspective in the development process.

(viii) Elimination of discrimination and all forms of violence against women and the girl child; and

(ix) Building and strengthening partnerships with civil society, particularly women's organizations.

POLICY PRESCRIPTIONS

Judicial Legal Systems

Legal-judicial system will be made more responsive and gender sensitive to women's needs, especially in cases of domestic violence and personal assault. New laws will be enacted and existing laws reviewed to ensure that justice is quick and the punishment meted out to the culprits is commensurate with the severity of the offence. At the initiative of and with the full participation of all stakeholders including community and religious leaders, the Policy would aim to encourage changes in personal laws such as those related to marriage, divorce, maintenance and guardianship so as to eliminate discrimination against women. The evolution of property rights in a patriarchal system has contributed to the subordinate status of women. The Policy would aim to encourage changes in laws relating to ownership of property and inheritance by evolving consensus in order to make them gender just.

Decision Making

Women's equality in power sharing and active participation in decision making, including decision making in political process at all levels will be ensured for the achievement of the goals of empowerment.

All measures will be taken to guarantee women equal access to and full participation in decision making bodies at every level, including the legislative, executive, judicial, corporate, statutory bodies, as also the advisory Commissions, Committees, Boards, Trusts etc. Affirmative action such as reservations/quotas, including in higher legislative bodies, will be considered whenever necessary on a time bound basis. Women–friendly personnel policies will also be drawn up to encourage women to participate effectively in the developmental process.

Development Process

Policies, programmes and systems will be established to ensure mainstreaming of women's perspectives in all developmental processes, as catalysts, participants and recipients. Wherever there are gaps in policies and programmes, women specific interventions would be undertaken to bridge these. Coordinating and monitoring mechanisms will also be devised to assess from time to time the progress of such mainstreaming mechanisms. Women's issues and concerns as a result will specially be addressed and reflected in all concerned laws, sectoral policies, plans and programmes of action.

ECONOMIC EMPOWERMENT OF WOMEN

Since women comprise the majority of the population below the poverty line and are very often in situations of extreme poverty, given the harsh realities of intra-household and social discrimination, macro economic policies and poverty eradication programmes will specifically address the needs and problems of such women. There will be improved implementation of programmes which are already women oriented with special targets for women. Steps will be taken for mobilization of poor women and convergence of services, by offering them a range of economic and social options, along with necessary support measures to enhance their capabilities

Micro Credit

In order to enhance women's access to credit for consumption and production, the establishment of new, and strengthening of existing micro-credit mechanisms and micro-finance institution will be undertaken so that the outreach of credit is enhanced. Other supportive measures would be taken to ensure adequate flow of credit through extant financial institutions and banks, so that all women below poverty line have easy access to credit.

Women and Economy

Women's perspectives will be included in designing and implementing macro-economic and social policies by institutionalizing their participation in such processes. Their contribution to socio-economic development as producers and workers will be recognized in the formal and informal sectors (including home based workers) and appropriate policies relating to employment and to her working conditions will be drawn up. Such measures could include: Reinterpretation and redefinition of conventional concepts of work wherever necessary e.g. in the Census records, to reflect women's contribution as producers and workers. Preparation of satellite and national accounts. Development of appropriate methodologies for undertaking (i) and (ii) above.

Globalization

Globalization has presented new challenges for the realization of the goal of women's equality, the gender impact of which has not been systematically evaluated fully. However, from the micro-level studies that were commissioned by the Department of Women & Child Development, it is evident that there is a need for re-framing policies for access to employment and quality of employment. Benefits of the growing global economy have been unevenly distributed leading to wider economic disparities, the feminization of poverty, increased gender inequality through often deteriorating working conditions and unsafe working environment especially in the informal economy and rural areas. Strategies will be designed to enhance the capacity of women and empower them to meet the negative social and economic impacts, which may flow from the globalization process.

Women and Agriculture

In view of the critical role of women in the agriculture and allied sectors, as producers, concentrated efforts will be made to ensure that benefits of training, extension and various programmes will reach them in proportion to their numbers. The programmes for training women in soil conservation, social forestry, dairy development and other occupations allied to agriculture like horticulture, livestock including small animal husbandry, poultry, fisheries etc. will be expanded to benefit women workers in the agriculture sector.

Women and Industry

The important role played by women in electronics, information technology and food processing and agro industry and textiles has been crucial to the development of these sectors. They would be given comprehensive support in terms of labour legislation, social security and other support services to participate in various industrial sectors. Women at present cannot work in night shift in factories even if they wish to. Suitable measures will be taken to enable women to work on the night shift in factories. This will be accompanied with support services for security, transportation etc.

Support Services

The provision of support services for women, like child care facilities, including crèches at work places and educational institutions, homes for the aged and the disabled will be expanded and improved to create an enabling environment and to ensure their full cooperation in social, political and economic life. Women-friendly personnel policies will also be drawn up to encourage women to participate effectively in the developmental process.

SOCIAL EMPOWERMENT OF WOMEN

Education

Equal access to education for women and girls will be ensured. Special measures will be taken to eliminate discrimination, universalize education, eradicate illiteracy, create a gender-sensitive educational system, increase enrolment and retention rates of girls and improve the quality of education to facilitate life-long learning as well as development of occupation/vocation/technical skills by women. Reducing the gender gap in secondary and higher education would be a focus area. Sectoral time targets in existing policies will be achieved, with a special focus on girls and women, particularly those belonging to weaker sections including the Scheduled Castes/ Scheduled Tribes/Other Backward Classes/Minorities. Gender sensitive curricula would be developed at all levels of educational system in order to address sex stereotyping as one of the causes of gender discrimination.

Health

A holistic approach to women's health which includes both nutrition and health services will be adopted and special attention will be given to the needs of women and the girl at all stages of the life cycle. The reduction of infant mortality and maternal mortality, which are sensitive indicators of human development, is a priority concern. This policy reiterates the national demographic goals for Infant Mortality Rate (IMR), Maternal Mortality Rate (MMR) set out in the National Population Policy 2000. Women should have access to comprehensive, affordable and quality health care. Measures will be adopted that take into account the reproductive rights of women to enable them to exercise informed choices, their vulnerability to sexual and health problems together with endemic, infectious and communicable diseases such as malaria, TB, and water borne diseases as well as hypertension and cardio-pulmonary diseases. The social, developmental and health consequences of HIV/AIDS and other sexually transmitted diseases will be tackled from a gender perspective.

To effectively meet problems of infant and maternal mortality, and early marriage the availability of good and accurate data at micro level on deaths, birth and marriages is required. Strict implementation of registration of births and deaths would be ensured and registration of marriages would be made compulsory. In accordance with the commitment of the National Population Policy (2000) to population stabilization, this Policy recognizes the critical need of men and women to have access to safe, effective and affordable methods of family planning of their choice and the need to suitably address the issues of early marriages and spacing of children. Interventions such as spread of education, compulsory registration of marriage and special programmes like BSY should impact on delaying the age of marriage so that by 2010 child marriages are eliminated.

Women's traditional knowledge about health care and nutrition will be recognized through proper documentation and its use will be encouraged. The use of Indian and alternative systems of medicine will be enhanced within the framework of overall health infrastructure available for women.

Nutrition

In view of the high risk of malnutrition and disease that women face at all the three critical stages viz., infancy and childhood, adolescent and reproductive phase, focussed attention would be paid to meeting the nutritional needs of women at all stages of the life cycle. This is also important in view of the critical link between the health of adolescent girls, pregnant and lactating women with the health of infant and young children. Special efforts will be made to tackle the problem of macro and micro nutrient deficiencies especially amongst pregnant and lactating women as it leads to various diseases and disabilities. Intra-household discrimination in nutritional matters vis-à-vis girls and women will be sought to be ended through appropriate strategies. Widespread use of nutrition education would be made to address the issues of intra-household imbalances in nutrition and the special needs of pregnant and lactating women. Women's participation will also be ensured in the planning, superintendence and delivery of the system.

Drinking Water and Sanitation

Special attention will be given to the needs of women in the provision of safe drinking water, sewage disposal, toilet facilities and sanitation within accessible reach of households, especially in rural areas and urban slums. Women's participation will be ensured in the planning, delivery and maintenance of such services.

Housing and Shelter

Women's perspectives will be included in housing policies, planning of housing colonies and provision of shelter both in rural and urban areas. Special attention will be given for providing adequate and safe housing and accommodation for women including single women, heads of households, working women, students, apprentices and trainees.

Environment

Women will be involved and their perspectives reflected in the policies and programmes for environment, conservation and restoration. Considering the impact of environmental factors on their livelihoods, women's participation will be ensured in the conservation of the environment and control of environmental degradation. The vast majority of rural women still depend on the locally available non-commercial sources of energy such as animal dung, crop waste and fuel wood. In order to ensure the efficient use of these energy resources in an environmental friendly manner, the Policy will aim at promoting the programmes of non-conventional energy resources. Women will be involved in spreading the use of solar energy, biogas, smokeless chulahs and other rural application so as to have a visible impact of these measures in influencing eco system and in changing the life styles of rural women.

Science and Technology

Programmes will be strengthened to bring about a greater involvement of women in science and technology. These will include measures to motivate girls to take up science and technology for higher education and also ensure that development projects with scientific and technical inputs involve women fully. Efforts to develop a scientific temper and awareness will also be stepped up. Special measures would be taken for their training in areas where they have special skills like communication and information technology. Efforts to develop appropriate technologies suited to women's needs as well as to reduce their drudgery will be given a special focus too.

Women in Difficult Circumstances

In recognition of the diversity of women's situations and in acknowledgement of the needs of specially disadvantaged groups, measures and programmes will be undertaken to provide them with special assistance. These groups include women in extreme poverty, destitute women, women in conflict situations, women affected by natural calamities, women in less developed regions, the disabled widows, elderly women, single women in difficult circumstances, women heading households, those displaced from employment, migrants, women who are victims of marital violence, deserted women and prostitutes etc.

VIOLENCE AGAINST WOMEN

All forms of violence against women, physical and mental, whether at domestic or societal levels, including those arising from customs, traditions or accepted practices shall be dealt with effectively with a view to eliminate its incidence.

Institutions and mechanisms/schemes for assistance will be created and strengthened for prevention of such violence, including sexual harassment at work place and customs like dowry; for the rehabilitation of the victims of violence and for taking effective action against the perpetrators of such violence. A special emphasis will also be laid on programmes and measures to deal with trafficking in women and girls.

RIGHTS OF THE GIRL CHILD

All forms of discrimination against the girl child and violation of her rights shall be eliminated by undertaking strong measures both preventive and punitive within and outside the family. These would relate specifically to strict enforcement of laws against prenatal sex selection and the practices of female foeticide, female infanticide, child marriage, child abuse and child prostitution etc. Removal of discrimination in the treatment of the girl child within the family and outside and projection of a positive image of the girl child will be actively fostered. There will be special emphasis on the needs of the girl child and earmarking of substantial investments in the areas relating to food and nutrition, health and education, and in vocational education. In implementing programmes for eliminating child labour, there will be a special focus on girl children.

Mass Media

Media will be used to portray images consistent with human dignity of girls and women. The Policy will specifically strive to remove demeaning, degrading and negative conventional stereotypical images of women and violence against women. Private sector partners and media networks will be involved at all levels to ensure equal access for women particularly in the area of information and communication technologies. The media would be encouraged to develop codes of conduct, professional guidelines and other self regulatory mechanisms to remove gender stereotypes and promote balanced portrayals of women and men.

OPERATIONAL STRATEGIES

Action Plans

All Central and State Ministries will draw up time bound Action Plans for translating the Policy into a set of concrete actions, through a participatory process of consultation with Centre/State Departments of Women and Child Development and National/State Commissions for Women. The Plans will specifically including the following:-

i) Measurable goals to be achieved by 2010.

ii) Identification and commitment of resources.

iii) Responsibilities for implementation of action points.

iv) Structures and mechanisms to ensure efficient monitoring, review and gender impact assessment of action points and policies.

v) Introduction of a gender perspective in the budgeting process.

In order to support better planning and programme formulation and adequate allocation of resources, Gender Development Indices (GDI) will be developed by networking with specialized agencies. These could be analyzed and studied in depth. Gender auditing and development of evaluation mechanisms will also be undertaken along side. Collection of gender disaggregated data by all primary data collecting agencies of the Central and State Governments as well as Research and Academic Institutions in the Public and Private Sectors will be undertaken.

Data and information gaps in vital areas reflecting the status of women will be sought to be filled in by these immediately. All Ministries/Corporations/Banks and financial institutions etc. will be advised to collect, collate, disseminate and maintain/publish data related to programmes and benefits on a gender disaggregated basis. This will help in meaningful planning and evaluation of policies.

Institutional Mechanisms

Institutional mechanisms, to promote the advancement of women, which exist at the Central and State levels, will be strengthened. These will be through interventions as may be appropriate and will relate to, among others, provision of adequate resources, training and advocacy skills to effectively influence macro-policies, legislation, programmes etc. to achieve the empowerment of women. National and State Councils will be formed to oversee the operationalisation of the Policy on a regular basis.

The National Council will be headed by the Prime Minister and the State Councils by the Chief Ministers and be broad in composition having representatives from the concerned Departments/Ministries, National and State Commissions for Women, Social Welfare Boards, representatives of Non-Government Organizations, Women's Organisations, Corporate Sector, Trade Unions, financing institutions, academics, experts and social activists etc.

These bodies will review the progress made in implementing the Policy twice a year. The National Development Council will also be informed of the progress of the programme undertaken under the policy from time to time for advice and comments.

National and State Resource Centres on women will be established with mandates for collection and dissemination of information, undertaking research work, conducting surveys, implementing training and awareness generation programmes, etc.

These Centres will link up with Women's Studies Centres and other research and academic institutions through suitable information networking systems. While institutions at the district level will be strengthened, at the grass-roots, women will be helped by Government through its programmes to organize and strengthen into Self-Help Groups (SHGs) at the Anganwadi/Village/Town level.

The women's groups will be helped to institutionalize themselves into registered societies and to federate at the Panchyat/Municipal level. These societies will bring about synergistic implementation of all the social and economic development programmes by drawing resources made available through Government and Non-Government channels, including banks and financial institutions and by establishing a close Interface with the Panchayats/Municipalities.

Resource Management

Availability of adequate financial, human and market resources to implement the Policy will be managed by concerned Departments, financial credit institutions and banks, private sector, civil society and other connected institutions. This process will include:

(a) Assessment of benefits flowing to women and resource allocation to the programmes relating to them through an exercise of gender budgeting. Appropriate changes in policies will be made to optimize benefits to women under these schemes;

(b) Adequate resource allocation to develop and promote the policy outlined earlier based on (a) above by concerned Departments.

(c) Developing synergy between personnel of Health, Rural Development, Education and Women & Child Development Department at field level and other village level functionaries'

(d) Meeting credit needs by banks and financial credit institutions through suitable policy initiatives and development of new institutions in coordination with the Department of Women & Child Development.

The strategy of Women's Component Plan adopted in the Ninth Plan of ensuring that not less than 30% of benefits/funds flow to women from all Ministries and Departments will be implemented effectively so that the needs and interests of women and girls are addressed by all concerned sectors.

The Department of Women and Child Development being the nodal Ministry will monitor and review the progress of the implementation of the Component Plan from time to time, in terms of both quality and quantity in collaboration with the Planning Commission.

Efforts will be made to channelize private sector investments too, to support programmes and projects for advancement of women.

Legislation

The existing legislative structure will be reviewed and additional legislative measures taken by identified departments to implement the Policy. This will also involve a review of all existing laws including personal, customary and tribal laws, subordinate legislation, related rules as well as executive and administrative regulations to eliminate all gender discriminatory references. The process will be planned over a time period 2000-2003. The specific measures required would be evolved through a consultation process involving civil society, National Commission for Women and Department of Women and Child Development. In appropriate cases the consultation process would be widened to include other stakeholders too.

Effective implementation of legislation would be promoted by involving civil society and community. Appropriate changes in legislation will be undertaken, if necessary. In addition, following other specific measures will be taken to implement the legislation effectively.

(a) Strict enforcement of all relevant legal provisions and speedy redressal of grievances will be ensured, with a special focus on violence and gender related atrocities.

(b) Measures to prevent and punish sexual harassment at the place of work, protection for women workers in the organized/unorganized sector and strict enforcement of relevant laws such as Equal Remuneration Act and Minimum Wages Act will be undertaken,

(c) Crimes against women, their incidence, prevention, investigation, detection and prosecution will be regularly reviewed at all Crime Review fora and Conferences at the Central, State and District levels. Recognised, local, voluntary organizations will be authorized to lodge Complaints and facilitate registration, investigations and legal proceedings related to violence and atrocities against girls and women.

(d) Women's Cells in Police Stations, Encourage Women Police Stations Family Courts, Mahila Courts, Counselling Centres, Legal Aid Centres and Nyaya Panchayats will be strengthened and expanded to eliminate violence and atrocities against women.

(e) Widespread dissemination of information on all aspects of legal rights, human rights and other entitlements of women, through specially designed legal literacy programmes and rights information programmes will be done.

Gender Sensitization

Training of personnel of executive, legislative and judicial wings of the State, with a special focus on policy and programme framers, implementation and development agencies, law enforcement machinery and the judiciary, as well as non-governmental organizations will be undertaken. Other measures will include:

(a) Promoting societal awareness to gender issues and women's human rights.

(b) Review of curriculum and educational materials to include gender education and human rights issues

(c) Removal of all references derogatory to the dignity of women from all public documents and legal instruments.

(d) Use of different forms of mass media to communicate social messages relating to women's equality and empowerment.

Panchayati Raj Institutions

The 73rd and 74th Amendments (1993) to the Indian Constitution have served as a breakthrough towards ensuring equal access and increased participation in political power structure for women. The PRIs will play a central role in the process of enhancing women's participation in public life. The PRIs and the local self Governments will be actively involved in the implementation and execution of the National Policy for Women at the grassroots level.

VOLUNTARY SECTOR ORGANIZATIONS

The involvement of voluntary organizations, associations, federations, trade unions, non-governmental organizations, women's organizations, as well as institutions dealing with education, training and research will be ensured in the formulation, implementation, monitoring and review of all policies and programmes affecting women. Towards this end, they will be provided with appropriate support related to resources and capacity building and facilitated to participate actively in the process of the empowerment of women.

International Cooperation

The Policy will aim at implementation of international obligations/commitments in all sectors on empowerment of women such as the Convention on All Forms of Discrimination Against Women (CEDAW), Convention on the Rights of the Child (CRC), International Conference on Population and Development (ICPD+5) and other such instruments. International, regional and sub-regional cooperation towards the empowerment of women will continue to be encouraged through sharing of experiences, exchange of ideas and technology, networking with institutions and organizations and through bilateral and multi-lateral partnerships.

7

Child Labour and Government

There are more children under the age of fourteen in India than the entire population of the United States. The great challenge of India, as a developing country, is to provide nutrition, education and health care to these children. Children under fourteen constitute around 3.6% of the total labour force in India. Of these children, nine out of every ten work in their own rural family settings. Nearly 85% are engaged in traditional agricultural activities. Less than 9% work in manufacturing, services and repairs. Only about 0.8% work in factories.

While child labour is a complex problem that is basically rooted in poverty, there is unwavering commitment by the Government and the people of India to combat it. Success can be achieved only through social engineering on a major scale combined with national economic growth. International policies and actions, therefore, must support and not hamper India's efforts to get rid of child labour.

India has all along followed a pro-active policy with respect to the problem of child labour, and has stood for constitutional, statutory and developmental measures to combat child labour. Six ILO conventions relating to child labour have been ratified,, three of these as early as the first quarter of this century. The first Act in India relating to child labour was the Enactment of Children (Pledging of Labour) Act of February 1933. Since then there have been nine different Indian legislations relating to child labour. The strategy of progressive elimination of child labour underscores India's legislative intent, and takes cognizance of the fact that child labour is not an isolated phenomenon that can be tackled without simultaneously taking into account the socioeconomic milieu that is at the root of the problem.

The Government of India is determined to eradicate child labour in the country. The world's largest child labour elimination programme is being implemented at the grass roots level in India, with primary education targeted for nearly 250 million. In this a large number of non-governmental and voluntary organizations are involved. Special investigation cells have been set up in States to enforce existing laws banning employment of children in hazardous industries. The allocation of the Government of India for the elimination of child labour was $10 million in 1995-96 and $16 million in 1996-97. The allocation for the current year is $21 million.

The International Programme on Elimination of Child Labour (IPEC) has the world's largest international initiative on child labour in India. The total outlay under this programme between 1992 and 1996 has been $4.15 million.

CHILD LABOUR AND CHILD ABUSE

Child labour and child abuse could be treated separately due to its magnitude and shame they leave on the society. But for convenience, they are being dealt with together. These are major problems of children which need special attention by development workers. Besides, the entire society has the responsibility to provide for the establishment of a better society where children are treated with care, bye and dignity. The suffering, despair and the resignation that are part of the children of slums are enormous and frightening. They have deep-seated lack of confidence in adults, even though they have great deal of patience in coping with tremendous adversity. They can overcome the existing social, educational and even economic chaos that can be immediately felt by a conscious person who visits any slum. Children are the future of the community. But child labour destroys the vitality of children and they become old without enjoying the charms and joys of childhood.

Child labour is a unaccounted force in unorganised sector and a by-product of industrial growth. When majority of the population in the slums are poor, it is only natural that children enter into labour force at a very early age and many children accept strenuous labour to escape starvation. Alarming sights of starvation problems had been visible to the social workers when they visited certain interior slum pockets when the Agency started its Projects. Girl children were severely affected than boys and adults. A starving body consumes itself, devour its own fat and muscles and a girl child has less fat to support the body, the skin begins to lose elasticity and sag. Loss of fat around the eyes starts to wringkle in. The protein-vitamin-mineral deficiency leads to swollen legs and ankles, caused by fluid leaking from blood vessels into the body starvation advances in a girl child, the body tries to conserve energy by limiting all but the most vital process. Because starving children are so severely disrupted, it takes more than good meals to revitalise them. They need constant care and love. But in an absolutely poor slum family, who would give them protection and care? Hence, they try to fetch for themselves and many children, including girl children, to escape from acute starvation, join labour force which is long, ardorous and back breaking. If work is not available, a number of them become rag pickers or lead a life of urchins and delinquents. Those who jointed the labour force would be treated like adults. So in a wider sense, child labour itself is child abuse; the society abuses the childhood without giving them an opportunity for intellectual and emotional growth, meaningful recreation, sufficient food and education.

In the given Projects, there were special programmes for the development of children under six years of age, in the way of proper health care programme, recreation and pre-school education. For children in the age group of six to twelve years, apart from getting them enrolled in schools, there were school dropouts education, casework and group work programmes. Little more than 80 per cent of school dropouts, belonging to this age group were helped to return to various schools and proper vigil was observed in retaining them in schools. When the Agency started its work, a large number of such children were found to be in the workforce.

They were also engaged in rag picking, construction work, fruit and vegetable vending, working in road-side tea-shops, various types of repairing, automobile and mechanic work, beedi manufacturing, etc. Most of them worked for 10 to 14 hours a day. The initial problem of the Agency was to meet them face to face, because most of the time they were not available in their huts or slum. The Agency tried to establish contact with them through community volunteers. In order to bring them together a community sports-*cum*-cultural programme for children was organised on a common festival day with various competitions and attractive prizes. Nearly 75 per cent of the children of these slums could participate in various events. Stopping them from work at that point without proper incentives and alternative help was found not appropriate by these Agency.

At the same time, they could not be left out of the process of sustainable development. Besides, most of them were from extremely poor families where the parents had no income or were not capable of supporting them due to illness, or destitution. To escape from starvation, it was necessary for them to start working at that tender age. It had also been observed that some of those children opted for a free life with runaway boys from schools. They were not giving their earning to their parents. They used to rob front their homes or neighbours and spent the money on gambling or any other mischievous activities. Such children were introduced to group work and group games by the social workers and regular recreational activities for atleast an hour had been organised every day. When they gradually developed interest in group activities and games, they began to spend more time with the social workers. Meanwhile a non-formal and vocational training programmes were started for them and the children were given nominal financial incentives. Simultaneously, the most needy families of these children were helped to take up self-employment or other income generation programmes. Such monetary incentives and economic benefits or improvement enabled them to be comparatively free from their work. This was the time when they were engaged to involve in other development efforts. Those who were getting regular income were encouraged to save a part of it. Some sort of non-formal education facilities were provided to them occasionally in the evening hours. A few of the elderly children were helped to learn certain skills such as operation of video cameras and shooting, T.V. and V.C.R. repairing and assembling, photography etc. By the end of the project work, nearly 80 per cent of working children could be brought under a network of regular recreational and cultural programmes in order to strengthen their future.

The agency also dealt with the problem of child abuse. Child abuse has various dimensions among the urban poor. The possibilities and actual incidents of a child being abused at home, neighbourhood, or in the slum itself is a very high. Due to misery and day to day struggle for a meal and proper work, the parents get less time or give insufficient attention to their children. The very nature of family environment creates untold tensions and either of the parents take out this tension on children. This is quiet true in this case of the girl child. The abuse of the girl child is very common among the slum dwellers where the Agency was working and the social workers undertook a detailed study on the problem. It was started in November 1985 and continued by the end of December 1990. The geographical area of the study comprised of nine slums in Nagpur City. The research team consisted of the authors and 10 other social workers, majority of them being women. The main objectives of the study were:

(a) To find out the extent of girl child abuse and to perceive what happens inside the home where the girl child abuse usually takes place.

(b) To know the personality characteristics and social background of girl children battered by their parents.

(c) To find out whether the parents could respond to treatment.

(d) To verify whether or not the family could be held together without further risk to the girl child.

(e) To demark the various ways through which the battered girl child can be helped.

An initial survey was carried out by the social workers in 1985 and identified 5208 households in these nine slums where girl child abuse had been occurring. 680 families and 720 girl children whose both the Parents were alive were randomly selected from these households for the present study for a duration of five years. Interview schedule and observation schedule were the main tools and interviewing and observing were the methods used for the study. The incidence of the girl child abuse was measured by the occurrence of any of the following acts during a six month period, such as kicking, striking with hand or an object, punching, burning, pouring hot water or oil, threatening with a weapon or tool, attacking with a stone, stick or dangerous material, physical assault, sexual molestation, rape, etc. Although the family by its very nature tends to be high in conflict, girl child abuse is only one method of dealing with conflict.

It has been observed that there was severe marital tension in most of the households in these slums. Little more than half the number of husbands studied were violent to their wives. About 64 per cent of the men consumed alcoholic drinks every day and 29 per cent of them had extra marital relations. 74 per cent of fathers themselves had suffered from severe physical maltreatment and rejection from their parents, severe disciplinc and resultant emotional breakdown. A great majority suffered from extreme poverty. The data show that in 53 per cent of households, psychological maladjustments and serious behavioural problems in one or both the parents contributed severe girl child abuse. Hence, parents were to a large extent responsible for girl child abuse. The study further reveals that 73 per cent of fathers and two third of mothers were aggressive. These parents had experienced rejection, cruelty, physical and mental maltreatment in their own childhood. 81 per cent of mothers who experienced cruelty from their mothers treated their girl children with gross forms or physical maltreatment. It shows that they usually took revenge upon their mothers by battering their girl children for the childhood abuses they experienced from their mothers.

The study revealed that 87 per cent of the mothers were married before they were 18 years of age and became mothers of an average five children with eight to nine years. The families were overcrowded and poor. Agonising incidents and deprivation of food, cloth, shelter and love and hunted their family life. Their parenthood reinforced their hatred towards others, especially on their own girl children. They lacked self-respect and understanding. The data indicate that becoming mothers of more than three children was not the need of 92 per cent of mothers, but they were forced to become mothers by their husbands. In their native villages in Chhattisgarh, Telangana, Chandrapur or Gadchiroli, they suffered due to material want, hence they migrated to the city and moved frequently in various slums. About 63 per cent of mothers realised that their husband did not love of support them, yet they had to feed many mouths; 69 per cent felt lack of emotional and/or physical support of loving consideration and care of husbands. About 53 per cent felt lonely even in crowd. These unfit mothers had an impaired ability to love and support their children and expected to be loved by the girl children rather than to love them. The data show that 81 per cent of the battered girl children were born to young mothers ill prepared for motherhood and who had not availed any accepted method of family planning programmes. It has also been observed that a particular girl child, handicapped, sickly and illiterate might be the scapegoat, but sometimes her sisters also suffered physical and psychological damage due to battering. It was found that frequent crying and continuous illness created frustration in about 53 per cent of parents. Regular waking at night leads to mother loss of sleep in 39 per cent. Feeding problems and vomiting after feeds created anger and dejection followed by battering in 66 per cent of cases.

Regular quarrel between father and mother and father's domination and physical torture often lead toward battering of the girl child by the mother in 62 per cent of the cases. It has been found that in a little more than three fourth of the cases, parents who suffered economic hardships, social and emotional stress, inferiority, extreme fatigue, suspicion, pervasive anxiety and depression, physically abused girl children. While immaturity and aggression were predominant personal characteristics of battered parents, fear anxiety, suspicion, submission and depression were the prominent psychological characteristics of the battered girl child.

It was found that separating a child, who suffered from traumatic battering from her parents was always beneficial if the substitute care provided adequately for the child needs. Social casework and or counselling with the immature and cruel parents was not sufficient. The battered children themselves required the social work intervention to understand

and experience that it was possible to trust an adult and that adult could love and care a child without selfish motives. A child needed professional help to inculcate the awareness that being a girl was nothing to be ashamed of or girl childrens always fell victims of adults. They also needed the help of a grown up person, who was a professional in coping with anger frustration, powerlessness, fear and loneliness which might often created much fear in the mind of the battered girl child.

Some of our social workers showed considerable sensitivity in helping the girl children by reducing the stresses in the total family situation and forming a helpful relationship with the parents. A few social workers showed varying degrees of authoritarianism.

Hence, they were not that successful in reducing the tension in the family and the resultant child abuse. Some others found it difficult to accept the reality if child abuse and reacted with anxiety which limited their ability to help the girl child or control the behaviour of her parents. But to a certain extent, the trained and skilful social workers could intervene successfully in reducing the incidents and severity of child battering, On the whole, much enthusiasms was shown by the social workers to initiate measures to protect the child from bruises, fractures, burns, or mental shocks. There was fear among some of' the social workers that their frequent visit and observation of battered girl children and their batterers could increase family stress and tension in the family and which may increase subsequent child abuse. Even after completing the present study, during our work, it has been observed that a good number of slum children were often left at the care of elder children and were totally neglected by parents.

In such situation, a problem child gets beaten up by the elder children. Anti-social elements also attack or abuse such a child. For some cases it was noticed that children, especially girl children were abused or sexually molested by adults or teenagers.

There had been cases of children under six years of age, raped by adolescents or adults when parents were away. Thus, children were kept at the mercy of persons who were not their parents often showed a tendency to abuse them. The problems of child abuse were tackled by creating general awareness among the people discussing with parents of vulnerable children under safe custody, forming conscious group of women in the locality keeping a watch on such situations and giving the overall responsibility to the mahila mandals. The grass-roots workers were also educated and equipped to report such cases of rape and assault or' children to the police or to prevent such victimisations. To equip the community to keep a close watch on anti-social youth and adults is a very import a at aspect of preventing and controlling child abuse.

CHILD LABOUR STUDY

According to the Indian census of 1991, there are 11.28 million working children under the age of fourteen years in India. Over 85% of this child labour is in the country's rural areas, working in agricultural activities such as fanning, livestock rearing, forestry and fisheries. This labour is outside the formal sector, and outside industry. Moreover, nine out of ten working children work within a family setting. Working in family-based occupations, these children also develop skills in certain traditional crafts, thus augmenting the human capital formation of India's developing economy.

India has all along followed a pro-active policy in the matter of tackling the problem of child labour. India has always stood for constitutional, statutory and development measures required to eliminate child labour. The Indian Constitution has consciously incorporated provisions to secure compulsory universal elementary education as well as labour protection for children. Labour Commissions in India have gone into the problems of child labour and have made extensive recommendations.

In India, the post-independence era has seen an unequivocal commitment of the government to the cause of children through constitutional provisions, legislation, policies and programmes. The Constitution of India in Article 39 of the Directive Principles of State Policy pledges that "the State shall, in particular, direct its policy towards securing... that the health and strength of workers, men and women, and the tender age of children are not abused, and that citizens are not forced by economic necessity to enter avocations unsuited to their age or strength, that children are given opportunities and facilities to develop in a healthy manner, and in conditions of freedom and dignity, and that childhood and youth are protected against exploitation, and against moral and material abandonment."

As a follow-up of this commitment, and being a party to the UN Declaration on the Rights of the Child 1959, India adopted the National Policy on Children in 1974. The policy reaffirmed the constitutional provisions and stated that "it shall be the policy of the State to provide adequate services to children, both before and after birth and through the period of growth to ensure their full physical, mental and social development. The State shall progressively increase the scope of such services so that within a reasonable time all children in the country enjoy optimum conditions for their balanced growth."

India has also ratified on December 2, 1992, the Convention on the Rights of the Child which came into force in 1990. This ratification implies that India will ensure wide awareness about issues relating to children among government agencies, implementing agencies, the media, the judiciary, the public and children themselves. The Government's endeavour is to meet the goals of the Convention and to amend all legislation, policies and schemes to meet the standards set in the Convention.

India is also a signatory to the World Declaration on the Survival, Protection and Development of Children. In pursuance of the commitment made at the World Summit, the Department of Women and Child Development under the Ministry of Human Resource Development has formulated a National Plan of Action for Children. Most of the recommendations of the World Summit Action Plan are reflected in India's National Plan of Action.

India's policy on child labour has evolved over the years against this backdrop and its present regime of laws relating to child labour has a pragmatic foundation, consistent with the International Labour Conference resolution of 1979. This ILO resolution calls for a combination of prohibitory measures and measures for humanizing child labour, wherever such labour cannot be eliminated altogether in the short turn.

It should also be mentioned that India is second to none in its commitment to and in the upholding of the core international labour standards such as freedom of association, collective bargaining, non-discrimination, etc. India is signatory to a record 36 ILO labour conventions.

The Child Labour (Prohibition & Regulation) Act, 1986 of India prohibits the employment of children below the age of 14 in factories, mines and in other forms of hazardous employment, and regulates the working conditions of children in other employment. India has announced a National Policy of Child Labour as early as 1987, and was probably the first among the developing countries to have such a progressive policy.

Through a notification dated May 26, 1993, the working conditions of children have been regulated in all employment not prohibited under the Child Labour (Prohibition and Regulation) Act. Further, following up on a preliminary notification issued on October 5, 1993, the government has also prohibited employment of children in occupations such as abattoirs/slaughter houses, printing, cashew de-scaling and processing, and soldering.

The announcement by the Prime Minister on India's Independence Day in 1994 that child labour would be abolished in hazardous occupations by the year 2000, reflects a national consensus and commitment. After this declaration, several far-reaching initiatives have been taken by the Government to effectively tackle the problem.

With the setting up of the National Authority for the Elimination of Child Labour (NAECL) under the Chairmanship of the Labour Minister, Government of India, a convergence of services and schemes for eliminating child labour is being achieved. The NAECL, comprising representatives from the Central Ministries, meets the need for an umbrella organization to coordinate the efforts of the different arms of the Government for the progressive elimination of child labour.

The child labour programme in India is national in character and involves the Government of India,, the governments of the States and the Union Territories of India, as well as such tripartite fora as the Indian Labour Conference and the Standing Labour Committee. A massive national and regional media campaign has been launched to sensitize society against child labour. Funds have been allocated to districts identified as child-labour endemic for surveys to identify child labour, and for awareness generation programmes among employers, parents and the working children themselves.

This paper covers the significant aspects of India's constitutional and legislative provisions relating to child labour, the enforcement of these provisions, and programmes being undertaken nationwide to eliminate child labour.

India's first act on the subject was the enactment of the Children (Pledging of Labour) Act of February 1933. This was followed by the Employment of Children Act in 1938. Subsequently, twelve additional legislations were passed that progressively extended legal protection to children. Provisions relating to child labour under various enactment such as the Factories Act, the Mines Act, the Plantation Labour Act etc. have concentrated on aspects such as reducing working hours, increasing minimum wage and prohibiting employment of children in occupations and processes detrimental to their health and development.

The Child Labour (Prohibition & Regulation) Act 1986 of India was the culmination of efforts and ideas that emerged from the deliberations and recommendations of various committees on child labour. Significant among them are the National Commission on Labour (1966-69), Gurupadaswamy Committee on Child Labour (1979), and the Sanat Mehta Committee (1984).

The Act aims to prohibit the entry of children into hazardous occupations and to regulate the services of children in non-hazardous occupations. The Act,, in particular,

- Bans the employment of children, *i.e.* those who have not completed their 14th year, in specified occupations and processes;
- Lays down a procedure to make additions to the schedule of banned occupations or processes;
- Regulates the working conditions of children in occupations where they are not prohibited from working;
- Lays down penalties for employment of children in violation of the provisions of this Act,, and other Acts which forbid the employment of children;

- Brings uniformity in the definition of the "Child" in related laws.

The protective legal provisions for working children in other laws are listed.

Government of India's Policies and Actions

The National Child Labour Policy: Increasing attention is now being paid to strengthening the enforcement machinery related to child labour.

Soon after the enactment of the comprehensive Child Labour (Prohibition & Regulation) Act, 1986, the Government of India adopted a National Child Labour policy in 1987, in accordance with the constitutional provisions and various legislation on child labour.

The idea of adopting a separate policy on child labour was not only to place the issue on the nation's agenda, but also to formulate a specific programme of action to initiate the process of progressive elimination of child labour. The policy consists of three complementary measures:

- *Legal Action Plan*: This policy envisages strict enforcement of the provisions of the Child Labour (Prohibition & Regulation) Act, 1986 and other child-related legislation.
- *Focus on General Development Programmes Benefiting Children Wherever Possible:* The policy envisages the development of an extensive system of non-formal education for working children withdrawn from work and increasing the provision for employment and income generating schemes meant for their parents. A special cell-Child Labour Cell-was constituted to encourage voluntary organizations to take up activities like non-formal education,-vocational training, provisions of health care, nutrition and education for working children.
- *Area Specific Projects:* To focus on areas known to have high concentration of child labour and to adopt a project approach for identification, withdrawal and rehabilitation of working children.

CENTRAL ADVISORY BOARD ON CHILD LABOUR

The Central Advisory Board on Child Labour was constituted on March 4, 1981. The following are the terms of reference of the Board:

- Review the implementation of the existing legislation administered by the Central Government.
- Suggest legislative measures as well as welfare measures for the welfare of working children.
- Review the progress of welfare measures for working children.
- Recommend the industries and areas where there must be a progressive elimination of child labour.

The Board was reconstituted last on November 2, 1994. The Union Labour Minister is the Chairman of the Board.

The other Members of the Board include representatives from the various sister ministries, Members of Parliament, non-governmental organizations, representatives of major trade unions and employers' organizations.

Child Labour Technical Advisory Committee: Under Section 5 of the Child Labour (P&R) Act 1986, the Government of India is empowered to constitute a Child Labour Technical Advisory Committee for the purpose of addition of occupation and processes in the Schedule to the Act. The Committee consists of a Chairman and members not exceeding ten. The Committee has been reconstituted on February 5,,1996 under the chairmanship of Director General of Indian Council of Medical Research.

National Child Labour Projects (NCLP): Under the action plan of the National Policy on Child Labour, there have been National Child Labour Projects (NCLP) set up in different areas to rehabilitate child labour. A major activity undertaken under the NCLP is the establishment of special schools to provide non-formal education, vocational training, supplementary nutrition etc. to children withdrawn from employment. Under the project based action plan of the policy, 12 NCLPs were started in the States of Andhra Pradesh (Jaggampet and Markapur), Bihar (Garwah), Madhya Pradesh (Mandsaur), Maharashtra (Thane), Orissa (Sambalpur),

Rajasthan (Jaipur), Tamil Nadu (Sivakasi) and Uttar Pradesh (Varanasi-Mirzapur-Bhadohi,, Moradabad, Aligarh and Ferozabad).

REHABILITATION OF HAZARDOUS OCCUPATIONS

A major programme was launched on 15th August 1994 for withdrawing child labour working in hazardous occupations and for rehabilitating them through special schools. Under the programme a total of two million children are sought to be brought out of work and put in special schools where they will be provided with education, vocational training, monthly stipends, nutrition and health-checks. As a follow-up, a high powered body, the National Authority for the Elimination of Child Labour (NAECL) was constituted on 26th September, 1994 under the Chairmanship of the Minister for Labour, Government of India. The functions of NAECL are:

- To lay down policies and programmes for the elimination of child labour, particularly in hazardous employment
- To monitor the progress of the implementation of programmes, projects and schemes for the elimination of child labour;
- To coordinate the implementation of child labour related projects of the various sister Ministries of the Government of India (to ensure convergence of services for the benefit of the families of child labour)

Secretaries to Government of India in the Ministries of Labour, Information & Broadcasting, Welfare, Rural Development, Textiles and the Departments of Expenditure, Education, Health, Family Welfare and Women & Child Development are members of the National Authority for the Elimination of Child Labour. The NAECL has already met five times on October 1, 1994, November 1, 1994, January 1, 1995, July 10,1995 and December 31, 1996.

Present Coverage Under National Child Labour Project: So far 76 child labour projects have been sanctioned under the National Child Labour Project Scheme for covering 150,000 children. Around 105,000 children are already enrolled in the special schools. The figures of the state-wise coverage of children under the National Child Labour Project.

Coverage under National Child Labour Project

State	*Districts*	*Sanctioned Schools*	*Coverage Children*	*Actual Schools*	*Coverage Children*
Andhra Pradesh	20	807	43550	610	36249
Bihar	08	174	12200	173	10094
Gujarat	02	040	2000	023	1254
Karnataka	03	100	5000	024	1200
Madhya Pradesh	05	138	9800	087	6524
Maharashtra	02	074	3700	024	1200
Orissa	16	430	33000	239	14972
Rajasthan	02	060	3000	054	2700
Tamil Nadu	08	379	19500	307	14684
Uttar Pradesh	04	150	11500	105	7488
West Bengal	04	219	12000	164	8250
Total	76	2571	155250	1810	104615

Assistance to Voluntary Organizations: Under the grant-in-aid scheme, voluntary organizations are being financially assisted to the extent of 75% of the project cost for taking up welfare projects for working children where the children are provided with education, supplementary nutrition, health care and vocational/skill training. The voluntary organizations, which were extended assistance under the scheme during 1996-97 (up to December 1996), are:

1. The Congregation of the Sisters of the Cross of Chavanad, Tiruchirapalli, Tamil Nadu
2. Indian Council for Child Welfare, New Delhi
3. Karnataka State Council for Child Welfare, Bangalore, Karnataka
4. India International Rural Centre, New Delhi
5. Vivekananda Education Society, Calcutta, West Bengal
6. Shramik Vikas Sewa Ashram, Allahabad,, Uttar Pradesh
7. Gramin Sansadhan Vikas Parishad, Buxur, Bihar
8. United Club, Ujini, Orissa
9. Jibaramjee Club, Orissa
10. Gram Vikas Seva Samity, Allahabad, Uttar Pradesh
11. Karimpur Social Welfare Society, District Nadia, West Bengal

12. Indian Council for Child Welfare, Tamil Nadu
13. ViJayapuram Praja Seva Samithi, Chittoor, Andhra Pradesh
14. Bandhuwa Mukti Morcha, New Delhi
15. Rafi Ahmed Kidwai Shiksha Samiti, Khurda, Bhopal, Madhya Pradesh
16. Gram Swaraj Abhiyan Sansthan, Baishali, Bihar
17. Mahatma Gandhi Khadi & Gramodyog Samity, Khurda, Orissa
18. Gopal Samaj Kalyan Pratishthan, Nalanda, Bihar
19. Mithila Gram Vikas Parishad, Darbhanga, Bihar
20. Navachaitanya Academy for Youth Advancement, Visakhapatnam, Andhra Pradesh
21. All India Santhan Welfare & Cultural Society, New Delhi
22. Unemployed Young Workers' Society, Burdwan, West Bengal
23. Village Reconstruction & Development Project, Salem, Tamil Nadu
24. Daroga Prasad Roy Mahila Prashikshan Avam Audogik Kendra, District Saran, Bihar
25. Manab Seva Sadan, Dhenkanal, Orissa
26. Bagmari Youth Progressive Association, Calcutta
27. Bhagra Diamond Club, Burdwan, West Bengal
28. Social Environmental and Rural Technology Council, Pallel, Manipur
29. Manorama Mahila Mandal, Vaishali

BUDGETARY SUPPORT

A plan provision of Rs. 150 million was made for child labour elimination programme in India's Eighth Five-Year Plan (1992-93 and 1996-97). The budgetary allocation was substantially stepped up after the launching of programme in August 1994 for the rehabilitation of child labour working in hazardous occupations. The allocation during 1995-96 and 1996-97 was of the order of Rs.344 million and Rs.560 million. As against this, the actual expenditure for these two years was of the order of Rs.343 million and Rs.338 million respectively. The allocation for 1997-98 is Rs.784 million. (In 1995-96 and 1996-97, \$1= Rs.35 approximately. In 1997-98, \$1 = Rs. 37 approximately).

STATUS OF FREE AND COMPULSORY EDUCATION

India's National Policy on Education, 1986 gives the highest priority to the programme of universal elementary education, and recommends that free and compulsory education of sufficient quality be provided to all children up to the age of 14 years before we enter the 21st century. The present thrust is on three aspects, namely, universal access and enrolment, universal retention of children up to 14 years of age, and substantial improvement in the quality of education to enable all children to achieve essential levels of learning. All these aspects have been incorporated in the various initiatives taken up by the Ministry of Human Resource Development.

All the State Governments have abolished tuition fees in government schools up to the upper primary level Education. In schools run by local bodies and private-aided institutions is almost free. However, unaided institutions (3 to 7%) do charge fees. Compulsory Education Acts have been enacted in 14 states and 4 Union Territories *viz.* Assam, Andhra Pradesh, Bihar, Delhi, Gujarat, Haryana, Jammu & Kashmir, Karnataka, Madhya Pradesh, Maharashtra, Punjab, Rajasthan, Tamil Nadu, Kerala, West Bengal, Chandigarh, Pondicherry and Andaman and Nicobar Islands.

SUPREME COURT DIRECTIONS

The Supreme Court of India, in its judgement dated 10th December, 1996 in Writ Petition (Civil) Number 465/1986, has given certain directions regarding the manner in which children working in the hazardous occupations are to be withdrawn from work and rehabilitated, and the manner in which the working conditions of children working in non-hazardous occupations are to be regulated and improved. The judgement of the Supreme Court envisages:

(a) Simultaneous action in all districts of the country;

(b) Survey for identification of working children (to be completed by June 10, 1997)

(c) Withdrawal of children working in hazardous industries and ensuring their education in appropriate institutions;

(d) Contribution of Rs.20,000 per child to be paid by the offending employers of children to a welfare fund to be established for this purpose;

(e) Employment to one adult member of the family of the child so withdrawn from work, and if that is not possible a contribution of Rs.5000 to the welfare fund to be made by the State Government;

(f) Financial assistance to the families of the children so withdrawn to be paid out of the interest earnings on the corpus of Rs.20,,000/25,000.00 deposited in the welfare fund as long as the child is actually sent to the schools;

(g) Regulating hours of work for children working in non-hazardous occupations so that their working hours do not exceed six hours per day and education for at least two hours is ensured. The entire expenditure on education is to be borne by the concerned employer;

(h) Planning and preparedness on the part of Central and State Governments in terms of strengthening of the existing administrative/regulatory/enforcement framework (covering cost of additional manpower, training, mobility, computerization etc.) implying additional requirement of funds.

Follow up Action on the Directions of the Supreme Court

As a follow up of the directions of the Supreme Court, all the State Governments were sent detailed guidelines on December 26, 1996 indicating the manner in which the directions of the Supreme Court were to be implemented. A meeting of the NAECL was convened on 31st December 1996 to discuss the directions of the Supreme Court on child labour. It was decided in the meeting that the Ministry of Labour should immediately release funds to the State Governments so as to enable them to conduct surveys of working children before June 10, 1997. A conference of the Labour Ministers of State/ Union Territories was convened on January 22,1997 to finalize an action plan for the implementation of the directions of the Supreme Court on withdrawal and rehabilitation of working children. In the conference, all the participating States and Union Territories welcomed the judgement and demonstrated their political will to eliminate child labour.

However, all the States pleaded for additional and liberal financial assistance from the Central Government for implementing the judgement of the Supreme Court. The following significant recommendations were made in the Conference:

- The survey envisaged in the judgement of the Supreme Court would be in two phases. In the first phase the survey would be conducted in all industries, establishments, shops, work places in urban and semi-urban catchment areas where hazardous processes will be identified. In the event of any child labour being found employed in any such process, simultaneous action would be taken to recover an amount of R.20,000/from the offending employer. Hazardous establishments in the rural areas would also be fully covered by the survey in the first phase. The door-to-door survey for the purpose of identification and enumeration of working children will be taken up in the second phase.
- While primarily it is the responsibility of the State Governments to provide necessary funds for taking up activities in compliance of the directions of the Supreme Court, funds for conducting the survey will be released by the Central Government to the agencies at the district level immediately. If the funds released for the first phase of survey fall short of the actual requirement in any district, the State Governments will provide the additional funds for this purpose. Since this first phase of the survey is concentrated on industrial establishments, the requirement of funds would be worked out by the Central Government and the same would be released immediately.
- Immediate action will be initiated by the State Governments for strengthening the enforcement machinery at various levels and for creation of a separate cell at the State level to monitor and coordinate the activities to be taken up in compliance of the directions of the Supreme Court. They will also send their

requirements of funds in this regard, if any, to the Planning Commission at the earliest.

- If the State Governments are not in a position to complete the survey by 10th June, they will apprise the Hon'ble Supreme Court about the reasons for delay and seek extension of time from the Hon'ble Supreme Court well in advance.
- If for some reason, the State Governments find it difficult to give effect to any one or more directions of the Supreme Court, they will seek necessary clarification/directions from the Hon'ble Supreme Court well in time.

As a follow-up of the decision taken in the State Labour Ministers' Conference, the Chief Secretaries of State and Union Territories have been sent detailed guidelines for carrying out the survey as per the directions of the Supreme Court. A copy of the child labour survey form has also been sent to the Governments of State and Union Territories. Funds have been released to all the State and Union Territories governments for the purpose of conducting the surveys. The Chief Secretaries were specifically instructed that if the State Governments could not complete the surveys in time, they should apprise the Supreme Court through an affidavit about the reasons for delay and seek extension of time from the Supreme Court well in advance.

INTERNATIONAL PROGRAMME FOR THE ELIMINATION OF CHILD LABOUR

The International Programme on the Elimination of Child Labour is a global programme launched by the International Labour Organization in December 1991. India was the first country to join it in 1992 when it signed a Memorandum of Understanding with the ILO. The long-term objective of IPEC is to contribute to the effective abolition of child labour. Its immediate objectives are:

- Elimination of the capability of ILO constituents and Non-Government Organizations to design, implement and evaluate programmes for Child Labour Elimination;
- To identity interventions at community and national levels which could serve as models for replication; and

- Creation of awareness and social mobilization for securing elimination of child labour.

At the international level, IPEC has a Programme Steering Committee consisting of representatives of the ILO, the donors and participating countries. At the national level in India,, there is a National Steering Committee of which the Labour Secretary is the Chairman. This is tripartite in its composition with representation from NGOs as well. There is a National Programme Coordinator based at New Delhi who coordinates IPEC work between the Ministry of Labour, the agencies receiving assistance and ILO Headquarters.

ILO has made an allocation of $4.15 million between 1992 and 1996 for the IPEC programme in India: State-wise projects under IPEC and number of children covered (92-97)

State	*Projects approved*	*No. of Children*
Andhra Pradesh	15	15455
Bihar	3	1340
Delhi	6	4200
Gujarat	5	1350
Haryana	1	300
Karnataka	2	1320
Kerala	2	2000
Madhya Pradesh	6	2050
Manipur	1	500
Maharashtra	7	1750
Orissa	4	1500
Rajasthan	7	5800
Tamil Nadu	17	6710
Uttar Pradesh	11	13939
West Bengal	19	22890
Regional	2	NA
All India Institutions	11	NA
Total	120	81154

As per the Memorandum of Understanding between the Government of India and the ILO, the IPEC programme was to continue till December 3 1, 1996. The MOU was extended on January 28, 1997, until December 31, 1997 in the first instance. Thereafter, the MOU continues with mutual agreement.

RISK FACTORS FOR SEVERE CHILD IN RURAL INDIA

Although the vulnerability of children to abusive practices is recognized in the Indian constitution, most research to date has focused on children's survival needs and societal abuses, such as malnutrition, child labour, child beggary, child marriage, and child prostitution (Banerjee, 1979; Bhattacharyya, 1979, 1983; Gupta, 1977; Jabbi, 1986; Mehta, Lokeshwar, Bhatt, Athavale, & Kulkarni, 1979). A few early clinical studies of child injuries suggested that some maltreatment of children may be the result of harsh discipline from family members (Bhattacharyya, 1983; Dave, Dave, & Mishra, 1982). At around the same time, Poffenberger (1981) offered one of the first candid observations of parental discipline practices in his report of child rearing in rural India.

In this qualitative investigation, parents described discipline practices they deemed acceptable and unacceptable. Whereas physical punishment was the norm and considered necessary for the socialization of children, the villagers spoke of punishments that they considered to be overly harsh including threats to send children away, invocations of ghosts and evil spirits to do the child harm, holding burning sticks to penises to control masturbation, branding, and hanging by hands or feet. Threats of death were also common.

Suman (1985), noting the paucity of systematic and quantitative data related to child physical and emotional abuse in India, called for research to document the prevalence of these phenomena and to identify the interacting factors that support or discourage child maltreatment within the family environment. In response, several investigators have conducted small studies investigating the extent to which harsh and abusive practices occur within the context of normal child rearing and socialization. Because there are no universal standards related to optimal child rearing or what might be considered child maltreatment, these early studies confronted the need to balance cultural norms against the well-being of children. Segal's progression of empirical studies has shed considerable light on the extent of harsh child discipline practices and the perceptions of the public and professionals regarding what constitutes abusive behaviour. Investigating cultural definitions of child abuse in India, Segal found very little difference in the perceptions of severity for different forms of child abuse among social workers, other human service workers, and other service workers (Segal, 1992). Cross-cultural comparisons with a similar U.S. study indicated that while both Indian and U.S. samples perceived sexual abuse as highest on an abuse scale and inadequate housing conditions as lowest, the rankings of the remaining forms of abuse were influenced by recognition of abuse, national norms, expectations, and the socioeconomic conditions of each country.

Although the U.S. sample ranked physical abuse second in severity in terms of its detrimental effects on the child, the Indian sample ranked it sixth, after sexual abuse, fostering delinquency, medical neglect, poor supervision, and exposing children to parental sexual mores.

A subsequent study that used the Conflict Tactics Scale (Straus, 1979) to investigate the discipline practices of middle-class professionals in India found that 57% engaged in "normal" corporal punishment (spanking, slapping), 42% in "abusive" forms of discipline (kicked, bit, or hit with fist; hit or tried to hit with something; beat up child), and 3% in "extreme" forms of violence (threatened with, or used, a knife or gun on child) (Segal, 1995). Segal observed that these relatively high rates of harsh discipline may reflect societal sanction of violence toward children and the perception that physical abuse has fewer detrimental effects than other forms of abuse.

Yet some parents, like those in Poffenberger's study (1981), may resort to practices that they feel are inappropriate and potentially harmful. Identification of risk and protective factors related to different levels of severity in discipline practices used in India may help address the question of whether severe practices are normative or whether they, at some point, cross a line to become unacceptable or abusive. In this study, risk and protective factors have been conceptualized using an ecological model that attributes family interactions (including child abuse and other family violence) to characteristics of the nested social ecology including the larger society, the local community, the family itself, and finally the characteristics of the involved individuals (Belsky, 1980; Cicchetti & Lynch, 1993; Garbarino, 1977). As in all societies, the treatment of children in India is likely a function of deep-seated cultural norms. Few would deny that there is societal tolerance for the use of corporal punishment, a cultural factor theorized as a risk factor for physical abuse (Zigler & Hall, 1989).

In addition, India is a patrilineal society in which the spiritual, economic, and social norms of everyday life reflect an extreme preference for male offspring and a corresponding denigration of female children. As a result, female children have been at higher risk for selective feticide, infanticide, poorer nutrition, poorer health care, poorer educational opportunities, kidnapping, and forced prostitution (Poffenberger, 1981; Wadley, 1993). However no data indicate that females are more likely to experience harsh parental discipline than their male counterparts. Although Singh and Kaur (1981) found that rural Indian mothers felt that girls need more instruction and discipline than boys, they did not analyze the harshness or severity of actual childrearing practices by gender.

In China, another country where sons are venerated because they are seen as insurance against old age and poverty, boys are more strictly disciplined, perhaps because the stakes connected to their behaviour and success are much higher (Ho, 1996; Tang, 1998; Wu, 1996). It is reasonable to expect that the same family dynamics might contribute to harsher punishment of sons in India.

At the community level, social isolation, lack of social support, and social change, such as migration away from family of origin, have been identified in the United States as risk factors for child abuse (Egeland & Brunquell, 1979; Garbarino & Gilliam, 1980; Starr, 1988). In studies outside the United States, Levinson (1989) found that child abuse is less likely in extended family households where child care responsibilities can be shared. Increasing mobility of Indian families and movement away from extended family structures may increase the parenting stresses once absorbed within the joint family (Sinha, 1984). Other types of stresses that occur at the family level (*e.g.*, alcohol abuse, marital conflict or violence, large family size, and parent psychological problems) have been shown to increase the probability of child abuse (Whipple & Richey, 1997). In a 1985 survey of American families, Straus and Gelles (1990) found that mothers who were victims of partner violence were at least twice as likely to physically abuse their children as mothers who were not.

Harsh discipline and child abuse have also been linked with family or parent socioeconomic characteristics, especially low income (Straus, 1980), low maternal education, closely spaced children, and a high household crowding index.

Characteristics of the child may increase the likelihood of severe discipline or abuse, especially when other risk factors are present. Wolfe has reported that the average age of abuse victims in the United States tends to be younger than the average age of all children (Wolfe, 1987). Others have found age related to discipline practices, with parents more likely to physically discipline younger children and more likely to use nonphysical discipline techniques including verbal abuse with older children (Jackson et al., 1999). Children perceived as being difficult to parent or manage have been identified as being at higher risk, especially when the mother is depressed and has few available supports (Hetherington, 1989). Poor health and handicapping conditions have also been found to be associated with child abuse, possibly because the child is perceived as different or as the source of increased stress (Kotelchuck, 1982). The goal of this study was to determine the type and severity of discipline practices used in this area of central India and to analyze how characteristics of the social ecology are associated with these practices. Based on ecological theory and previous studies, we expected that high levels of family stress (characterized by household crowding, high numbers of children in the household, low numbers of adults in the household, domestic violence, and alcohol abuse) and low levels of community support (characterized by having lived in the community for less than 5 years and by maternal perceptions of poor support from neighbours) would be associated with more severe discipline practices. At the individual level, low parent education, child gender (male), younger child age, child disobedience, and child health problems were also expected to be risk factors for more severe discipline practices.

Method—Study Design and Development

This investigation was a rural pilot study for a larger multiregion study that will ultimately collect data from 10,000 mothers across India. In turn, the Indian project is part of a larger international collaboration, called WorldSAFE (World Studies of Abuse in the Family Environment), which is using a common research protocol to address questions related to family violence and risk factors in the social ecology. WorldSAFE's conceptual framework and study methods have been formulated over a period of years by an international multidisciplinary group of investigators from the International Clinical Epidemiology Network who are dedicated to reducing family violence in countries around the world by advancing understanding of its etiology and impact. Although the core survey instrument focuses primarily on child discipline practices and spousal/partner violence, demographic characteristics and other characteristics of the social ecology hypothesized to be related to family violence (*e.g.*, husband's alcohol abuse, residential stability, neighbourhood support, child disobedience, child health problems, and maternal depression) are also included. The instrument for this study was formulated in English, translated into Marathi, the local language, and then back-translated, by a different professional. Comparisons were made with the original version and modifications implemented wherever necessary to ensure equivalence in meaning between the English and translated version.

Focus Groups

Prior to the development of the survey and the field procedures, focus group discussions were conducted in an attempt to anchor our research methodology to the culture of rural Maharashtra. As others have noted, focus groups and other qualitative methods can enhance quantitative studies by providing direct access to the language and the concepts that participants use in thinking about and describing their experiences. The principal investigator (DJ) conducted the focus groups in three rural villages that were close in proximity to those selected for the survey and believed to be similar in sociodemographic characteristics. Each focus group was composed of a convenience sample of 10-16 mothers recruited from a list of mothers identified by village leaders. The goal of the focus groups was to discover who typically disciplines children in the village, the range of discipline practices employed, and opinions about the acceptability of these practices.

In addition, participants were asked to comment on proposed field procedures for recruitment and data collection. We expected that the discussions would provide access to the language and concepts that these mothers used to describe their interactions with their children and thus inform the final terminology used in the survey questionnaire. A structured discussion guide specifying the order in which topics were to be introduced was prepared by the research team. While the principal investigator served as the moderator in each group, the field interviewers sat on the outside of circle and transcribed the discussions. The data were analyzed by identifying themes that emerged across groups that related to common discipline practices and the perceived appropriateness of these practices.

Procedure

The study was conducted in five villages in the Saoner district of northern Maharashtra in central India. Villages in this district were stratified into two sizes: large (2,000) and small (<2,000). Five villages were randomly selected and proportionately sampled. Households were approached up to three times, to screen for eligibility. Households that included a married woman who had at least one coresiding child under 18 years old were considered eligible. After obtaining permission from the village authorities, trained interviewers approached homes from a standardized starting point, screening for eligible households from all four quadrants until the sample size for that village was reached.

At each eligible household, a census was conducted and names of all residents and their relationships to each other were recorded on a standardized form. When more than one eligible woman resided in the household, the interviewer randomly selected one for interview by using tables of randomly generated numbers that conformed to the number of possible eligible women that might be encountered in a household (2-5 women). For example, for a household that contained three eligible women, the interviewer would use the numerals 1, 2, and 3 listed in random order. She would use the first available number on the list to indicate which woman she should select from among those identified as eligible on the census form. She would then strike through the "used" number, so that in the next household of three eligible women, she would choose the next number on the list. When the selected mother had more than one eligible child, one was randomly selected as the referent child in a similar fashion, using a different set of tables (for 2-10 children). The field supervisor and interviewers were female social workers with prior experience in rural villages. They received extensive standardized training in all aspects of study protocol prior to entry into the field. Following training, the instrument was pretested in 25 households resulting in minor modifications. Because illiteracy was a concern in targeted villages, the informed consent procedure was verbal. Eligible women were invited to participate in a study related to maternal and child health that consisted of an interview on private and sensitive family matters. After receiving consent, all face-to-face interviews were conducted privately, either within or close to the woman's residence. Study methodology was reviewed and received approval by the Ethical Review Board of the Government Medical College in Nagpur.

Measures

Child disciplinary practices were assessed using a modified version of the Parent-Child Conflict Tactics Scale (Straus, Hamby, Finkelhor, Moore, & Runyan, 1998). This has been one of the more commonly used measures of discipline and abusive practices in the United States and it has been previously used in India (Segal, 1995) and in other Asian countries (Tang, 1998). The time frame for self-report was reduced from 1 year to 6 months and the range of response options was condensed from an 8-point scale (ranging from never to more than 20 times in past year) to a 3-point scale (not at all, sometimes, or many times in the last 6 months).

The scale itself was expanded to include 12 additional practices identified by the focus groups as among the strategies employed by mothers in the villages of this area. For this investigation, the discipline practices were classified as belonging to one of five different categories: nonviolent discipline (four items), moderate verbal/psychological aggression (four items); severe verbal/psychological aggression (three items); minor physical aggression (ten items); and severe physical aggression (eight items). Two items (putting chili pepper in the mouth and tying to something) were not classified because the relative severity of these actions was difficult to assess.

The discipline classification schemes were consistent overall with those used by both Straus et al. in U.S. studies (1998) and Segal in Indian studies (1995). For the analyses, the values for the categories of discipline practices were dichotomized (by combining response options, sometimes and many times) to simply indicate whether that mode of discipline was used or not used within the specified time period. Maternal depression was assessed using the 20-item Centre for Epidemiologic Studies-Depression Scale (CES-D) (Radloff, 1977). The standard cutpoint for "caseness" (a score of 16 or higher) was used to classify the mothers as depressed or not depressed.

If the husband was reported to get drunk at least 1-3 days a month, then husband drunkenness was classified as present. Spousal abuse of the mother was classified as present if the mother said she had been slapped, kicked, hit, or beaten by her husband. Neighbourhood support was measured using a 5-item scale (In this neighbourhood... people help each other out, people watch out for each other's children, there are people I can count on, there are people who care about me, and there are people I can talk to about my problems.) These items were scored on a 4-point Likert scale ranging from very much to not at all. For analysis purposes, mothers who responded very much or somewhat to all five items were scored as having "high" support. Mothers who responded very little or not at all to all five items were scored as having "low" support. All others were classified as having "moderate" support.

Mothers were asked to rate the referent child's health on a 3-point scale. In addition, they were asked if the child had any of seven chronic health problems or conditions, including hearing problems, speech problems, vision problems (not corrected by glasses), physical handicap or deformity, mental retardation, chronic condition like asthma or tuberculosis, and polio. A health problem index was created by summing all endorsements from this list. A global rating of poor health was counted as one point on the health problem index; thus, the range for the index extended from 0-8. Child disobedience was examined with one global question: "Compared to other children of the same age, how obedient is s/he?" Response options were more obedient, about average, and less obedient. Demographic data including household characteristics, residential stability, mother's age, mother's and father's level of education, religion, child age, and child gender were based on the mother's response to structured questions within the interview.

Data Analysis

Prior to analyses of data, the internal consistency reliability of the CES-D and the Neighbourhood Support scale (both with unknown psychometric properties in this population) was evaluated by calculating Cronbach's alpha coefficient for each scale. Subsequent analyses included generating descriptive statistics for the variables of interest and conducting univariate tests for association between the dependent variables and the demographic and social context variables considered as potential risk factors. Chi-square tests were used to test for significant associations between categorical variables, and Pearson correlation coefficients and Kruskal-Wallis tests were used for continuous variables. Independent variables that demonstrated a relationship with a dependent variable (at $p < .20$) were selected for further testing in multivariate models. Logistic regression was used to estimate the odds of having used each type of discipline for each predictor variable, while simultaneously controlling for the other variables in the model. Selected independent variables were entered into the model simultaneously, and a backward elimination procedure was used to select the "best" model. Odds ratios (ORs) were calculated to estimate the strength of the association between the different categories of discipline practice and the sociocontextual risk factors.

Results

Focus Group Results: There was consensus in all three focus groups that within local villages mothers are the primary disciplinarians of their children and that scolding, slapping, and beating with a broom, shoe, or stick are the most common punishments. The mothers described a range of other practices also used in their villages, including: threatening the child with ghosts or evil spirits, tying the child's hands and feet, hanging the child by hands or feet, forcing chili pepper into child's mouth, threatening to burn, threatening to beat, pulling hair, kicking, withholding food, calisthenics, and forced kneeling for a period of time with some added burden, such as in hot sand or holding a brick in each hand.

Although scolding, slapping, and spanking were considered both appropriate and necessary for the socialization of children, some mothers felt that beating should be reserved for only the most severe offenses. There was general agreement that hanging, burning, kicking, threatening abandonment, and threatening with evil spirits are not appropriate strategies, and some mothers expressed remorse at having resorted to such severe practices. Even though not a focus group topic, reasons for harsh discipline were occasionally volunteered and seemed to be related to the mother's stress, the child's escalating misbehaviour, or both. In one group, the mothers agreed that children who were difficult to manage required harsher methods of discipline. They also said that as children get older it is easier to correct their behaviour with verbal explanations without having to resort to physical punishment.

Reliability of Measurement Scales: Internal consistency reliability of the CES-D in this sample was very acceptable (Cronbach's alpha =.93). Only two of the items had low item-total correlations: "I felt I was as good as other people" (r =.28) and "I felt hopeful about the future" (r =.27). All other item-total correlations ranged from 45 ("I talked less than usual") to 77 ("I felt sad" and "I felt depressed"). The alpha coefficient for the Neighbourhood Support scale was 86, also quite satisfactory given the relative shortness of the scale (five items). Item-total correlations ranged from 58 to 76.

Bibliography

Benjamin, J.: *Socio-religious Status of Girl Child in India*, New Delhi, Ashish Publishing, 1991.

Calman, J.: *Toward Empowerment: Women and Politics in India*, Colorado, Westview Press, 1992.

Carr, Marilyn: *Speaking Out: Women's Economic Empowerment in South Asia,* London, 1996.

Chandra Mowli, V.: *'Jogin'. Girl-Child Labour Studies*, New Delhi, Sterling 1992

Dak, T.M.: *Women and Work in Indian Society*, Delhi, Discovery, 1988.

Erikson, E. H.: *Childhood and Society,* New York, W. W. Norton, 1993.

Flavia Agnes: *Law and Gender Inequality : The Politics of Women's Rights in India,* Oxford University Press, 1999,

Ghadially, Rehana: *Women in Indian Society*, New Delhi. Sage Publication, 1988.

Hashemi, Syed M.: *Defining and Studying Empowerment of Women: A Research Note from Bangladesh,* Washington, John Snow, 1993.

Jordan, J. V.: *Women's Growth in Diversity,* New York, Guilford Press, 1997.

Lipking, Lawrence: *Abandoned Women and the Poetic Tradition.* Chicago: Univ. of Chicago Press, 1988.

Mathur, B.B.: *Women and Depressed Class Population in India*, Allahabad, Chugh, 1994.

Nair, Janaki: *Women and Law in Colonial India*, New Delhi, Kali, 1996.

Narayan, Deepa : *Empowerment and Poverty Reduction,* Washington, World Bank, 2002.

Nussbaum, Martha: *Women and Human Development: The Capabilities Approach*, New York, Cambridge Press, 2000.

Ross, J.A.: *Family Planning and Child Survival Programs as Assessed in 1991*, New York, Population Council, 1992.

Selliah, S.: *The Self-Employed Women's Association, Ahmedabad*, Geneva, ILO, 1989.

Sharma, Arvind : *Women in World Religion,* New York Press, New York, 1990.

Tinker, I.: *Persistent Inequalities: Women and World Development*, New York, OUP, 1990.

Vicinus, Martha: *Suffer and be Still: Women in the Victorian Age*. London: Macmillan, 1972.

Vyas, A. & Singh, S.: *Women's Studies in India. Information Sources, Services and Programmes*, New Delhi, Sage, 1993.

Ware, H.: *Prepared for the Expert Group Meeting on Population and Women*, Gaborone, Botswana, 1992.

Index

❑❑❑